Towards a more accountable United Nations Secu

Legal Aspects of International Organizations

VOLUME 61

The titles published in this series are listed at *brill.com/laio*

Towards a more accountable United Nations Security Council

By

Carolyn M. Evans

BRILL
NIJHOFF

LEIDEN | BOSTON

Library of Congress Cataloging-in-Publication Data

Names: Evans, Carolyn M., author.
Title: Towards a more accountable United Nations Security Council / by Carolyn M. Evans.
Description: The Netherlands : Koninklijke Brill NV, [2021] | Series: Legal aspects of international organization, 0924-4883 ; volume 61 | Includes index.
Identifiers: LCCN 2020054300 (print) | LCCN 2020054301 (ebook) | ISBN 9789004444294 (hardback) | ISBN 9789004444300 (ebook)
Subjects: LCSH: United Nations. Security Council. | Security, International.
Classification: LCC KZ5036 .E93 2021 (print) | LCC KZ5036 (ebook) | DDC 341.23/23–dc23
LC record available at https://lccn.loc.gov/2020054300
LC ebook record available at https://lccn.loc.gov/2020054301

Typeface for the Latin, Greek, and Cyrillic scripts: "Brill". See and download: brill.com/brill-typeface.

ISSN 0924-4883
ISBN 978-90-04-44429-4 (hardback)
ISBN 978-90-04-44430-0 (e-book)

This book is printed on acid-free paper and produced in a sustainable manner.

Contents

Acknowledgements

Since this book started its life as a doctoral dissertation, no small thanks are due to my thesis supervisors: Professor Martin Krygier, who patiently prompted me to improve my writing over the course of my research, and Associate Professor Christopher Michaelsen, who originally prompted my interest in international law over a decade ago.

I am also indebted to the examiners of my thesis, Professor Simon Chesterman and Professor Jan Klabbers, whose feedback was so illuminating and who each provided some of the impetus for developing the thesis into this book.

Of course, a long list of family, friends, and colleagues, inspired me towards this research in the first place, then goaded and encouraged me along the way in roughly equal parts—even as they always nurtured belief that it should be done, and did not cease their efforts when the PhD was in hand and possibilities of a book arose.

First among all, I put my late mother, who *knew* the world could become a better place—if we each took action to pay our share on that account.

In memory of her, this book is for all those women disparaged as 'difficult', simply for not bowing to an inadequate, incomplete, or uninclusive, status quo—who instead wanted to take a step towards seeing that better place become a reality. More power to their arms, I say, and to those of any others who choose to work with such women in furtherance of their aspirations.

Carolyn M Evans
Sydney, June 2020

Figures

CHAPTER 1

Introduction

The weight of reform discourse about the United Nations Security Council, especially in the post-Cold War geopolitical environment, gives reason to believe that the Council is not as productive as it could be in pursuing its Functions under the *Charter of the United Nations*.[1] That is, the Council is certainly busy, perhaps busier than ever,[2] and generates voluminous documentation, perhaps more than ever, but there is a great deal more at stake than just doing this work. In fact, progress on its raison d'être is quite unclear, and doubts continue to linger on the extent to which the Council should be counted as productive of salutary outcomes.[3]

The *Charter* does provide UN member states with the means by which to amend its provisions to address related concerns, but the record on such formal change is sparse—so far involving the Council by just one increase in its membership.[4] In any event, the world continues to evolve, so reforming the

1 *Charter of the United Nations*, opened for signature 26 June 1945, 1 UNTS XVI (entered into force 24 October 1945) ('*Charter*'). On Council Functions, see Article 24.

2 Though consultations are not on the public record, close observers of the Security Council have noted, for example: 'In 1990, the Council held 69 meetings and 80 consultations. In 2017, there were 296 meetings [and] 137 consultations'—*In Hindsight: What's wrong with the Security Council?* (29 March 2018) Security Council Report <https://www.securitycouncilreport.org/monthly_forecast/2018-04>. As discussed later, COVID-19 has also had a non-trivial impact on how the Council does its work, with its activities less accessible due to the happenstance of New York City being both the home of the UN and an epicentre in the pandemic. At the time of writing, what—if any—change this will bring over the longer term is an open question.

3 In ordinary language, 'productiveness' speaks to whether a thing is producing or capable of producing desired results, for which 'effectiveness' is commonly a synonym. This appears to be the usage of 'effectiveness' by some scholars (for example, see Peters, below Chapter 2, n 16 and associated text, or Chesterman, below Chapter 5, n 160) and practitioners (such as UN member states, see below Chapter 2, n 36 and Chapter 3, n 83, and associated text). In similar contexts 'effectiveness' may also be used more specifically: for example, see Salvatore Zappalà 'Can Legality Trump Effectiveness in Today's International Law?' in Antonio Cassese (ed) *Realizing Utopia: The Future of International Law* (Oxford, 2012). While certainly not irrelevant, in this book 'effectiveness' and 'effective' are not meant so specifically, and thus have largely been avoided in favour of 'productiveness' and 'productive', as discussed in Chapter 2, and these are used in shorthand, portmanteau terms (beneficially productive, usefully productive, productive of salutary results).

4 An increase achieved by adding non-permanent members—see below n 97 and Chapter 2, n 26.

 | DOI:10.1163/9789004444300_002

Council to meet today's challenges would not be enough. Tomorrow brings fresh developments—importantly, and inevitably, including some that are unanticipated. The potential need for adjustment, adaptation, or addition, thus never entirely passes. Of course, the Council is by no means alone in this as 'it is common knowledge that international law lacks an efficient institutional mechanism for the abolition of outdated legal rules and the formation of more modern and adequate prescriptions'.[5]

Such concerns are unlikely to evaporate. With an eye to the laudable Purposes of the United Nations, and the effort and resources invested in the Council and its endeavours, attention turns from lack of reform, per se, to the potential impact this may have on the Council's capacity and capability to do what it is there to do. In broad terms, is the Council as productive as it might be in maintaining or restoring international peace and security, via the decisions or recommendations that it makes and, presumably, wishes to see implemented? Or are there ways to better equip it than the legal and institutional arrangements under which the Council labours presently?

There are many and various reasons advanced for Council reform.[6] The central concern in this book is, however, quite specific: whether being more accountable would improve the Council's capacity to discharge its *Charter* responsibilities.

Of course, more is needed than institutional devices that are aimed at 'accountability' in a general sense.

To begin with, one should clarify why one thinks accountability might be worth having, or what the point of accountability is thought to be in the context examined. My particular question in this is whether there are reasons to make, and possibilities for making, the Council more accountable for its actions, *in the interests of the Council becoming more 'productive'*. That would stand to shape to whom, for what, and according to what standard, an account would be rendered.

This might, however, still be seen in different ways: for one example, accountability could be cast as a state of affairs, or shaped into a process—perhaps a broad 'virtue' of decision making, as distinct from the manner or means by which

5 Antonio Cassese 'Introduction' in Antonio Cassese (ed) *Realizing Utopia: The Future of International Law* (Oxford, 2012), xviii. The same might be said of the reform process itself—see discussion in Chapter 2.2.

6 As discussed further in Chapter 2, and these are also faced by just as many hurdles and complexities: in terms of the legal accountability, for example, the state of the international legal order means that immunities to prosecution would need to be overcome to hold the Council accountable, which is no small thing, but such immunities are also thought to be integral to the proper functioning of international relations.

pertinent questions can be articulated, a response devised, and so on.[7] To do more than revisit ongoing reform debate, where many such divergences have been mooted, my interest is in addressing how accountability might actually be brought to bear on the Council in its idiosyncratic circumstances.

The vantage point for examining possibilities on this has been taken as international law because, though born of war and politics, the UN and its Security Council are legal constructs: they were created by an international treaty, the *Charter*, and thus in the context of international law. Then again, with due regard to the time and place of their birth, it is also noteworthy that a considerable period has passed in which the design in their constituent document might have been amended, but has not been. Since that continues to appear out of reach, suggesting proposals premised on *Charter* amendment would quite likely stall alongside the reform debate. As an aid to productiveness of the Council, a scheme for greater Council accountability thus probably has healthier prospects if devised under the *Charter* as it stands.

This highlights a defining feature of the backdrop to discussion in this book: international organisations operate in a socially constructed space for cooperative intergovernmental processes and activities, usually termed 'international organisation' if formalised in treaties,[8] and made manifest in institutions.[9] The 'international community',[10] however, may have money for such endeavours, but not a room of its own in which to write—to some deliberate design, for example, or even generally towards outcomes agreed as desirable. Instead, added workspace is carved out as each sui generis entity is created, gradually aggregating into 'international organisation' by addressing specific circumstances—via a peculiar breadth and depth of purposes, combined with an extent of consent to participate in that endeavour that is obtained from sovereign states.

---

7 For example, Mark Bovens 'Two Concepts of Accountability: Accountability as a Virtue and as a Mechanism' (2010) 33(5) *West European Politics* 946.

8 For an overview, see for example José E Alvarez 'International Organizations: Then and Now' (2006) 100 *American Journal of International Law* 324; see also generally Inis L Claude *Swords into Ploughshares: The Problems and Progress of International Organization* (Random House, 4th ed, 1971).

9 As opposed to less formalised activities such as holding international conferences or meetings, even where these become a series but still without institutions being associated with them.

10 To the extent that there is one—see, for example, Dino Kritsiotis 'Imagining the International Community' (2002) 13(4) *European Journal of International Law* 961; Bardo Fassbender *The United Nations Charter as the Constitution of the International Community* (Martinus Nijhoff, 2009). See also Monica Hakimi 'Constructing an International Community' (2017) 111(2) *American Journal of International Law* 317; cf Evgeny Roshchin

One effect of this idiosyncrasy is that even if space may be added by giving a venue legal personality, as the UN is said to have,[11] this may never sum to a room in which an 'international community' resides—and yet all the world may have an interest in what happens there. Another is that this space is not immune to influence from entities which are short of that legal status,[12] or merely a network or informal grouping of states,[13] or which do not even involve nation states per se.[14]

Importantly, such other entities shape opinions about what it is that international organisations do, or should do, and how they should do it—while technological change continues to lower barriers to mobilising these views in contemporary geopolitics.[15]

'The Hague Conferences and "international community": a politics of conceptual innovation' (2016) 43(1) *Review of International Studies* 177.

11 Though different to the legal personality accorded to a state—see *Reparation for Injuries Suffered in the Service of the United Nations* (*Advisory Opinion*) [1949] ICJ Reports 174, 179. See also David J Bederman 'The Souls of International Organizations: Legal Personality and the Lighthouse at Cape Spartel' (1996) 36 *Virginia Journal of International Law* 275.

12 Such as the the Organization for Security and Co-operation in Europe (OSCE) which engages the equivalent of a third of the UN's members—see Organization for Security and Co-operation in Europe *Where We Are* <http://www.osce.org/where>. It is not in full flower as an international organisation—see Organization for Security and Co-operation in Europe *Who We Are: History* <http://www.osce.org/history>. For example, the underpinning document is 'non-legally binding'—Jan Klabbers 'International institutions' in James Crawford and Martii Koskenniemi (eds) *The Cambridge Companion to International Law* (Cambridge, 2012), 228, 236.

13 Such as the G20, a 'condominium of big states from both the G8 and the Global South'—see Andrew F Cooper and Bessma Momani 'Re-balancing the G-20 from Efficiency to Legitimacy: The 3G Coalition and the Practice of Global Governance' (2014) 20(2) *Global Governance* 213, 226. The G20 came to the fore in the aftermath of the 2008 global financial crisis, and is influential in the Council's province as far as global economic stability is a component of international security. It does not have formalised structure, legal personality, or even a fully constant group of participants—see Peter Holcombe Henley and Niels M Blokker 'The Group of 20: A Short Legal Anatomy from the Perspective of International Institutional Law' (2013) 14(2) *Melbourne Journal of International Law* 550; see also Charis Palmer and Emil Jeyaratnam 'The G20 economies explained in 12 charts' on *The Conversation* (12 November 2014) <http://theconversation.com/the-g20-economies-explained-in-12-charts-33887>.

14 For example, the C40 skirts around national and sub-national government to network cities as influential actors on climate change, now recognised as a security issue (see, for example, below Chapter 2, n 109 and associated text). See C40 Cities *About C40* <https://www.c40.org/about>.

15 Including in ways that that are not without ramifications for the Security Council (and perhaps also the international legal order), such as the '1 for 7 Billion' campaign on finding a UN Secretary-General—see below Chapter 4, n 119 and n 120, and discussion in

Tracing the heritage of international organisations from early 'public international organizations functioning as institutions [in] essentially a development of the late nineteenth century',[16] shows a march from river commissions for managing shared waterways, and for interchange of services via transport and communications unions,[17] to the proliferation of international institutions of myriad purposes, or 'functions',[18] through the twentieth century.[19]

As history, this bears the stamp of law: just for a few examples, scholars contend that international organisations are empowered and obliged by the law;[20] that they are 'legal communities in a threefold sense—they are created by law, they use law as a means of governance, and they should be governed by the rule of law';[21] and that organisational relationships engage multiple 'legal dynamics'—with constituent members, with staff and between organs, and with the world.[22]

Centred on cooperation between states, the processes and activities of international organisation are, however, also inherently political and interest-laden from their outset, and these institutions cannot help but be similarly enmeshed. Thus, while constituted in international law, both the conception of

---

Chapter 6 2.3. Similarly, both the call from the Secretary-General for a global ceasefire during the COVID-19 pandemic, and the Council's inability to respond in support of the call, became widely known without noticeable delay. The Council's failure to obtain a result at that time could hardly be said to have reflected well on the productiveness of the Council, which is not much offset by a resolution after months of delay, and therefore is something for which an explanation would no doubt be welcomed. For more on this, see below Chapter 5, n 105.

16 C F Amerasinghe *Principles of the Institutional Law of International Organizations* (Cambridge, 2nd ed, 2005), 1.

17 For a brief overview, see Dapo Akande 'International Organizations' in Malcolm D Evans (ed) *International Law* (Oxford, 4th ed, 2014), 248.

18 See Jan Klabbers 'Theorizing International Organizations' in Anne Orford and Florian Hoffmann (eds) *The Oxford Handbook of the Theory of International Law* (Oxford, 2016).

19 See David Kennedy 'The Move to Institutions' (1987) 8(5) *Cardozo Law Review* 841.

20 Michel Virally 'La notion de fonction dans la théorie de l'organisation internationale' in Michel Virally *Le Droit International En Devenir* (Graduate Institute Geneva, 1990), [51] <https://books.openedition.org/iheid/4398?lang=en>. See also generally Jorge E Viñuales '"The Secret of Tomorrow": International Organization through the Eyes of Michel Virally' (2012) 23(2) *European Journal of International Law* 543.

21 Anne Peters 'International Organizations and International Law' in Jacob Katz Cogan, Ian Hurd and Ian Johnstone (eds) *The Oxford Handbook of International Organizations* (Oxford, 2016), 33.

22 Jan Klabbers *An Introduction to International Organizations Law* (Cambridge, 3rd ed, 2015), 3.

international relations at the time when it is formed, and the pragmatic adjustments enforced by geopolitics then and since, serve to shape and re-shape the societal context for any international organisation, including the legal context.

How an international organisation functions as a legal entity thus is intertwined with its political character: this appears all the more so in the UN, given the scope of its interests and almost universal membership. This is a factor which is elemental in understanding the nature of the Security Council and how the question I sought to answer is addressed in this book.

1.1 The United Nations Security Council

During World War II, the 'United Nations' alliance came to contemplate the unthinkable prospect of another such war, along with egregious conduct by states, such as war crimes, genocide, or crimes against humanity.

Those states resolved to foster future prevention of such calamities via an organising mechanism for international efforts, as expressed in Article 1(1) of the *Charter*:

> The Purposes of the United Nations are:
>
> 1. To maintain international peace and security, and to that end: to take effective collective measures for the prevention and removal of threats to the peace, and for the suppression of acts of aggression or other breaches of the peace, and to bring about by peaceful means, in conformity with the principles of justice and international law, adjustment or settlement of international disputes or situations which might lead to a breach of the peace ...[23]

Also fresh in the memory of statesmen was the less-than-satisfactory experience with the League of Nations, the first international organisation overtly directed towards maintaining international peace and security.[24]

Such considerations are evident in millions of pages of documents generated by the 'United Nations Conference on International Organization' (UNCIO),[25] which gave birth to the UN. As World War II ground to a close, negotiations ran

23 See also below Chapter 2, n 7 and associated text regarding the rest of Article 1.

24 For an overview, see, for example, Qizhi He 'The Crucial Role of the United Nations in Maintaining International Peace and Security' in Christian Tomuschat *The United Nations at Age Fifty: A Legal Perspective* (Kluwer, 1995).

25 Ian Hurd *After Anarchy: Legitimacy & Power in the United Nations Security Council* (Princeton, 2007), 83, citing Ruth B Russell *A History of the United Nations Charter: The*

from April to June 1945 in San Francisco, involving most of the 51 states known as the 'original members'.[26] Perusing UNCIO materials highlights a legacy of historical realities from when and how the United Nations came to be: this was transmitted in the Purposes and persona given to the UN by its original members, and how these would be addressed by the new endeavour.

One innovation, for example, was intended to improve the prospects for making *any* collective decision. Institutionalising deciding by majority vote was to replace the traditional requirement for unanimity in international co-operation,[27] the effect of which up until that time had been to afford a veto to any dissenting state.[28]

Another was to bolster Security Council capacity for meeting its responsibility, under Article 24(1), for maintaining or restoring international peace and security. Becoming a member of the UN entails becoming party to the *Charter*, while Article 25 obliges UN members to act at Council direction in some circumstances. These provisions together mean each UN member has a treaty obligation that they will 'accept and carry out the decisions of the Security Council'.[29]

Beyond that, the UN was to embody the ideal of universal membership, but a desire to better engage the 'great powers' of those times was pivotal in how the Council was constructed as a principal organ of the UN.[30] The guiding aim was to avoid the League's ineffectiveness between the wars, often linked to incomplete engagement with the 'great powers' of its day—such as the United States, which stayed out of the League, and the USSR, which joined late and participated but briefly.[31]

Role of the United States, 1940–1945 (The Brookings Institution, Washington DC, 1958), 625 n 1.

26 United Nations *Growth in United Nations membership, 1945-present* https://www.un.org/en/sections/member-states/growth-united-nations-membership-1945-present/index.html.

27 See, for example, *Charter* Article 18(2) in relation to the General Assembly. For one historical perspective on development of this 'majoritarian' approach, see Claude, above n 8, 120.

28 See below Chapter 5, n 90 and n 99, and associated text.

29 Though not an absolute or unmitigated obligation—see Bruno Simma, Daniel-Erasmus Khan, Georg Nolte and Andreas Paulus (eds) *The Charter of the United Nations: A Commentary* (Oxford, 3rd ed, 2012), Volume 1, 790.

30 Under Article 7 of the *Charter*, the UN's principal organs also include the General Assembly, the International Court of Justice, the Economic and Social Council, the Trusteeship Council, and the Secretariat. References herein to 'the Council' always mean the Security Council.

31 Such that, at the time, eyewitnesses observed a prevailing disinclination to even connect the two endeavours overtly—see, for example, Leland M Goodrich 'From League of Nations to United Nations' (1947) 1(1) *International Organization* 3, 3.

The design of the Council itself thus may be the clearest response to the League's legacy. Its structure and procedures privilege certain states by permanent Council membership,[32] and by their vote having the potential to be a veto.[33] At the time, there was also tremendous pressure to facilitate nimble Council decision-making by limiting its size, to be a 'small and efficient body',[34] where military power, standing by for enforcement action, was supposed to be concentrated among those states set to be made permanent members of the Council.[35]

Of course, that is not to deny that the Council's design, as put forward to UNCIO,[36] was strongly debated in San Francisco.[37] On the contrary, an array of schemes—to similar ends, but with less privilege for the so-called 'great powers'—is quite visible in the chunk of official records generated by the Commission tasked with addressing this part of the treaty negotiations.[38]

---

32 *Charter*, Article 23. See discussion in Simma et al, above n 29, 753.

33 *Charter*, Article 27(3). For a comprehensive discussion, see Bardo Fassbender *UN Security Council Reform and the Right of Veto: A Constitutional Perspective* (Kluwer, 1998).

34 *Report of the Rapporteur of Commission III (Celso R. Velazquez, Paraguay) to the Plenary Session* UNCIO Doc 1170 (23 June 1945), 4.

35 Ibid, noting that later, in due course of Council discussions, France proffered the view that the permanent members might provide around 75 per cent of the forces needed—this was brought up in the process of the Military Staff Committee making some estimates on the size of the forces, and noted in the Council session: see UN SCOR, 149th mtg, UN Doc S/PV.149 (30 June 1947), 1175 (Australia). However, the reality was that if called upon, supplying this need may substantially have fallen to the USSR and the USA, recalling that the Republic of China was engaged in a long running civil war; France was unstable in re-emerging from its wartime Vichy France era, seeing 16 prime ministers before the Fourth Republic collapsed in 1958; and World War II had left the UK with quite a fragile economy, including that it was 'the world's greatest debtor'—see George C Peden 'Recognising and Responding to Relative Decline: The Case of Post-War Britain' (2013) 24(1) *Diplomacy & Statecraft* 59, 61.

36 For background on the Dumbarton Oaks (1944) and Yalta (1945) sessions which led to convening of the San Francisco Conference, and the draft treaty put to it, see Hurd, above n 25, 85.

37 For an eyewitness narrative which is evocative of the Conference atmosphere, how it was created by that mindset, and some of the implications of it, see Herbert Vere Evatt *The United Nations* (Harvard, 1948), especially Part I. See also below Chapter 3, n 120 as to his particular involvement in these matters.

38 Commission III at UNCIO addressed the Security Council, working as Committee 1 (Structure and Procedure), Committee 2 (Peaceful Settlement), and Committee 3 (Enforcement Arrangements). A collection of 21 volumes of UNCIO documents is available online from the UN Bibliographic Information System—one is devoted to summary reports from Committee 1 and runs to over 800 pages, and another similarly to Committees 2 and 3, which approaches 900 pages. See United Nations Bibliographic Information

This highlights some things that—at least in retrospect—might have been debated but were not.[39] For example, what Council members must, may, or might, consider, when casting their votes in Council decisions, does not appear to have been on the agenda. One by-the-way remark, possibly linked to that theme, was that 'the members of the Security Council should be regarded as trustees of the whole Organization',[40] but this is not reported as having been specifically taken up in formal debate. This hints that the topic was not on the geopolitical radar at the Conference or, if it was, this summary was not contentious.[41]

Contemporaneous geopolitics can thus be found threaded into the socio-legal framing of the composition, obligations, and tasks, of the Council, as a creature of its time. Such contexts do not remain static, however, any more than do the problems that the organisation may face. This has enduring implications for work by, and productiveness of, UN organs, how they relate to member states, whether UN members choose to duly deliver their contribution to UN endeavours,[42] and to what extent the contributions made by states ultimately prove to help or hinder realisation of the UN's raison d'être.[43]

That said, a socially constructed entity always has the opportunity to change, by activating the initiative to develop within its social 'ecosystem': such an entity always stands to be shaped by the actors and context comprising it, though the process involved may be complicated and not entirely within the control of those actors.[44]

System *Documents of the United Nations Conference on International Organization, San Francisco, 1945* (UNBISNET Call Number UNX.341.13 U51).

39 Perhaps in favour of giving full vent to issues relating to the Council's composition and powers per se.

40 In the course of discussion that culminated in the 'equitable geographical distribution' element of Article 23(1), drawing a contrast with being representatives of a particular region—*Summary Report of Seventh Meeting of Committee III/1* UNCIO Doc 338 (16 May 1945), 3.

41 Of course, there is a third option—that it was so contentious that delegates *all* chose to avoid the matter entirely, but this seems quite improbable given how enthusiastically many other contentious matters appear to have been debated over the course of time devoted to UNCIO.

42 When said to be obliged to do so, or otherwise as requested by or through its organs.

43 Where, for example, notorious misconduct by some peacekeepers might well be seen as counter-productive—see below Chapter 3, n 75, 76, and 77, and associated text.

44 So it may seem to take a 'crisis' to move things along—see, for example, Gabrielle Marceau 'IGOs in Crisis? Or New Opportunities to Demonstrate Responsibility?' (2011) 8(1) *International Organizations Law Review* 1.

Beyond that, the scope and scale of challenges before an organisation, and thus the need for change, naturally depend partly on the complexities of its purposes. For example, even when technological change is embraced unevenly around the world, working to adapt interchange of infrastructure services (telecommunications, banking, mail handling, and so on) is probably less challenging than restoring or maintaining international peace and security. Moreover, *maintaining productiveness by finding a direction in which to evolve, and navigating towards that evolution*, is impacted upon simply by the number of states that must agree.

On the whole, it is safe to say that the UN begins with more challenges than most organisations from an unparalleled combination of circumstances, in the breadth of its Purposes and almost universal membership. Others then arise from questions about governing pursuit of its Purposes within the frame that the *Charter* provides, and what may now be encompassed by the broad sweep of 'governance issues'.[45] Some were known and actioned in the *Charter*, while others, though known, were not actioned. Perhaps more importantly, some could not have been known to the drafters, but a range of such things have variously proven to be relevant to maintaining international peace and security. All such things are potentially germane to both matters on which the Council may make decisions, and the process by which those decisions might be made.

Firstly, in terms of the substantive business of the Council, questions about how to respond to non-state actors, for example, emerged later in the twentieth century, and they remain moot in the state-centric world of international law and international relations.[46] No surprise, then, that the *Charter* does not stipulate the Council response to non-state actors, including those whose malice is armed by modern technology—so the question arises about *how the Council is to develop that capacity*.

On the other hand, the need to develop some relevant capacity applies no less to known issues either not addressed, or addressed imperfectly, in the *Charter* design. In terms of interpreting the *Charter*, for example, debate at UNCIO included the possibility of contention, conflict, or cross-purposes,

---

45 Where 'disagreement on the definition of global governance is the rule'—Alessandro Mulieri 'Can we democratise global governance? Two guiding scenarios based on a narrative approach' in Jan Wouters, Antoon Braeckman, Matthias Lievens and Emilie Bécault (eds) *Global Governance and Democracy: A Multidisciplinary Analysis* (Edward Elgar, 2015), 15.

46 See, for example, Math Noortmann, Cedric Ryngaert and August Reinisch (eds) *Non-State Actors in International Law* (Hart, 2015); see also Bob Reinalda (ed) *The Ashgate Research Companion to Non-State Actors* (Routledge, 2013); Antonio Cassese 'States: Rise and Decline of the Primary Subjects of the International Community' in Bardo Fassbender and Anne Peters (eds) *The Oxford Handbook of the History of International Law* (Oxford, 2012).

among UN organs, but the drafters opted to leave this lay—declining, for example, to adopt proposals to confer on the International Court of Justice powers and authority to resolve such disagreements.[47] Consequently, along with new issues arising, various matters of treaty interpretation relating to the Council still remain open, potentially affecting Council productiveness—the latter group including, by no means least, the nature and extent of Article 25 obligations for states to 'accept and carry out the decisions of the Security Council in accordance with the present Charter'.

Then, in relation to process, including due engagement with UN members, one self-evident example is the outgrowth of what was unknown (or, at least, largely unknown) to the drafters. This rapidly became a cause célèbre in the UN: the passing of the colonial era, seen in some of the earliest agenda items coming before the Council,[48] and in the burgeoning independence and self-determination of former colonies which helped to triple UN membership by the mid-1970s.[49]

Beyond obvious consequences for the geopolitical makeup of the 'international community',[50] this also had the effect of greatly diversifying the UN's membership and opinions voiced about a range of matters. For example, the concepts of, and views on, options for how to maintain or restore international peace and security, and states' capacity to support those options; or why and how the Council can or should pursue these in relation to the *Charter*, under Chapter VI (pacific settlement of disputes) and/or Chapter VII (threats to the peace, breaches of the peace, and acts of aggression).

For the reader more accustomed to seeing accountabilities appear in legal instruments, another process feature from the post-World War II era legacy is what is *not* there—such as standards for governing the Council's work.[51] Again: this is hardly surprising when the idea that international organisations might do harm was largely yet to come forward,[52] and today's notions of accountability were barely on the horizon.[53]

---

47 See generally Claude, above n 8, 166. The Court's advisory jurisdiction gives the possibility of assisting, but it has not often been called upon in this way. See also below Chapter 4, n 9.

48 Such as on Indonesia—see below Chapter 6, n 45 and associated text.

49 See above n 26.

50 As far as there is one—see above n 10 and associated text.

51 Or that of other UN organs.

52 See below Chapter 2, n 11 and 13, and associated text. See also Jan Klabbers 'Checks and Balances in the Law of International Organizations' in Mortimer Sellers (ed) *Autonomy in the Law* (Springer, 2007).

53 For an example illustrating the contemporaneous freshness of that debate, see Herman Finer 'Administrative Responsibility in Democratic Government' (1941) 1(4) *Public Administration Review* 335. See also below Chapter 2, n 48 and associated text.

On the whole, however, given the passage of time these examples speak less to the *Charter* per se, and rather more to the organic, institutional capacity of the UN to work well and productively at the junction of its Purposes and its organisational circumstances (with all of the exigencies that these entail), and *continuing to do so as they both unfold over time.*

Equally, processes for organisational learning, development, and evolution, to ensure that the organisation continues to work well and productively, depend partly on how, and how effectively, the organisation detects and recognises alterations in its own peculiar situation. For the UN, such changes include seismic political shifts, such as the breakup of the former USSR, as well as creeping increments of social evolution, such as the accretion of geopolitical agency by non-government organisations.[54] Within the social ecosystem in which an institution exists, responding as may befit its stated objects or purposes thus begins with detecting alteration in its circumstances, or recognising some gap, or deficit, in its results, that may hold potential for material impact on future endeavours. For international organisations, possible responses then include formal change, usually amendment to its constituent treaty, or otherwise by less formal means such as by adjusting internal rules adopted, practices followed, understandings shared, and so on.

Among various inputs, it is such responses that being accountable may serve to inform, towards preserving or improving institutional productiveness.

1.2 Accountability

My interest in accountability of the Security Council is closely linked to its functioning and what this may add to the institutional capacity of the UN. Thus the main question asked in this book is—in the interests of making the Council more productive, are there possibilities for making it more accountable, and could a scheme to such effect be devised under the *Charter* as it stands?

54 See, for example, Simon Chesterman 'How "Public" Is Public International Law? Toward a Typology of NGOs and Civil Society Actors' (2018) 24 *Global Governance* 159; Steve Charnovitz 'Nongovernmental Organizations and International Law' (2006) 100 *American Journal of International Law* 348. There is also the question of evolving an understanding of what helps or hinders international peace and security, and thus with what the Council should be concerned—including when circumstances deliver unexpected opportunities that the Council might respond to towards advancing that, as seen in the call by the Secretary-General for a global ceasefire during the COVID-19 pandemic on which the Council failed to make a productive response (see below Chapter 5, n 105).

The nature of the Council is clouded by being a legally-constituted entity with powers to create binding obligations on states, towards a mission of undeniably political character. Equally, any analysis of its accountability is dogged by the fact that the idea sits where international law intersects with international relations, and neither yet offers a generally accepted definition, nor even an uncontested conceptualisation.[55] In international legal scholarship, it remains to be settled whether accountability may equate to responsibility for internationally wrongful acts,[56] for example, while in international relations there is, for example, more than one school of thought on the role of (legal) accountability in 'global governance' (however that is defined),[57] and habits vary on interdefining democracy and accountability.[58] Both wrestle with what contribution 'sanctions' may make.[59]

What is clear, nevertheless, is that accountability originates in a relationship that carries with it the capacity for one actor to make judgements on the conduct of another. Why accountability is relevant, to whom an account is owed to 'explain or justify conduct',[60] to what conduct (and a related standard) accountability pertains, and how it might actually be obtained, are all matters of necessary situational detail about being accountable: why, to whom, for what, and how, are four corners of concerns about any actor that another would wish to see held accountable.

Seen from outside that square, answers to those questions hinge on the idea that accountability is not an end in itself: it is a means to the ends of the relationship, and being accountable should thus be arranged to contribute to achieving ends for which the relationship exists.

Accordingly, my approach is premised on the idea that whatever one takes accountability to consist of depends first on why one seeks it—what the overarching point of accountability is thought to be in the circumstances. I take this to be that accountability may contribute to productiveness by encouraging desired conduct, and discouraging conduct that is shown to as unproductive, counter-productive, or otherwise deleterious to the existential reasons for the relationship. Then prevailing concerns are more about dialogue aimed at

55 See discussion in Chapter 2.3.
56 See below Chapter 2, n 53 and 87, and associated text.
57 See above n 45 and below Chapter 2, n 67, and associated text.
58 See below Chapter 2, n 65 and 66, and associated text.
59 Or 'consequences'—see below Chapter 2, n 63 and associated text.
60 As a bare bones idea of accountability is commonly put—see, for example, Mark Bovens 'Analysing and Assessing Accountability: A Conceptual Framework' (2007) 13(4) *European Law Journal* 447, 450.

identifying and agreeing changes that may need to be sought, and less about devising means by which to compel an actor to make change. In short, to aid productiveness accountability begins by addressing the purposes the actor is supposed to serve and then progress in that direction, after which change would show 'learning' or 'development'—as evidenced in amended conduct.[61]

This logic underpins my unifying theme about whether the Council is as well equipped as it might be to deal with what it faces, and how that changes over time, as an integral element of where the UN stands in realising the Purposes for which it exists.

Importantly, the Council faces more, plus rather more complex, matters than it did in the wake of World War II.[62] Such escalating complexity further highlights the need to preserve or improve institutional productiveness by learning and development, some contributions to which may be had from the Council being accountable for its conduct. Thus, to what extent the Council is evolving—keeping pace with changing circumstances and ensuring it is well-equipped to play its part under the *Charter*—is central to discussion in this book. To that point, and as discussed further in Chapter 2, accountability always relates to conduct of a (legal) person,[63] but there are diverse ways in which to approach that in concept and in practice, and the overarching point is to assess what modification of conduct is required (if any).

The next step is that, in pragmatic terms, accountability is circumscribed by how such change is to be obtained, distinct from how that may be compelled (by 'sanctions' or 'consequences'). This recalls the Council's character as a legal construct, located in the international legal order but not, by any stretch of imagination, hermetically sealed off from international politics. Formal (treaty-based) or informal (internal and/or practice-based) avenues exist for change consistent with international law, but any such change in Council conduct will also need to be achievable in the light of the UN's geopolitical operating realities.

61 Where 'learning' is used in the common use sense of the word—for example, where some would see that the 'purpose of public accountability is to induce the executive branch to learn'—ibid, 463; 'development' is used as, for example, Inis Claude uses the term in his discussion of evolution of the *Charter*—see Claude, above n 8, 167. See also below Chapter 7, n 16, as to what is not 'dialogue'.

62 In some ways, these may even surpass those in a relatively state-centric political and legal reality at the height of the Cold War—where, for example, threats to international peace and security from armed non-state actors was yet a marginal issue.

63 Whether a natural person, or a juristic/juridical person (that is, a result of legal construction).

The UN's sparse track record on *Charter* amendment is there for all to see.[64] Indeed, the Council's design has experienced just one treaty change since 1946, when its total membership was expanded to 15 by increasing the non-permanent (elected) members from six to ten.[65] Accordingly, treaty-based reform of the Council's capacity is relevant, but, in terms of how to obtain change in the Council, largely left aside here as an unlikely prospect.

On the other hand, the UN does have a rich body of adjustments made to its internal rules and to its practice over the course of some 75 years, suggesting that this offers the (relatively) more likely avenue for future change. Further, it is already clear that the sui generis nature of international organisations is key to their politico-legal relationships, so that nature remains fundamental to any characterisation of their accountability.[66]

Thus, part of the story of international organisations is that they are what they each are—none provides a precedent or even a model for any other, except in a broad advisory sense of showing one case of how such interstate purposes could be furthered, or how related work might be done. While true, that also remains a far cry from saying 'and thus they shall always be', especially since the same rich body of adjustments seen in the UN is also seen to a varying breadth and depth elsewhere in international organisations.

Importantly, such adjustments evidence that these institutions are better understood as works in progress. That work progresses at various speeds, certainly, and with uneven results animated by political will(s) that may not be predictable in quantum, or even consistent in direction from time to time.

On the whole, however, this is not a story carved in stone, once and for all—even for the Security Council, or for those that may, in turn, learn from what the Council does in future.

1.3 Towards (Greater) Security Council Accountability

In terms of the approach I have taken in this book, it is worth recalling that law is the origin of, and underpinning for, the UN as a treaty-based organisation

64 See discussion in Chapter 2.2.

65 Which took effect from 1966—see below Chapter 2, n 26 and associated text.

66 As canvassed again in recent years, in the politico-legal discussion following on from work by the International Law Commission to develop articles on the legal responsibility of international organisations. For example, the idea is variously addressed by contributors to a volume devoted to considering the draft articles: Maurizio Ragazzi (ed) *Responsibility of International Organizations: Essays in Memory of Sir Ian Brownlie* (Martinus Nijhoff, 2013).

whose mission is, in part, to 'establish conditions under which justice and respect for the obligations arising from treaties and other sources of international law can be maintained'.[67] In the Council forming part of the UN, it is thus created and framed by law, but, in its specific role, the Council is challenged to address some of the most complex, contested, and fraught, problems of international politics and international law.

Accordingly, though there are many ways in which to consider the Council's accountability, my approach in this book is primarily legal and institutional. The point is not to suggest that being accountable would itself be able to deliver some part of 'maintaining or restoring international peace and security' as the Council is charged to do. Nor is it to assert that related changes could alone achieve actual accountability in the interest-laden arena of international politics. Rather, the purpose of this approach is to identify what could better equip the Council for its *Charter* purposes than the legal and institutional arrangements under which it labours presently, including to better afford capacity to continue developing in that vein in the future.

In seeking possibilities for obtaining a more 'productive' Council by means of making it more accountable for its actions, the chapter structure of this book reflects my approach to the task. After taking a look at the literature in Chapter 2, I address why, to whom, and for what, the Council should be accountable, and how this could then be brought to bear on the Council.

In a little more detail: to begin with, seeing accountability as a means to other ends tends to beg the question of why accountability under international law is desirable in this context, as distinct from a narrower view about why accountability might be entailed in (legal) relationships that the Council has with other actors. As Chapter 3 notes, the first approach may be cast more as what ought to be, the second as what is now the case, but each involves the other. Discussion of that interconnection highlights that the Council is a unique politico-legal actor, under no compulsion to adopt a political style (such as democratic) or legal approach (perhaps to mimic the law-making parts of government in a state's judiciary or its legislative assembly)—though there may well be merit in such suggestions.

Thus, my approach is not about asserting some actor's right to hold the Council accountable, for example, or arguing the potential merits of accountability as one part of emulating a preferred form of government. Instead, I tackle this directly by asking how the UN might be made more productive in its own cause, which acknowledges both the UN's sui generis character, and the

67 *Charter*, third preambular paragraph.

Council's peculiar role in the UN's activities. Accordingly, themes in this book centre on seeking possibilities for strengthening realisation of the UN's raison d'être by rendering the Council more accountable.

Accountable to whom is the next concern. Conventionally this is approached by looking at how accountability may be entailed in, or attached to, one actor's interactions with another, which calls for some conception of the relationship.[68] If set within the narrow confines of (legal) responsibility for internationally wrongful acts, legal accountability would thus likely be limited to matters that arise from formal legal instruments and which, on that basis, are justiciable in a relevant venue. As discussed in Chapter 4, though, there may be reason to believe it could or should go further. If so, who may expect the Council to be accountable in the international legal order is a wider, more multi-faceted contingent of actors, encompassing states that empower the Council and many other actors that are affected by its work. My interest here is that recognising this politico-legal reality may also open up options for answers towards the Council being more productive in its own cause.

In conceptualising accountability, specificity is needed to account for conduct—in particular, a scope for that conduct, and some related standard by which to assess it. Discussion in Chapter 5 shows, however, some of the difficulties involved in setting a scope or standards, given the manifest and manifold intricacies of Council work. For example, international peace and security is a high stakes realm in which action has consequences, but, then again, so does inaction—are these both things the Council should 'explain and justify'? Similarly, if decisions are the bread and butter of that work, are these limited to those taken positively (or negatively) by the Council, such as by adopting (or not adopting) a formally-proposed resolution? Might they also include decisions by default—when no overt decision means the Council somehow, in effect, 'decides not to decide'?[69] Chapter 5 highlights that this is not just a question of identifying a thing for which the Council should account, or one characteristic which the Council perhaps ought to explain or justify. Rather, this is about having some means to work through such questions—*now and whenever they arise in the future*—and to do so effectively and promptly (or at least reasonably so).

---

68 Such as a principal-agent connection, for example.

69 So potentially encompassing when a proposal is tabled but lapses without attention, or, behind the scenes, a formal proposal is prepared but held back, or, more recently, when the Council makes a Presidential statement or a media release without a draft, or proposed, or successful, resolution—see discussion in Chapter 5.2.

Establishing 'why, to whom and for what' still leaves the question of how to actually obtain greater Council accountability. Mindful of *Charter* imperfections and idiosyncrasies, in Chapter 6 I revisit the *Charter* to that end, seeking options for the key to a scheme, or model, of Council accountability without necessarily resorting to *Charter* reform. Noting that various approaches to accountability would heed those empowering an entity and/or those affected by what it does, I find the key is being accountable to those empowering the Council (UN member states), by explaining or justifying what the Council does, including in the course of doing it.[70] This calls for such actors to have more voice in Council doings, in part as international peace and security is now impacted upon by a larger, and rather more variegated, array of state and non-state actors than could have been imagined when designing the UN.[71] If acceptable that such voice can, at least in part, be achieved indirectly, this means there appears to be more 'representative' work to do on behalf of those states empowering the Council—that is, more to say, and, quite probably, more need to say it. Retailed via contemporary journalism and social media, this also stands to better inform 'those affected' by consequences of the Council's work, not least those who do not feel well-served by their state and for whom civil society continues to play a crucial role in highlighting their situation.

That being the case, one possible scheme is articulated in the first section of Chapter 7, and modelled as a 'future-scape' in the second, before my conclusions are summarised in the final section.

The scheme turns on a key conclusion from this research: that the UN General Assembly is a relevant venue in which to hear the collective view of states empowering the Council. Not the least reason is that the Council has significant power under the *Charter*, but can wield such power only if allowed to do so by its constituent membership—which is drawn from those states empowering the Council. Options under the *Charter* for that *collective* to be represented in Council workings thus vest in that constituent membership,[72] which

70 Which may elsewhere be obtained by what are often termed 'checks and balances'—see Klabbers, above n 52. See also below Chapter 2, n 55 and 86.

71 Even if particulars of, or imperfections in, the *Charter* design now appear as part of the problem—see discussion in Chapter 2.2.

72 From the *Charter* and in established Council practice, individual states already have various options for making their views known to the Council. The point here is that an individual state does not empower the Council, it is the combined effect of the *Charter* as the enabling treaty and the electoral process conducted in the Assembly to provide 10 of the 15 constituent members, without which the Council cannot function.

always includes some members elected by the Assembly.[73] To such ends, the five permanent (P5) and ten non-permanent, elected (E10) members have rights in Council decision-making,[74] and it is open for them to speak on a wider front than their own interests. Any or all of the P5 may choose not to and, in all probability, no actor has the means to compel them. Elected members are, however, conventionally cast as 'representing' the wider UN membership due to the *manner* of their election.[75] To my eye, the *process* of their election opens up options for the UN membership to act collectively to create obligations, duties, tasks, hurdles to election, and so on, that are to be associated with this elected office.

As I see it, taking this path has opportunities to make E10 members 'representatives' in more than just name, and the 'future-scape' then is a speculative image embodying sample elements of more accountable practice in the UN sphere from a potentially more productive Council—if the E10 will wear the mantle of 'representatives' (including via engendering fresh Council working methods).[76]

My conclusion is that the vehicle for Council accountability could be an omnipresent voice for the UN membership in Council workings, to be found in E10 members speaking, not monolithically, but jointly or severally, as suits

73 Since 11 votes are needed for any decision, a mix of permanent and non-permanent members is always required to provide the capacity to make a decision. See generally Chapter 5.2; see also below Chapter 5, n 70 and associated text, in relation to the question of a quorum for Council proceedings.

74 Though the *Charter* does not set out concomitant duties—as Kishore Mahbubani puts it: 'What the UN Charter fails to spell out are the responsibilities associated with membership of the Council, permanent or elected. Nor has a consensus developed in practice on what those responsibilities are. The absence of a widely shared understanding [on this] has developed into a serious weakness of the organization.' See Kishore Mahbubani 'Permanent and Elected Council Members' in David M Malone (ed) *The UN Security Council: From the Cold War to the 21st Century* (Lynne Rienner Publishers, 2004), 253, 256.

75 See discussion in Chapter 6.2, noting that what 'representing' means in this context is not a given.

76 Such as by more 'penholding'—see, for example, UN SCOR, 8175th mtg, UN Doc S/PV.8175 (6 February 2018): in a discussion of working methods, six E10 members spoke to this and more than a dozen other states also intervened to similar effect. For an example of practice, see below Chapter 5, n 161 and associated text. For background—*In Hindsight: The Security Council Penholders* (30 September 2016) Security Council Report <https://www.securitycouncilreport.org/monthly_forecast/2016-10>. There is also more to be learned from the Council being challenged to meet the Article 28(1) requirement to 'function continuously' when finding itself located in one epicentre of the COVID-19 pandemic (see below (Chapter 5, n 80) and what this suggests about the prospects for success in seeing others take a greater share of penholding as discussed in Chapter 7.

the occasion and purpose. In turn, this would provide leverage for having E10 members adopt modes of conduct consistent with the idea that at least part of their function is to be a voice in its workings for those empowering the Council—where they should not be insensible to voices raised by, or on behalf of, those affected by what the Council does, even if such voices emanate from entities other than states.

Put another way, whatever any or all of the P5 may choose to do, if the UN's membership collectively persuades the E10 to 'explain and justify' the Council conduct as an element of their 'representative' role, the E10 will, in effect, become arbiters of Council accountability within the *Charter* design. Despite various imperfections in that design, their concerted efforts could provide a measure of accountability in aid of the Council's productiveness, and thus enhance the Council's capacity to fulfil its *Charter* remit. While acknowledging that any change will be challenging, this approach also leaves open the possibility that formal change to the *Charter* may prove to be possible in the future, and could further enhance such endeavours.

Because the documentary backdrop for this book is so important, it is worth noting that research involved collating empirical evidence by extensive perusal and analysis of Council deliberations and decisions (in light of when and how the Council came to be), and then framing and scoping Council accountability while drawing on the *Charter* in the context of international law. For these purposes, primary sources of international law in treaties and cases are not numerous, and primary authorities, such as Council resolutions, help but do not tell a complete story. Accordingly, additional sources included, for example, verbatim transcripts of all formal Council meetings (plus records of some Assembly proceedings); associated documents such as correspondence, draft resolutions, and the like; materials compiled by the UN Secretariat, including serial reporting such as the *Summary Statement by the Secretary-General on the matters of which the Security Council is seized and on the stage reached in their consideration*,[77] and periodical publications such as the *Repertoire of the Practice of the Security Council*;[78] plus scholarship and publications where international law and international relations intersect.

---

77 *The Summary Statement by the Secretary-General on the matters of which the Security Council is seized and on the stage reached in their consideration* has been issued by the Secretary-General since 1946 in accordance with the Council's *Provisional Rules of Procedure* (see below Chapter 2, n 112). On the referencing convention used herein, see below Chapter 5, n 22.

78 The *Repertoire of the Practice of the Security Council* 'provides comprehensive coverage of the Security Council's interpretation and application of the United Nations Charter and its own Provisional Rules of Procedure since 1946'—United Nations Security Council

Some relevant materials are quite readily gathered, but others rather less so. Empirical material relating to the Council's formal meetings, for example, is available from the UN's Official Documents System;[79] the Dag Hammarskjöld Library provides a digest of Council meetings and outcomes (with enumerated voting on proposed resolutions), for my purposes covering over 5,300 official meetings from 1994 to 2019 inclusive;[80] resolutions adopted are available from the Council's web site.

On the other hand, garnering data on non-veto defeat of a proposal before 1994 is quite challenging, and called for trawling verbatim records of more than 3,300 official meetings held from 1946 to 1993.[81] There is, of course, a wealth of information also associated with the Council's official meetings which is even less accessible: knowledge of all of those things that happen off the record, behind closed doors, in political processes that attend creation of decisions, determinations, recommendations, and other outputs of the Council. These things can now feature heavily in discerning its workings, but, arguably, did so rather less in the Council's early years—when verbatim meeting transcripts display the colour and texture of actual debate and unscripted results.

If the primary, or principal, focus of this book was, for example, accountability for the conduct of individual states in Council decision-making, that could be crucial. Here it is informative without being crucial, because the Council is a distinct actor in its own right, and my focus is on what the Council does along with whether and how to account for that. This is essentially in line with its status under law: the Council has powers as an entity, something more than the sum of its parts and not reducible simply to the interests of the states that constitute the Council from time to time. No doubt, what states are said to have done (and what is observed about that, or the reasons ascribed thereto), has explanatory value in probing how the Council works, for example, but what the Council has done is evidenced by *Council* actions and inactions as shown in official records and associated documents.[82]

About the Repertoire https://www.un.org/securitycouncil/content/repertoire/structure. This is published by the Secretariat as authorised by the General Assembly: see *Ways and means for making the evidence of customary law more readily available* GA Res 686(VII), UN GAOR, 7th sess, 400th plen mtg, UN Doc A/Res/686 (VII) (5 December 1952), [1(b)].

79 See United Nations *Official Documents System* <http://documents.un.org>.

80 See Dag Hammarskjöld Library *Security Council—Quick Links* <http://research.un.org/en/docs/sc/quick/meetings/2019>.

81 Which was done while this book was still a draft doctoral thesis, as part of reading the Council's entire history of formal deliberations in its meeting transcripts.

82 In any case, works by scholars and publicists who tap 'unofficial' and off-the-record information were considered as part of this research. Such sources include monographs based

Perusal of such materials shows that the Council's unparalleled place in the world, together with the intrinsically sui generis nature of the UN and its organs, mean that there are few analogies that might be drawn about the Council's governance, performance, or accountability, that are not (strongly) contested. Material limitations arise even in comparing the Council to other decision-making bodies in the international arena. Accordingly, to understand 'productiveness' as it applies to the Council, scope its accountability, and design a model to be articulated from this research, illustrative episodes serve to explore possibilities—in particular to compare the Council to itself over time.

To make this research accessible, guided by an interdisciplinary perspective on the territory over which Council decision-making ranges I selected various case examples to portray important legal and/or institutional angles on empirical material analysed. Intentionally not comprehensive in the usual manner of a case study,[83] these cases highlight pervasive and enduring themes observable in well over 70 years of Council activities.

---

on first-hand experience or drawing on close knowledge of Council events and/or practice. For example, on forming the UN, see Evatt, above n 37, and Dulles, below Chapter 2, n 73; for the case example on Timor, see Galvão Teles (with Canelas de Castro), below Chapter 6, n 46, and Robinson, below Chapter 6, n 92; as background on post-Cold War peacekeeping, see David Malone *Decision-Making in the UN Security Council: The Case of Haiti, 1990–1997* (Oxford University Press, 1998). Also relevant on this point are edited collections that feature insiders well versed and directly experienced in Council work, such as: David M Malone (ed) *The UN Security Council: From the Cold War to the 21st Century* (Lynne Rienner, 2004); Sebastian von Einsiedel, David M Malone and Bruno Stagno Ugarte (eds) *The UN Security Council in the 21st Century* (Lynne Rienner, 2016). To these were added materials based on close observation of the Council and put out by others, such as the nonprofit think tank, Security Council Report: Security Council Report *About Security Council Report* https://www.securitycouncilreport.org/about-security-council-report; plus reports funded by states using observations, both on and off the record, from states involved in the Council, including, for example:

a) the report by Simon Chesterman, *The UN Security Council and The Rule of Law—The Role of the Security Council in Strengthening a Rules-based International System: Final Report and Recommendations from the Austrian Initiative, 2004–2008*, appended to *Letter dated 18 April 2008 from the Permanent Representative of Austria to the United Nations addressed to the Secretary-General* A/63/69-S/2008/270 (7 May 2008); and

b) the series of reports submitted to the Security Council by the Government of Finland from sessions with Council members—the first session being in 2004 and the most recent result presently being *Letter dated 11 February 2020 from the Permanent Representative of Finland to the United Nations addressed to the President of the Security Council* S/2020/116 (11 February 2020).

83 Therefore sometimes known among practitioners as 'case cameos', acknowledging the briefer and more limited, possibly even one-sided, nature of the discussion.

Empirical material was oriented to factors pervasively likely to influence the Council's conduct as a decision-making body,[84] taken as the Council's size, and its constituent composition.[85] Constituting the Council by the *Charter* means that both the number of members, and the P5 as named, are factors usually assumed to be constant, while composition of the E6 (until 1965) or the E10 (since then) obviously could be assumed to be variable. But, in practice, are these reasonable assumptions?

Turning first to non-permanent members, terms of office are for two years and consecutive terms are not allowed under Article 23(2) of the *Charter*. The elected membership thus is variable in composition, but could, nevertheless, be a constant influence on decision-making practice of the Council, if either of the following were true:

(a) All UN member states seek election and, at some point, will serve on the Council, tending to randomise that influence.

(b) Time served on the Council is evenly distributed among states that do serve, tending to homogenise such influence—at least insofar as more time would allow a state to assert more influence than another serving less time.

The first proposition is readily dismissed as implausible: UN records highlight that, even after more than 70 years, over 50 states have not yet served on the Council.[86] That is, well over one in four current UN members either have not sought election, or were unsuccessful when they did.[87] The second proposition may also be dismissed after a moment of attention: analysis of UN records shows membership is not spread evenly over those states that are elected, looked at *independent* of when the state gained membership of the UN. For example, 'frequent members' of the Council include Japan (to 2019 inclusive, 22 years of elected membership despite not being an 'original member' of the UN), Brazil (20) and Argentina (18), followed by Colombia, India and Pakistan (14 years each).[88]

84 Again, as distinct from the question of factors affecting the decision-making behaviour of individual states when a member of the Council.

85 Including, for example, the state identities of the permanent members mandated under the *Charter*, but excluding features potentially influential while they lasted—such as the state identity of elected members, and/or the appointed representatives of any member.

86 See 'members': United Nations *United Nations Security Council* https://www.un.org/securitycouncil/.

87 Noting that one did, and was successful, but then did not take up office when elected—see below Chapter 4, n 97.

88 Looked at *relative* to when the state gained UN membership, some (again, such as Japan) also show more of a 'habit' of Council membership by spending more time on the Council

Thus, elected membership of the Council is variable, but perhaps not so much as it appears to be on first blush.

Turning to the assumed constants of the Council as a collective, the size is set by the *Charter* and so change in this factor is as likely as changing the *Charter*. This has happened only once, in the twilight of colonial power in the 1960s,[89] meaning that this is as constant as expected. The other assumed constant is the permanent members, and one view is that they have been unchanged since the UN's inception. However, this papers over cracks from potential political exigencies, because the *Charter* simply does not provide for changing the P5. This is more than a mere historical curiosity,[90] as events since indicate actual exigencies with potential to scupper a P5 membership. For example:

- Lithuania, Latvia, and Estonia, were annexed while the USSR was aligned with Nazi Germany, and this clouded the precise identity of the USSR when forming the UN.[91] Largely not recognised by western powers, these annexations had latent potential for ructions until those states re-asserted their independence in what proved to be an early signal towards the demise of the USSR.[92]
- World War II left the UK with quite a fragile economy and it was then 'the world's greatest debtor', so its post-war political survival was not a foregone conclusion.[93]

---

proportional to their time as a UN member. This perhaps facilitates the accretion of relevant experience and thus the development of a greater capacity to influence the workings of the Council (see also below Chapter 7, n 50). Compare, for example, Australia (an original UN member) and Germany (based on the membership of West Germany before 1973)—until the end of 2018, each had served ten years on the Council, but Germany has accumulated that over a noticeably shorter UN membership period (and is again elected for the period 2019–2020).

89 See below Chapter 2, n 26.

90 Which wrangling over the representation of China (by the nationalist or the communist regimes) may now be, since an accommodation was reached in this in 1971—see below Chapter 4, n 64, Chapter 5, n 69 and associated text, and Chapter 6, n 122 and associated text.

91 See the comprehensive discussion in Lauri Mälksoo *Illegal Annexation and State Continuity: The Case of the Incorporation of the Baltic States by the USSR* (Martinus Nijhoff, 2003).

92 That is: 'The United Kingdom and other States refused to recognise the illegal annexation by the Soviet Union in 1940 of the Baltic States (Estonia, Latvia and Lithuania) as *de jure*. Instead, they merely recognised that the Soviet Union exercised control of the three States *de facto*'—Anthony Aust *Handbook of International Law* (Cambridge, 2nd ed, 2010), 26; for more detail see Peter Van Elsuwege 'State Continuity and its Consequences: The Case of the Baltic States' (2003) 16(2) *Leiden Journal of International Law* 377.

93 Peden, above n 35, 61. After several years of the 'Brexit' debate, one might also be moved to speculate about its long term implications now that 'Brexit' looks set to become a reality.

- The collapse of France's Fourth Republic in 1958 did lead to the Fifth Republic, but some other outcome may not have provided a successor state.[94]
- After disintegration of the USSR, an internal agreement amongst Soviet republics saw the Russian Federation 'succeed' the USSR in positions of public power. For the Council seat, the change was between the 3024th and 3025th Council meetings in late 1991—the representative's new allegiance appearing unremarked in the verbatim meeting record.[95] Regarded as 'legally suspect',[96] only the distance of history confirms that Russia remained seated.

The overarching point here is that what may change in the Council, and what is widely presumed not to, are themselves more fluid than they initially appear. This means, amongst other things, that where there is sufficient will, a way might well be found to change what first appears unchanging and so is assumed to be unchangeable—even just in prosaic matters of work practice, where the exigencies forced upon it during the COVID-19 pandemic show again that when needs must, a way can be found even in the Council.

Although some attention is given to the entire history of the Council, such considerations suggested that more attention in this book be paid to:

(i) the initial period, to the end of 1965, during which time the Council had 11 members,[97] established many of the patterns of its decision-making conduct, and grappled with a first surge in UN membership arising in significant part from the passing of the colonial era; and

(ii) the post-Cold War period, from 1990, during which time the Council has been far more active and there has also been a second, post-colonial era surge in newly independent states seeking UN

94 See also above n 35.

95 See UN SCOR, 3024th mtg, UN Doc S/PV.3024 (23 December 1991), 1 (President); UN SCOR, 3025th mtg, UN Doc S/PV.3025 (31 December 1991), 1 (President).

96 Yehuda Z Blum 'Russia Takes Over the Soviet Union's Seat at the United Nations' (1992) 3(2) *European Journal of International Law* 354, 361. It is worth recalling that succession to the USSR membership was a problem for multiple international organisations, and state continuity and succession is also a broader problem in the history of the UN—see generally Rein Mullerson 'The Continuity and Succession of States, By Reference to the Former USSR and Yugoslavia' (1993) 42(3) *International and Comparative Law Quarterly* 473.

97 Until change became effective as a consequence of *Question of equitable representation on the Security Council and the Economic and Social Council* GA Res 1991 (XVIII) A, UN GAOR, 1285th plen mtg, UN Doc A/Res/1991 (XVIII) A (17 December 1963). See also below Chapter 2, n 26.

> membership and further diversifying the issues that may affect matters of international peace and security.

That attention is seen in the case examples highlighted in Chapters 3, 4, 5, and 6, but also in a variety of other illustrations sprinkled through this book.

The process of selecting these suggested some overall themes as texture in this discussion. For example, whether or not the ends of international peace and security might be said to justify the means used by the Council, what the Council does still appears inseparable from how it is done: as by no means the least consideration, both affect 'conditions under which justice and respect for the obligations arising [from] international law can be maintained'.[98]

Consequences of, or associated with, Council decisions are also far-reaching in both geography and time, underscoring why (legal) accountability remains important: all the world may benefit if the Council pursues its role in the international legal order productively, but, equally, all the world may suffer from misuse, abuse, disrepair, or desuetude, of its powers under the *Charter*, or neglect of its *Charter* obligations, especially where these activities or inactivities prove to be unproductive, counter-productive, or even deleterious, in relation to UN Purposes.

Overall, case examples, and research involved in selecting them, highlight that the world may—not at all unreasonably—hold expectations that the Council ought to make decisions that matter to its Functions under the *Charter*. Those Functions matter greatly to all the world, and how they are addressed very likely will continue to affect many generations yet to come.

Interrelating accountability and the capacity of the Council to fulfil its *Charter* Functions, the case examples further show the Council's formidable tasks are certainly endless, but need not be futile—since those things arise in important part from the actions of the Council itself.

Of course, navigating a productive path through that morass is certainly something of a balancing act between hope that is not unreasonably naïve, and pragmatism that is not unduly cynical. How so begins in the next chapter, looking at literature informing context for the Council and its conduct, its productiveness as an organ of an international organisation, and accountability as a potential aid to supporting that.

98 *Charter*, third preambular paragraph.

CHAPTER 2

Security Council Productiveness & Accountability

In ordinary language, the notions of productiveness and accountability intersect in relation to understanding the conduct of an actor. Both ideas speak to how the actor comports itself, but there is a key difference: an actor is productive to the extent that it did what it was supposed to do, whether or not another observes that, but accountability calls for an external viewpoint on what was done and whether that measured up to relevant standards for that conduct. As interrelated notions that are not uncommonly interdefined, productiveness and accountability thus remain distinct ideas: productiveness concerns what the actor was supposed to do in purposive terms, and to what extent they did it; accountability concerns assessment by another of what an actor did (or did not) do, compared to standards for the particulars of its conduct. Realisation of outcomes that the actor was anticipated to obtain (that is, productiveness in broad terms) is now likely to be recognised as one such standard for conduct.

Productiveness and accountability of international organisations present conceptual issues of this kind, but also many practical issues. There is no model that might be drawn from 'like' actors, as international organisations are said to be sui generis in nature, and are actually noticeably diverse in a range of practical dimensions. Equally, definition of such notions is not usually to be found in the organisation's constituent document, and the international legal order does not provide a general case that might be applied instead. If a relevant treaty is informative, it is very likely imperfectly so, and well-known challenges of treaty reform then loom as one part of the puzzles to be solved. Discourse about these notions may guide their application in a specific case, such as is seen in discussions of Council reform, but there are multiple ways in which that might unfold.

Accordingly, what scholars and practitioners have had to say about the Council's productiveness, and the necessity of, and possibilities for, its reform, give context for considering possibilities for bolstering Council productiveness via being accountable.

2.1 Productiveness

In his discussion of how international organisations have so far been theorised, Jan Klabbers notes that the dominant logic for explaining international

 | DOI:10.1163/9789004444300_003

organisations has been 'functionalism': states create them 'to do things they are unable or reluctant to do on their own, yet consider inherently useful'.[1] It is said that functionalism is 'a school with many rooms',[2] depending on how one perceives the power relationships involved, but a formally created international organisation may nonetheless benefit from object(s) stipulated in a constituent treaty, because 'productiveness' then is, inter alia, a matter of interpreting evidence about the extent to which object(s) may have been realised.

A 'productive' international organisation would, in very general terms, thus be expected to evidence that it was effective in addressing the purposes for which it was established.[3] One measure of it doing so is the extent to which it was seen to be producing salutary contributions towards those ends—especially if one accepts, broadly, that international organisations are 'obliged' to perform their functions as Michel Virally suggests.[4]

The work of international organisations typically is far from finite, however, and, in any case, they may be conceived of in differing ways. This will affect how 'productiveness' is understood in relation to a politico-legal actor—to be seen, perhaps, in some combination of talk and action. That is, from one perspective it may be clear that the UN and its organs ought to be something more than a 'mere debating chamber, a contemptible talk-shop',[5] but it is contestable how much more is needed—or what blend of talk and action would suffice.[6] For example, Article 1(1) of the *Charter* concerns the maintenance of

1 Klabbers, above Chapter 1, n 18, 624.
2 Alvarez, below n 70, 17.
3 Including as that may be agreed to evolve over time and experience—that is, it is not unreasonable for established purposes to be reshaped along the way, but those reshaped purposes still must be addressed to be productive in some fashion. The main point to note is the mutuality involved in reshaping, which is not sufficiently evident when changes in its purposes continue to be strongly contested. That mutuality is perhaps most clearly visible when amended Purposes are adopted to change a constituent document, but that is not the only way that may legitimately embody what its constituency comes to think that the organisation should do.
4 See Virally, above Chapter 1, n 20, [73].
5 Inis L Claude 'Collective Legitimization as a Political Function of the United Nations' (1966) 20(3) *International Organization* 367, 372.
6 For example, see Jan Klabbers 'Two Concepts of International Organization' (2005) 2 *International Organization Law Review* 277; Kenneth Anderson 'United Nations Collective Security and the United States Security Guarantee in an Age of Rising Multipolarity: The Security Council as the Talking Shop of the Nations' (2009) 10(1) *Chicago Journal of International Law* 55; see also Leo Gross 'Voting in the Security Council and the PLO' (1976) 70 *American Journal of International Law* 470, 490. See also generally Adam Roberts and Benedict Kingsbury *Presiding Over a Divided World: Changing UN Roles, 1945–1993* (Lynne Rienner, 1994), Chapter 4.

international peace and security,[7] at no time a simple matter, but that Article goes on to other Purposes—and on these it is certainly not hard to imagine debate on the productiveness of *any* amount of talk and action:

> 2. To develop friendly relations among nations based on respect for the principle of equal rights and self-determination of peoples, and to take other appropriate measures to strengthen universal peace;
> 3. To achieve international co-operation in solving international problems of an economic, social, cultural, or humanitarian character, and in promoting and encouraging respect for humans rights and for fundamental freedoms for all without distinction as to race, sex, language, or religion; and
> 4. To be a centre for harmonizing the actions of nations in the attainment of these common ends.

Constituent documents also remain subject to interpretation: the *Charter* is not unusual in that its clarity of expression is not unreasonable in context, but complexities arise because, firstly, its provisions are cast widely, and, secondly, its drafters deliberately omitted judicial review and left each principal organ to its own interpretation devices.[8]

For international organisations, productiveness is a relatively recent issue anyhow. In looking at why states may choose to act via international organisations, Kenneth Abbott and Duncan Snidal summarise that by 'taking advantage of [their] centralisation and independence ... states are able to achieve goals that they cannot accomplish on a decentralised basis',[9] and as Jan Klabbers points out, for much of the twentieth century the tradition was portraying international organisations as 'innately good, socially beneficial creatures'.[10] On the other hand, Michael Barnett and Martha Finnemore observe that international relations theories have paid 'little attention to how [international organisations] actually behave after they are created',[11] and 'normative evaluation of

7 See above Chapter 1, n 23 and associated text.

8 See above Chapter 1, n 47 and associated text.

9 Kenneth W Abbott and Duncan Snidal 'Why States Act through Formal International Organizations' (1998) 42(1) *Journal of Conflict Resolution* 3, 29.

10 Jan Klabbers 'Unity, Diversity, Accountability: The Ambivalent Concept of International Organisation' (2013) 14(1) *Melbourne Journal of International Law* 149, 153.

11 Michael N Barnett and Martha Finnemore 'The Politics, Power, and Pathologies of International Organizations' (1999) 53(4) *International Organization* 699, 699. See also below Chapter 2, n 100 and associated text.

[their] behaviour should be an empirical and ethical matter, not an analytic assumption'.[12] Klabbers also notes that as the twentieth century wore on, 'practical developments [such as] collapse of the International Tin Council'[13] meant that these institutions 'started to lose some of their glamour'.[14] Further, in an overview of the 'state of the art of legal thought about [international organisations] as legal entities in a legal environment',[15] Anne Peters assesses that:

> In the post-1989 legal landscape, a need was felt to adapt international organizations to a new political, military, economic and legal surrounding, and to respond to new demands on their effectiveness and legitimacy. Effectiveness deficits stem not only from waste or mismanagement, but also from legal design.[16]

Of course, even taking it that member states intend these creations to do things—that is, to be productive in some way—'productiveness' is hardly a simple variable. The nature of geopolitical purposes allotted to such institutions makes complexity unavoidable, if more so in maintaining international peace and security than in exchanging of infrastructure services (telecommunications, mail, and so on). So 'productiveness' may not be measurable in meaningful terms, or at all, and a qualitative assessment will be challenging to agree in relevant dimensions: how well the thing was done, what was foregone to get it done and if that proved to be worthwhile, if it suited those involved, its cost-effectiveness,[17] the nature and extent of complaints, and so on. Still, seeking to understand the extent to which the Council has, or is seen to have, maintained or restored international peace and security, might start, for example, with exploring the Council's involvement in wars, as John Dunbabin has done. Dunbabin concludes that the Council 'is seldom the medium through

12 Ibid, 727.

13 Klabbers, above Chapter 1, n 18, 623. For background, see Romana Sadurska and C M Chinkin 'The Collapse of the International Tin Council: A Case of State Responsibility?' (1990) 30(4) *Virginia Journal of International Law* 845.

14 Klabbers, above Chapter 1, n 18, 624.

15 Peters, above Chapter 1, n 21, 33.

16 Peters, above Chapter 1, n 21, 38. See also discussion in Richard Collins and Nigel D White 'Moving Beyond the *Autonomy-Accountability* Dichotomy: Reflections on Institutional Independence in the International Legal Order' (2010) 7(1) *International Organizations Law Review* 1 (emphasis in original).

17 Or 'efficiency', speaking broadly to the effort and resources required to deliver whatever was actually delivered, rather than whether that was the appropriate thing to deliver in achieving the purposes at hand (the concern of 'productiveness'/'effectiveness').

which high profile conflicts are addressed'.[18] In his contribution to a volume on the future of international law, Bardo Fassbender similarly looks briefly at how the Council has carried out its mandate or lived up to the expectations of the UN's founders. On that point, he concludes that:

> [What] can safely be said (in perhaps overly moderate language), [is] that the Security Council accomplished its object of maintaining "international peace and security" (understood as global peace) only very inadequately.[19]

As a sample practitioner's perspective, prior to becoming UN Secretary-General António Guterres repeatedly highlighted the Council's inability to assist in resolving, or even progressing, the situation in Syria since 2011. In April 2013, for example, when briefing the Council on the situation in his capacity as UN High Commissioner for Refugees:

> [He] was almost tempted to limit his statement to just 10 seconds because everything he had said in February remained true, "but, it all got much worse". If nothing politically dramatic happens, "things will go on getting worse".[20]

As is well known, the Council did not find a compromise, Syria proving to be a serious bone of contention among the Council's permanent members for years, even as the situation continued to deteriorate.[21] Having already assessed that 'there is more and more impunity for those starting conflicts [but a] seeming utter inability of the international community to work together

18 J P D Dunbabin 'The Security Council in the Wings: Exploring the Security Council's Non-Involvement in Wars' in Vaughan Lowe, Adam Roberts, Jennifer Welsh and Dominik Zaum (eds) *The United Nations Security Council and War: The Evolution of Thought and Practice since 1945* (Oxford, 2008), 494, 514. He does confirm that it is ' "seldom", though not "never" '. See also below Chapter 6, n 16 and associated text.

19 Bardo Fassbender 'The Security Council: Progress is Possible but Unlikely' in Antonio Cassese (ed) *Realizing Utopia: The Future of International Law* (Oxford, 2012), 55. See also Edward C Luck 'Why the United Nations Underperforms at Preventing Mass Atrocities' (2018) 11(3) *Genocide Studies and Prevention: An International Journal* 32.

20 United Nations Security Council 'Top UN Official Says Situation in Syria "Humanitarian Catastrophe", Calls on Security Council to Take Actions Needed to End "Brutal Conflict" ' (Meetings Coverage, SC/10981, 18 April 2013).

21 Security Council Report 'Syria: A Council Divided' on *What's in Blue* (17 April 2018) <http://www.whatsinblue.org>.

to stop wars and build and preserve peace',[22] in April 2018 Guterres, by then speaking as UN Secretary-General, stated to the Security Council that 'Syria represents the most serious threat to international peace and security in the world today', and he was moved to 'remind [UN] Member States that there is an obligation, particularly when dealing with matters of peace and security, to act consistently with the Charter … and with international law in general.'[23]

On the point of avoiding wars by peaceful settlement of disputes—that is, maintaining rather than needing to restore international peace and security—the observations of practitioners are routinely no more positive. As reported by the highly regarded nonprofit think tank, Security Council Report,[24] for example, a member of the Security Council said that conflict prevention is 'the most important thing we do, but the thing we are worst at'.[25]

No (reasonably) ready or (moderately) uncomplicated basis thus arises from the *Charter* for evidencing a 'productive' Council, but there appears good reason to believe that the Council is not as productive as it should be, or as circumstances call on it to be. Accordingly, revisiting discussion of *Charter* reform may provide more clues as to what scholars and practitioners find important in Council performance, and which would therefore be interesting in terms of its productiveness.

22 United Nations High Commissioner For Refugees 'Worldwide displacement hits all-time high as war and persecution increase' (UNHCR News, 18 June 2015).

23 UN SCOR, 8233rd mtg, UN Doc S/PV.8233 (14 April 2018), 2. For a potted history of related events since 2011, see Security Council Report 'Chronology of Events: Syria' Security Council Report (2 April 2018) <https://www.securitycouncilreport.org/chronology/syria.php>; see also Security Council Report *The Rule of Law: Retreat from Accountability?* (Research Report No. 3, Security Council Report, 23 December 2019). The story of Syria is picked up again in later chapters—in particular, see below Chapter 5, n 163 to 170, and associated text, and below Chapter 6, n 188 and 189, and associated text.

24 For example, UN SCOR, 8175th mtg, UN Doc S/PV.8175 (6 February 2018)—when the Executive Director of Security Council Report was afforded an opportunity to brief the Council.

25 Security Council Report *Can the Security Council Prevent Conflict?* (Research Report No. 1, Security Council Report, 20 February 2017), 16. The view expressed corresponds to what others have reported about views from Council members: 'in the back of their minds they felt that they were failing', because 'a series of conflicts in which the Council was not doing well' could give 'reason to doubt the relevance of the Council'—see *Letter dated 26 May 2016 from the Permanent Representative of Finland to the United Nations addressed to the President of the Security Council* S/2016/506 (2 June 2016), 10.

2.2 Reform

In terms of formal change to the UN's *Charter*, so far the sole amendment to the Council's design was to increase the non-permanent members from six to ten. That change took effect from its first meeting in 1966,[26] and the Council has operated since then with 15 members.

It is not the change itself which is informative here, so much as reasons advanced for making it. As captured in the General Assembly's resolution, the rationale was that a larger UN called for a larger Council. The increase would provide 'for a more adequate geographical representation of non-permanent members and making it a *more effective organ* for carrying out its functions under the Charter'.[27]

Despite that desire for a more productive Council, as is well-known it was Cold War divisions that proved to be the more profound influence on its capacity, for quite some time by curtailing what the Council could do at all.

Interest in whether the Council was doing what it was put there to do was rekindled, however, by a significant upswing in the Council's activity from the early 1990s, after the Cold War was seen to be passing with the breakup of the USSR.

In 1993, the General Assembly resolved to create a Working Group to address concerns about the Council.[28] The Working Group has since debated various questions that are relatable to how, and how well, the Council does its work (productiveness, in broad terms)—issues such as the size and composition of the Council, voting arrangements (including, but not only, the veto power),

---

26 As a consequence of *Question of equitable representation on the Security Council and the Economic and Social Council* GA Res 1991 (XVIII) A, UN GAOR, 1285th plen mtg, UN Doc A/Res/1991 (XVIII) A (17 December 1963). After entering into force as a treaty variation, this first applied to elections for the term of office beginning 1 January 1966, meaning the Council functioned with only 11 of 15 members from September to December in 1965: the treaty variation came into force on 31 August 1965, when it had (in accordance with the *Charter*, Article 108) been ratified by two-thirds of the UN member states including all of the Council's permanent members, but the Assembly opted not to fill the new seats out of synchronisation with the usual pattern of elections (see discussion in Simma et al, above Chapter 1, n 29, 752).

27 Ibid, second preambular paragraph (emphasis added).

28 Created by *Question of equitable representation on and increase in the membership of the Security Council* GA Res 48/26, UN GAOR, 48th sess, 26th plen mtg, UN Doc A/Res/48/26 (3 December 1993). For background, see Bardo Fassbender 'Pressure for Security Council Reform' in David M Malone (ed) *The UN Security Council: From the Cold War to the 21st Century* (Lynne Rienner Publishers, London, 2004), 341, 342.

and day-to-day working methods.[29] With that debate ongoing, the Working Group has been, to an extent, reconfigured into an inter-governmental negotiation process in September 2008, by the Assembly's Decision 62/557.[30] Tangible *Charter* reform outcomes remain a work in progress.[31]

A decade into the Working Group's activities, another push for *Charter* change was instigated by then UN Secretary-General Kofi Annan, leading to vigorous discourse in UN circles about needs and possibilities for significant change to the organisation. Reform of the Council was said to be the 'lynchpin'[32] of Annan's wider intention to address 'how our existing policies and institutions have done'.[33] In particular, he asked a High-Level Panel on Threats, Challenges and Change to 'make recommendations for strengthening the United Nations so that it can provide collective security for all'. In reporting back, the Panel put forward 101 recommendations,[34] including that the Council be enlarged (but without altering the veto arrangements).[35] Council productiveness surfaced when the Panel said reform should, inter alia, 'not impair [its] effectiveness',[36] and in an overarching remark that the Council 'needs greater credibility, legitimacy and representation to do all that we demand of it'.[37]

---

29 For a synopsis, see, for example, Joachim Müller *Reforming the United Nations: A Chronology* (Brill Nijhoff, 2016), Chapter 2.

30 *Resolutions and Decisions adopted by the General Assembly during its sixty-second session: Volume III 23 December 2007–15 September 2008* 62nd sess, UN Doc A/62/49(Vol.III) (2008), 106.

31 It may be too generous to allow that the discussion prompted in and around the Working Group itself has a value despite there being no tangible output, but the airing of such opinion does have a place if one accepts the purpose of a related forum—such as the General Assembly—to be in some part talk and some part action. In any case, the UN is not alone here—see, for example, Peters, above Chapter 1, n 21, 38.

32 Spencer M Zifcak 'United Nations Reform: Heading North or South?' (2006) 18(3) *Global Change, Peace & Security* 135, 138.

33 *Note by the Secretary-General* 59th sess, Agenda Item 55, UN Doc A/59/565 (2 December 2004), 1.

34 Ibid: this enclosed the report: *A more secure world: our shared responsibility* (*Report of the High Level Panel on Threats, Challenges and Change*).

35 The Panel proffered two models for specific reconfiguration of the Council: for further discussion, see for example Zifcak, above n 32; Yehuda Blum 'Proposals for UN Security Council Reform' (2005) 99(3) *American Journal of International Law* 632; Bardo Fassbender 'On the Boulevard of Broken Dreams: The Project of a Reform of the UN Security Council after the 2005 World Summit' (2005) 2(2) *International Organizations Law Review* 391. See also Müller, below n 38.

36 See above n 34, 88.

37 Ibid, 64.

In so saying, the Panel's report did not manage to inspire actual reform of the Council, but it did signal staple themes about the Council since then.[38] Taken together, those themes strongly suggest a desire to improve Council productiveness, to be obtained, or at least facilitated, by amending its constituent document—but the amount of effort invested to date contrasts rather starkly with a paucity of results. Cooperation between states is enabled in a legal framework, but this is a reminder that the endeavour remains inherently political and interest-laden: such frustrated reform efforts may show little more than that international cooperation struggles to surpass being 'just a collection of states pursuing their own interests',[39] or, in the words of Edward Luck:

> To put it crudely, much of the reform debate, at its basest level, is a struggle over political turf, over who is perceived to gain or lose influence within the Organization if the proposed changes are enacted or implemented.[40]

Such realities may matter less if the rationale or reasoning given for reforms still held water. However, scholarly investigation suggests they more show an untidy intersection of ideas linking productiveness and accountability, such as what could be said to show the Council delivering on its remit, and what standards apply to the Council—not least so that meeting those standards would reinforce its legitimacy. In analysing Council legitimacy, for example, Ian Hurd finds that behind 'every proposal for Council reform is a different model for how legitimacy, effectiveness, and membership fit together'.[41] Importantly, Hurd identifies 'five distinct claims about the connection between membership and legitimacy, [but each] is either logically inconsistent or empirically implausible',[42] as each 'ultimately relies on prior assumptions that are themselves questionable'.[43]

---

38 See, for example, Joachim Müller *Reforming the United Nations: The Struggle for Legitimacy and Effectiveness* (Martinus Nijhoff, 2006); Sabine Hassler *Reforming the Security Council Membership: The illusion of representativeness* (Taylor & Francis, 2012); Peter Nadin *UN Security Council Reform* (Taylor & Francis, 2016).

39 Joel E Oestreich 'Intergovernmental Organizations in International Relations Theory and as Actors in World Politics' in Bob Reinalda (ed) *The Ashgate Research Companion to Non-State Actors* (Ashgate, 2011), 172.

40 Edward Luck 'Reforming the United Nations: Lessons from a History in Progress' in Jean E Krasno (ed) *The United Nations: Confronting the Challenges of a Global Society* (Lynne Rienner, 2004), 359, 364.

41 Ian Hurd 'Myths of Membership: The Politics of Legitimation in UN Security Council Reform' (2008) 14(2) *Global Governance* 199, 200.

42 Ibid, 199.

43 Ibid, 213.

Thus it may be a little generous to credit UN reform debate with identifying specific changes needed from the Council and why, but such credit is, anyhow, offset substantially by the inability to find a way to negotiate how that change might be realised. While discourse may have a value of its own, change cannot possibly help unless it actually occurs.

In any case, while unsuccessful reform initiatives mean the Council is working to a 1945 design, time continues to march on—so successfully resolving original deficiencies would not necessarily bring the Council closer to a design suitable for addressing the world as it may soon be in 2025, or then be in 2035. That is, even if one of the many reform proposals had been adopted, such as to enfranchise a contemporary power by permanent membership (and so recognise its capacity to contribute to the UN), that says nothing about how long that power might last in evolving geopolitics, or to what extent it may prevail over up-and-coming others—and then what is to be done if or when the wheel of fortune turns again.

Accordingly, the enduring point from reform efforts to date is that they will never be enough on their own. If those headlines can provide a direction in which to evolve, however, other means may be found to better navigate and negotiate the needed evolution. On that score, Joachim Müller's chronological narrative of Council reform highlights that 'the longest negotiation process in UN history' has been associated with changes to practice—such as the move for the Council to more often meet in open session, or, on peacekeeping, to consult (to some extent) with troop-contributing countries.[44]

With that in mind, the question becomes whether being (more) accountable would somehow better inform the rules adopted, practices followed, and understandings shared, and, by the form that accountability takes, continue to do so over time.

2.3 Accountability

From a bare bones idea of explaining or justifying conduct,[45] several strands of issues have been noted that impact upon how accountability might be understood, and the forms that it might take,[46] in relation to an actor such as the Council. These include that:

---

44 Plus some more mundane measures such as publication of the provisional agenda and the monthly forecast of the work programme—see Müller, above n 29, 38.

45 See above Chapter 1, n 60 and associated text.

46 Where one form of accountability connected to the law is being held accountable in court.

(a) accountability, as it is now understood, post-dates creation of the UN and is not applied systematically as a term in international law or international relations;
(b) the idiosyncratic nature of international organisation itself weighs heavily in characterising how notions of accountability may be relevant, and dealing with limitations on how they may be applied; and
(c) recent attempts to formally articulate related legal concepts in UN circles have not met with notable success (yet).

Addressing each of these in turn, accountability is, to begin with, a comparatively modern concept. When assessing its scope and meaning in public administration,[47] Richard Mulgan notes that accountability is a 'word which a few decades or so ago was used only rarely and with relatively restricted meaning [but it now] crops up everywhere'.[48] In setting out a conceptual framework, Mark Bovens highlights that:

> Since the late twentieth century, the Anglo-Saxon world in particular has witnessed a transformation of the traditional bookkeeping function in public administration into a much broader form of public accountability [noting that various other languages] have no exact equivalent and do not (yet) distinguish semantically between "responsibility" and "accountability".[49]

In discussing ways to conceptualise accountability, Bovens finds it is used as 'a synonym for many loosely defined political desiderata, such as good governance, transparency, equity, democracy, efficiency, responsiveness, responsibility and integrity'.[50] He sees it as a term which is 'an essentially contested and contestable concept *par excellence*',[51] which accords with views that accountability is 'chameleon-like'.[52] In international law scholarship, Jutta Brunnée

---

47 Noting that: '"Publicness" is immanent ... increasingly in global governance, where it applies to public entities rather than to identifiable global publics'—Benedict Kingsbury 'The Concept of "Law" in Global Administrative Law' (2009) 20(1) *European Journal of International Law* 23, 23.

48 Richard Mulgan '"Accountability": An Ever-Expanding Concept?' (2000) 78(3) *Public Administration* 555, 555. See also above Chapter 1, n 53.

49 Bovens, above Chapter 1, n 60, 449.

50 Bovens, above Chapter 1, n 7, 946.

51 Ibid, 949.

52 Mulgan, above n 48, 555; then see, for example, Robert O Keohane 'The Concept of Accountability in World Politics and the Use of Force' (2003) 24(4) *Michigan Journal of International Law* 1121; Philippe C Schmitter 'The Ambiguous Virtues of Accountability' (2004) 15(4) *Journal of Democracy* 47; David Held 'Democratic Accountability and

similarly points out that despite 'increasingly frequent invocation by international lawyers, the concept of "accountability" has not acquired a clearly defined legal meaning'.[53] Observing that 'focus of contemporary legal thought on international organizations [has shifted] from constituting and enabling organizations to constraining them',[54] Anne Peters notes 'the new buzzword is "accountability" ', interest in which arises in part because:

> The functionalist paradigm [focused] exclusively on the relationship between the organization and its members states [so it] is thus inherently unsuited to take note of the interests of affected outsiders [and] tends to lend acceptance to the idea that the ends justify the means. There is little or no room for the rule of law, for checks and balances, and for legal constraints.[55]

In particular, functionalism addresses only one of three 'legal dynamics', as Jan Klabbers phrases it—the interaction of the organisation with member states, but not that between its organs or with its staff (internal), or with the rest of the world (external).[56]

Such scholarship underscores a key aspect of accountability: it arises in a relationship between (legal) persons,[57] presumably to serve purposes associated with that relationship. Accountability thus takes its primary character from the societal nature of the relationship in which it is present, and then is a means to the relationship's ends. How accountability is to be obtained—the use of means and forms—should therefore be coherent with the purposes that accountability is intended to serve in that relationship.[58]

Political Effectiveness from a Cosmopolitan Perspective' (2004) 39(2) *Government and Opposition* 364.

53 Jutta Brunnée, 'International Legal Accountability through the Lens of the Law of State Responsibility' (2005) XXXVI(1) *Netherlands Yearbook of International Law* 21, 22.

54 Peters, above Chapter 1, n 21, 41.

55 Peters, above Chapter 1, n 21, 42. She adds that neglect of accountability has, inter alia, prompted revisiting global constitutionalism to focus on its 'constraining and checking' function (ibid, 43)—see, for example, Erika de Wet 'The Constitutionalization of Public International Law' in Michel Rosenfeld and András Sajó (eds) *Oxford Handbook of Comparative Constitutional Law* (Oxford, 2012); and considering possibilities for global administrative law (ibid, 44)—see, for example, Benedict Kingsbury, Nico Krisch and Richard B Stewart 'The Emergence of Global Administrative Law' (2005) 68(3) *Law and Contemporary Problems* 15.

56 See Klabbers, above Chapter 1, n 18, in his introduction and in discussion of 'functionalism'; see also above n 1 and associated text.

57 Whether a natural person, or a juristic/juridical person (a result of legal construction).

58 Though interest in accountability, and the purposes to which it is bent, are now so omnipresent one could well sympathise with the view that accountability 'has gradually

Looking at forms that accountability might take, others emphasise its dialogic quality—for example, Andreas Schedler says that this 'makes both parties speak and engages them both in public debate [being] opposed not only to mute power but also to unilateral speechless controls of power'.[59] In their 'widely regarded' article on accountability and abuses of power in world politics,[60] Ruth Grant and Robert Keohane say accountability characteristically requires that:

> [Some] actors have the right to hold other actors to a set of standards, to judge whether they have fulfilled their responsibilities in the light of these standards, and to impose sanctions if they determine that these responsibilities have not been met.[61]

Mark Bovens takes a similar approach, where 'the possibility of sanctions [is] a constitutive element [which differentiates] non-committal provision of information and being held to account'.[62] Bovens also, however, sees that:

> … the term sanction would bias towards negative forms of scrutiny. Many accountability arrangements are not focused on finding fault with actors [so he uses] a somewhat more neutral expression: the actor may *face consequences*.[63]

Concerned with controlling powerful actors, Grant and Keohane model accountability based on power relationships in national politics. They distinguish between a basis in *participation*, by those affected by the actions of the powerful ('direct democracy' and 'populist' approaches), or a basis in *delegation*,

become a goal in itself [and] one of those evocative political words that be used to patch up a rambling argument, to evoke an image of trustworthiness, fidelity and justice, or to hold critics at bay' (Bovens, above Chapter 1, n 60, 449).

59 Andreas Schedler 'Conceptualizing Accountability' in Andreas Schedler, Larry Diamond and Marc F Plattner (eds) *The Self-Restraining State: Power and Accountability in New Democracies* (Lynne Rienner Publishers, Boulder, 1999), 15. His point is admittedly linked to democracy, but remains relevant in a wider variety of cases related to (public) powerholders. There is no intention to prioritise democracy in considerations taken up here. See also below Chapter 7, n 16.

60 Michael Goodhart 'Democratic Accountability in Global Politics: Norms, not Agents' (2011) 73(1) *Journal of Politics* 45, 46.

61 Ruth W Grant and Robert O Keohane 'Accountability and Abuses of Power in World Politics' (2005) 99(1) *American Political Science Review* 29, 29.

62 Bovens, above Chapter 1, n 60, 451.

63 Ibid, 452 (emphasis in original).

which entrusts the powerful with a particular capacity (via 'principal-agent' or 'trustee' connections).[64] Looking at the extent to which opportunities for these arise in world politics, they discuss seven types of accountability, including legal accountability in the usual sense of an actor being held accountable in a court. That much said, Grant and Keohane do not, for their part, assume that accountability need necessarily be interdefined with democracy. Instead, noting weaknesses that concern others on the 'democratic' accountability of actors,[65] they observe that:

> Recognizing new possibilities for accountability requires abandoning the belief that global accountability, to be genuine, must conform to abstract, maximal principles of democratic organization. Such a belief prevents us from recognising specific opportunities for limiting abuses of power.[66]

In all of these forms and descriptions, and consistent with the work of what is now a host of scholars (including those mentioned below), being accountable is somehow interactive and dialogic, and originates in a relationship carrying the capacity for one actor to make judgements about the conduct of another: an agent might be expected to 'explain or justify' its conduct in response to a principal who empowered them, the elected official to those who did the electing, and so on.

Beyond those general concerns, however, idiosyncrasies of international organisation bring other burdens when developing an understanding of accountability from a burgeoning, multi-disciplinary literature. There is, for example, a substantial body of scholarship around the concept of global governance, although what that concept may signify is itself contested.[67] For

64 Grant and Keohane, above n 61, 31. See also, for example, Mathias Koenig-Archibugi 'Accountability' in Jacob Katz Cogan, Ian Hurd and Ian Johnstone (eds) *The Oxford Handbook of International Organizations* (Oxford, 2016).

65 Noting that the *Charter* provides little indication that democratic operation of the Council was intended by its drafters, this line of discussion concerns, for example, a 'democracy deficit' plus a confounding lack of a demos: Robert A Dahl 'Can International Organizations be Democratic? A Skeptic's View' in Ian Shapiro and Casiano Hacker-Cordón (eds) *Democracy's Edges* (Cambridge, 1999); Joseph S Nye Jr 'Globalization's Democratic Deficit: How to Make International Institutions More Accountable' (2001) 80(4) *Foreign Affairs* 2; cf Joshua Cohen and Charles F Sabel 'Global Democracy?' (2005) 37 *New York University Journal of International Law and Politics* 763.

66 Grant and Keohane, above n 61, 41. See also, for example, Mark Philp 'Delimiting Democratic Accountability' (2009) 57(1) *Political Studies* 28, 47.

67 In his article referring to a wide cross section of relevant scholarship, Mulieri notes that 'disagreement on the definition of global governance is the rule … First, there is no agreement on the extent to which global governance succeeds, as an explanatory category, in

example, Anne-Marie Slaughter examines accountability of networks engaged in such purposes,[68] and some models for global governance.[69] Others, notably José Alvarez, argue that international organisations do make law though they 'are not intended to be proto-states or governments in the making'.[70] Alvarez also clearly demonstrates the wider, and definitely non-trivial, effects such institutions have had on the international legal order,[71] even though it is states' practice that is usually taken to be the basis for customary international law.

While adopting a model of accountability will be fundamentally hampered by disagreement on the nature of the power relationships involved,[72] such discussion connects to Council productiveness wherever accountability may strengthen its capacity to have its decisions implemented. This arises with regard to the lawfulness of Council decisions, for example, where states may resist decisions that appear unlawful, even without an effective avenue for that to be determined in court. Similarly, legitimacy accorded to Council decisions by states may be impacted upon by the decisions it makes as well as how it makes them—and by how states understand the nature of the power relationships involved.

Whatever way that relationship may be understood, not enough lawfulness or legitimacy thus stands to be unproductive, counter-productive, or deleterious, for results that the Council is seeking, but how much of those things is enough is an unfinished conversation. John Foster Dulles, a member of the USA delegation to UNCIO in San Francisco in 1945, later famously asserted that it is 'not a body that merely enforces agreed law [but] is a law unto itself';[73] on

describing the transformations that have followed the end of the Cold War [and second,] to the extent that we can distinguish an analytical and normative concept of global governance, disagreements also abound on which institutional design global governance should take, and whether this idea is desirable to foster productive reflection on the "democratic" transformations of agency at the global level'—see Mulieri, above Chapter 1, n 45, 15.

68 Anne-Marie Slaughter 'The Accountability of Government Networks' (2001) 8(2) *Indiana Journal of Global Legal Studies* 347.

69 Anne-Marie Slaughter 'Disaggregated Sovereignty: Towards the Public Accountability of Global Government Networks' (2004) 39(2) *Government and Opposition* 159; Anne-Marie Slaughter *A New World Order* (Princeton, 2004).

70 José E Alvarez *International Organizations as Law-makers* (Oxford, 2005), 15.

71 José E Alvarez *The Impact of International Organizations on International Law* (Brill Nijhoff, 2017).

72 Similarly, discussion of 'checks and balances' also faces this—see, for example, Klabbers, above Chapter 1, n 52.

73 John Foster Dulles *War or Peace* (Harrap, London, 1950), 194. For comprehensive discussion of this point, see Mohammed Bedjaoui *The New World Order and the Security Council: Testing the Legality of Its Acts* (Martinus Nijhoff, 1994).

the other hand, the International Criminal Tribunal for the Former Yugoslavia has more recently said:

> The Security Council is ... subjected to certain constitutional limitations, however broad its powers under the constitution may be [and] neither the text nor the spirit of the charter conceives of the Security Council as *legibus solutus* (unbound by law).[74]

As well as a body of scholarship on this point in international organisation,[75] and on the role played by legitimacy in obtaining compliance in the international legal order,[76] scholars such as Ian Hurd particularly examine the role and contribution of legitimacy in the Council's work: appearing more legitimate may be an active strategy for increasing compliance, pursued while 'many other actors are working to delegitimize international organizations to reduce their power'.[77] Others probe contributions to the rule of law from, or by, the Council.[78] The UN is an organisation created, in part, to 'establish conditions under which justice and respect for the obligations arising from treaties and other sources of international law can be maintained',[79] so accountability may be important for UN and Council 'productiveness' as an inherent element of,[80] or somehow promoting,[81] the rule of law.

---

74 *Prosecutor v Dusko Tadic a/k/a 'Dulé'*, (*Appeal on Jurisdiction*) (International Criminal Tribunal for the Former Yugoslavia, Appeals Chamber, Case No. IT-94-1-AR72, 2 October 1995), (1996) 35 *International Legal Materials* 32 [28].

75 For an overview, see Jeffrey L Dunoff 'The Law and Politics of International Organizations' in Jacob Katz Cogan, Ian Hurd and Ian Johnstone (eds) *The Oxford Handbook of International Organizations* (Oxford, 2016).

76 See, for example, Harold Hongju Koh 'Why Do Nations Obey International Law?' (1997) 106(8) *Yale Law Journal* 2599; Thomas M Franck 'Legitimacy in the International System' (1988) 82 *American Journal of International Law* 705; Abram Chayes and Antonia Handler Chayes 'On compliance' (1993) 47(2) *International Organization* 175. See also Louis Henkin *How Nations Behave: Law and Foreign Policy* (Columbia, 2nd ed, 1979); 'How Are Nations Behaving?' (2002) 96 *Proceedings of the Annual Meeting* (*American Society of International Law*) 205. See also the overview of models in Mulieri, above Chapter 1, n 45.

77 Ian Hurd 'Legitimacy and Authority in International Politics' (1999) 53(2) *International Organization* 379, 383. See also generally Hurd, above Chapter 1, n 25.

78 Jeremy Farrell and Hilary Charlesworth (eds) *Strengthening the Rule of Law through the UN Security Council* (Routledge, 2016).

79 *Charter*, third preambular paragraph.

80 See generally Jeremy Matam Farrall *United Nations Sanctions and the Rule of Law* (Cambridge, 2007).

81 Jeremy M Farrall 'Rule of Accountability or Rule of Law? Regulating the UN Security Council's Accountability Deficits' (2014) 19(3) *Journal of Conflict & Security Law* 389, 404.

Of course, there are much-mooted issues of defining the rule of law,[82] and no simple continuum runs from adherence to it and productiveness, through to non-adherence and unproductiveness. There is a wider problem, however, as put by Steven Wheatley:

> The difficulty with the reliance on a concept of law developed at the level of the state, and based ultimately on an idea of law as a system of coercive, institutionalised norm enforcement, is that the concept proves problematic when applied in other contexts.[83]

Put another way, the international legal order is part of a societal ecosystem surrounding collectives of sovereign states, a situation diverging significantly from the legal system of a state: dynamics for accountability are shaped by the voluntaristic nature of states' participation in such institutions and, on the other hand, by those institutions typically lacking the accoutrements of law-making and law-enforcement within a state—such as legal competence (and practical capacity) to legislate routinely on a plenary basis, or to compel judicial or other authoritative review of alleged wrongdoing,[84] or otherwise to coerce specific conduct, or changes to conduct, by means of enforceable sanctions.[85] The strengthening of such institutions by amending their constituent document is not readily done, as has certainly proven to be the case with the UN. So one might need to engage with the principles behind rules, or reinforce available institutions using preventative and post-operative measures, as Philip Selznick suggests in his approach to the rule of law.[86]

---

82 For an overview, see Brian Tamanaha 'The History and Elements of the Rule of Law' [2012] *Singapore Journal of Legal Studies* 232.

83 Steven Wheatley 'A Democratic Rule of International Law' (2011) 22(2) *European Journal of International Law* 525, 531.

84 When judicial review remains challenging to obtain and there are multiple other hurdles, including the operation of immunities—see below n 97 and 98, and associated text, and complexities of control and attribution of conduct—see, for example, Security Council Report *Sexual Exploitation and Abuse by UN Peacekeeping Personnel* (Update Report No. 3, Security Council Report, 20 February 2006); Terry D Gill 'Legal Aspects of the Transfer of Authority in UN Peace Operations' (2011) 42 *Netherlands Yearbook of International Law* 37. For an informative synopsis of the history of international courts, see Benedict Kingsbury 'International courts: uneven judicialisation in global order' in James Crawford and Martti Koskenniemi (eds) *The Cambridge Companion to International Law* (Cambridge, 2012).

85 See, for example, Bovens (2010), above Chapter 1, n 7; Grant and Keohane, above n 61; Brunnée, above n 53; see also Mulgan, above n 48; Antonios Tzanakopoulos *Disobeying the Security Council: Countermeasures against Wrongful Sanctions* (Oxford, 2011).

86 See Philip Selznick 'Legal Cultures and the Rule of Law' in Martin Krygier and Adam Czarnota (eds) *The Rule of Law after Communism: Problems and Prospects in East-Central*

Moving ahead, more is now under way in UN circles to share understanding on legal accountability. In his analysis of how states might respond to unlawful sanctions imposed by the Council, for example, Antonios Tzanakopoulos suggests that 'the most objective and effective process for holding the Council to account' will coincide with its responsibility for internationally wrongful acts.[87] Whether this results in some measure of legal accountability will only be determined in the future: it was as recently as 2003 that the Assembly 'took note' that the International Law Commission had put 'responsibility of international organizations' in its work program;[88] draft articles were discussed during the Assembly's 66th Session,[89] again in the 69th session,[90] and the 72nd session;[91] and they are slated for further consideration during the 75th session.

It is also noteworthy is that states have not, to date, been so enthusiastic in their responses,[92] and complexities arise as to how any such articles might be applied.[93]

Such institutions may, in any case, have no identifiable requirement to create the necessary rules by which their conduct could be assessed, unless, for example, they could be said to be obliged in a fashion suggested by Clyde

---

Europe (Ashgate Dartmouth, 1999), 26. Preventative measures would potentially also speak to issues raised by Jan Klabbers—see above Chapter 1, n 52.

87 Antonios Tzanakopoulos 'Strengthening Security Council Accountability for Sanctions: The Role of International Responsibility' (2014) 19(3) *Journal of Conflict & Security Law* 409, 411. See also his longer discussion—Tzanakopoulos (2011), above n 85.

88 *Report of the International Law Commission on the work of its fifty-fourth session* GA Res 57/21, UN GAOR, 57th sess, Agenda Item 156, 52nd plen mtg, UN Doc A/Res/57/21 (21 January 2003).

89 *Responsibility of international organizations* GA Res 66/100, UN GAOR, 66th sess, Agenda item 81, 82nd plen mtg, UN Doc A/Res/66/100 (27 February 2012), adopting unamended the substance of a document from the International Law Commission: International Law Commission *Draft articles on the responsibility of international organizations, with commentaries* (2011).

90 *Responsibility of international organizations* GA Res 69/126, UN GAOR, 69th sess, Agenda item 85, 68th plen mtg, UN Doc A/Res/69/126 (18 December 2014).

91 *Responsibility of international organizations* GA Res 72/122, UN GAOR, 72nd sess, Agenda item 87, 67th plen mtg, UN Doc A/Res/72/122 (18 December 2017).

92 As reflected in related scholarly discussion—see for example, Jean d'Aspremont 'The Articles on the Responsibility of International Organizations: Magnifying the Fissures in the Law of International Responsibility' (2012) 9(1) *International Organizations Law Review* 15; Nataša Nedeski and André Nollkaemper 'Responsibility of International Organizations "in connection with acts of States"' (2012) 9(1) *International Organizations Law Review* 33; José E Alvarez 'Revisiting the ILC's Draft Rules on International Organization Responsibility' (2011) 105 *Proceedings of the Annual Meeting (American Society of International Law)* 344.

93 For a cross section of views, see Ragazzi, above Chapter 1, n 66.

Eagleton. In delivering the 'International Organization and The Law of Responsibility' course at the Hague Academy of International Law in the UN's early years, his discussion of legal responsibility was premised on the idea that international organisations could not be held legally responsible.[94] However, Eagleton also argued that:

> It is a fundamental principle of international law that a state—a legal person under that law—must provide itself with the means of meeting its international obligations. If laws, or courts, or other means are needed, then the state must have them. [The *Alabama* Claims Award and] hundreds of cases have attested that a state cannot escape responsibility by pleading the lack of legal or governmental means for performing its duties. *If the United Nations is a legal person having obligations and responsibility for their performance, the United Nations will be expected to have the means at its disposal for so doing.*[95]

From that perspective, international organisations could be seen to be obliged to create their own rules, simply because they ought to provide themselves with whatever means are necessary to perform their duties as legal persons, at least in accordance with their constituent treaty. If such an analysis was accepted, though, it seems clear that states are yet some way from agreeing that the draft articles should be adopted, in some fashion, into the practice of international organisations.

Armed with such rules, as is well known an aggrieved actor would still face the hurdles of finding a legal forum,[96] and not being stumped by other features of the international legal order, such as immunities.[97] Here, immunities highlight an important dilemma about how far to go in seeking accountability.

---

94 See Jan Klabbers 'The Paradox of International Institutional Law' (2008) 5 *International Organizations Law Review* 151, 159.

95 Clyde Eagleton 'International Organization and The Law of Responsibility' (1950) 76 *Collected Courses of the Hague Academy of International Law* 385, 402 (emphasis added). For a contemporary review of the *Alabama* case, see Tom Bingham 'The Alabama Claims Arbitration' (2005) 54(1) *International and Comparative Law Quarterly* 1.

96 Though also noting there are 'well over 100 international courts and tribunals functioning'—see Jan Klabbers 'Law, Ethics and Global Governance: Accountability in Perspective' (2013) 11(2) *New Zealand Journal of Public International Law* 309, 311.

97 For example, the UN may claim, or anyhow be accorded, immunity from prosecution (even absolute immunity)—see for example Mara Pillinger, Ian Hurd, and Michael N Barnett 'How to Get Away with Cholera: The UN, Haiti, and International Law' (2016) 14(1) *Perspectives on Politics* 70; *Mothers of Srebrenica et al v State of the Netherlands and the United Nations*, Supreme Court of the Netherlands, 10/04437, 13 April 2012.

They are taken to be essential for the functioning (productiveness) of international cooperation by protecting an institution from undue influence of, or control by, states. On the other hand, while that protection is intended to allow the UN to do its job, for example, in practice that can also lead to perverse outcomes and related conduct that are, broadly speaking, unproductive, counterproductive, or deleterious, and for which accountability is also lacking.[98]

Being accountable thus may stand to contribute to enhancing institutional and legal arrangements under which the Council labours, but, equally, relevant scholarship and practice confirms that it will be essential to devise some bespoke approach to accounting for Council conduct. Whatever forms and means that approach might take, challenges certainly include balancing the components and adjusting them to meet the Council's purposes in non-static geopolitical conditions.

The greater hurdle is, however, likely to be finding the political will to move the Council to a point of balance, somewhere between too much accountability and approaching none at all, by means that, crucially, will also allow that balance to be maintained over time and evolving circumstances.

2.4 Powers for a Purpose

The Council is without peer in its potential leadership role in maintaining or restoring international peace and security, for which it is obliged under the *Charter*—at least, it is if one takes Michel Virally's point that international organisations empowered by law to pursue their functions may also be obliged by law to perform them.[99] In the sense of being purposive, the Council thus was given its powers to a purpose, that being to pursue its Functions and contribute towards the UN's Purposes. To what extent the Council is productive of salutary outcomes can, accordingly, be associated with how adequately and sufficiently it responds to international peace and security issues by deploying the powers bestowed upon it, perhaps especially on matters falling within its exclusive purview where no other actor is comparably enabled by law to respond.

---

98 For a discussion in relation to the UN, see Ai Kihara-Hunt *Holding UNPOL to Account: Individual Criminal Accountability of United Nations Police Personnel* (Brill Nijhoff, 2017); for background on immunities, see August Reinisch 'Privileges and Immunities' in Jacob Katz Cogan, Ian Hurd and Ian Johnstone (eds) *The Oxford Handbook of International Organizations* (Oxford, 2016).

99 See above n 4.

In the context of international organisation, one concern about productiveness thus is whether core Council activities of deliberating and deciding strike the right balance of talk and action, as needed to maintain or restore international peace and security. At least some of its decisions also create legal obligations for other actors, or give policy to guide their actions, so another concern is that implementation of Council directions is essential to (at least potentially) have the anticipated effect. These concerns connect to the broad sentiment of a question posed by Michael Barnett and Martha Finnemore: 'Do international organizations really do what their creators intend them to do?'[100]

Beyond issues over what, specifically, the Council is intended to do, UN member states have no clear means of agreeing an answer to whether that was done, thereby assessing the extent to which the Council could be counted as 'productive'. Reform initiatives, for example, appear hamstrung without an orderly and (reasonably) finite means of articulating, investigating, and analysing, the Council's activities and/or results, the better to devise change that would address gaps or shortfalls in Council productiveness. Moreover, if an answer were agreed among states, such reform of the Council may still not be enough to make the Council as productive as it might be, for at least two reasons.

First, whatever the Council does, decides, or directs, may still be perceived as somehow not entirely lawful (even without review by a court), and so prove to be less-than-sufficiently productive. As Antonios Tzanakopoulos points out, disobedience to its directions is one way of defeating the Council that is always open to states—a tactic that may, not unreasonably, be deployed when states do not agree that the Council has acted lawfully or directed lawful action by states.[101] Then, there are also other 'legal dynamics' to consider, such as Jan Klabbers points to,[102] between the Council and the world at large. In a contemporary setting, it is not just that the Council affects this much wider audience by its actions or failure to act—the concern here is that the favour may also be returned, by that audience mobilising to affect what it is that the Council is there to do and thus its (potential) productiveness.[103]

---

100 Barnett and Finnemore, above n 11, 699. Their focus was on what the bureaucracy of such institutions does but the point holds.

101 See Tzanakopoulos, above n 85 and further discussion of Resolution 1267 in Chapter 6.2.2.

102 See above Chapter 1, n 22 and above n 56.

103 For example, in making a recommendation about appointing a Secretary-General—see below Chapter 4, n 119 and 120, and discussion in Chapter 6.2.3.

The historical record, from the creation of the Council during World War II through to present day, does little to allay such concerns: it more highlights that these questions remain fresh. For example, published in June 1947, the inaugural journal-style cover of the *Bulletin of the Atomic Scientists* famously shows the 'Doomsday Clock'.[104] An icon for how closely the world is said to be approaching destruction from man-made technologies,[105] the image could hardly have been more poignant for the Council. With the UN not two years old and the Cold War developing in the wake of World War II, the Council was grappling with its allotted 'primary responsibility' for maintaining or restoring international peace and security.[106] The Council's agenda already included, for example, cases in Iran, Egypt and the Balkans, a recalcitrant regime in Spain, and the treaty obligation for negotiating agreements to create armed forces for the UN, as it was obliged to do under Article 43 of the *Charter*. The agenda also included tasks such as appointing a Governor for the Free Territory of Trieste,[107] clarifying its own voting methods,[108] and finalising rules of procedure to answer Article 30 of the *Charter*. After waxing and waning between two and 17 minutes to midnight since then, in January 2020 the Doomsday Clock was set closer to midnight than at any point since its creation, because:

> Humanity continues to face two simultaneous existential dangers—nuclear war and climate change—that are compounded by a threat multiplier, cyber-enabled information warfare, that undercuts society's ability to respond. The international security situation is dire, not just because these threats exist, *but because world leaders have allowed the international political infrastructure for managing them to erode*.[109]

---

104 Originally a mimeographed newsletter, this was established in 1945 by those who had created the atomic bomb as part of the Manhattan Project. The publication now has an associated entity of the same name. See Bulletin of the Atomic Scientists *Mission and History* <https://thebulletin.org/about-us/>.

105 Bulletin of the Atomic Scientists *Timeline* <https://thebulletin.org/doomsday-clock/past-announcements/>.

106 *Charter* Article 24(1).

107 Per the Italian peace treaty after World War II—see Budislav Vukas, Jr 'The Free Territory of Trieste as a Subject of International Law' in Budislav Vukas and Trpimir M Šošić (eds) *International Law: New Actors, New Concepts—Continuing Dilemmas* (Martinus Nijhoff, 2010).

108 Which at this early stage quite literally meant how, exactly, to record voting in meetings—practice over taking a show of hands, and recording which representatives voted in what way, emerged gradually over the early months. See also below Chapter 4, n 52 and Chapter 5, n 79.

109 Bulletin of the Atomic Scientists 'Closer than ever: It is 100 seconds to midnight' (2020 Doomsday Clock Statement, 23 January 2020) <https:// thebulletin.org/doomsday-clock/current-time/> (emphasis added). It is also noteworthy that this announcement pre-dated

Correspondingly, little seems to have changed for the work of the Council.

Its agenda still includes situations in Iran, Egypt and the Balkans, along with myriad others around the globe, all of which ebb and flow in their urgency and seriousness. Recalcitrant regimes now include an array of 'failed' or 'failing' states, plus those implicated in contemporary threats (such as international terrorism and its financing), or latter day eventualities (such as displacement of populations on a vast scale—for example as a consequence of the situation in Syria since 2011). Discussion on Article 43 stalled in 1947, leaving visions of 'UN Armed Forces' unrealised and enforcement by military means a vexed question.[110] Also, the Council never chose a Governor for Trieste;[111] its voting practices remain contested, especially the Article 27(3) 'veto' power of permanent members; and its rules of procedure remain 'provisional', though unamended for approaching four decades.[112]

On the other hand, an unremittingly long agenda for the Council possibly shows not much more than that the world has many problems which are complicated and difficult to ameliorate, let alone resolve. Of course, the Council cannot be the sole author of necessary action—that needs states and other actors to play their part, where, in particular, UN member states have obligations under Article 2(3) to 'settle their international disputes by peaceful means'.[113]

---

the COVID-19 pandemic, and that prior announcements have put focus on whether world leaders can respond 'with the speed and on the scale' necessary to address global peace and security in the present day: see, for example, Bulletin of the Atomic Scientists 'January 2015 Doomsday Clock Annual Statement: Three Minutes and Counting' (2015 Doomsday Clock Statement, January 2015) <https://thebulletin.org/sites/default/files/2015%20Clock %20Statement.pdf>.

110 The matter was last discussed, inconclusively, on 15 July 1947—see UN SCOR, 157th mtg, UN Doc S/PV.157 (15 July 1947). See also further discussion in Chapter 3.1.

111 With the Security Council unable to progress the matter, it was overtaken by other arrangements: firstly a memorandum of understanding in 1954, between Italy, Yugoslavia, the USA and the UK, and then a treaty between Italy and Yugoslavia in 1975—see Vukas, above n 107, 154–155. For additional discussion, see Glenda Sluga 'Trieste: Ethnicity and the Cold War, 1945–54' (1994) 29(2) *Journal of Contemporary History* 285.

112 *Provisional Rules of Procedure of the Security Council* UN SCOR, 2410th mtg, UN Doc S/96/Rev.7 (21 December 1982) ('*Provisional Rules of Procedure*'). It is also worth noting that despite remaining 'provisional' for 'flexibility' (see below Chapter 4, n 114 and 115, and associated text), a raft of new arrangements were nonetheless necessitated in the face of COVID-19, for example, which had to be pursued outside or alongside the *Provisional Rules of Procedure* (see below Chapter 5, n 80) as, indeed, many others have been (see below Chapter 4, n 117 and 118).

113 Of course, the *Charter*, in Chapter VIII, also recognises that others such as regional organisations will have a vital role to play, but the issue is larger: see, for example, discussion

There is also the question of states' obligations to comply with Council decisions, or help that may be had from implementation of Council directions, even if not expressed so as to carry obligations under Article 25 of the *Charter*.

Ultimately, however, the Council was given power and powers to fulfil its Functions as part of the UN's Purposes, and this grant was not unconditional. This is the sense of the *Charter* conveyed by perusal of documents generated in its design, reflected in opinions of states voiced—at length and often—in Council proceedings, and, not least, embroiled in extensive debate over Council reform.

On the whole, then, while the Council does not seem as productive in its own cause as it might be, or as relevant audiences urge that it should be, the dimensions in which its institutional and legal arrangements might be modified to obtain improved productiveness have escaped majoritarian support, and so need clarification. These prevailing questions are taken forward into considering four corners of discussion: why, to whom, and for what, the Council may benefit from being accountable in aid of its productiveness, and then, pivotally, how that might be realised in the functioning of the Council under the *Charter* as it stands.

in Philip Alston 'The United Nations: No Hope for Reform?' in Antonio Cassese (ed) *Realizing Utopia: The Future of International Law* (Oxford, 2012), 38, 41–42.

CHAPTER 3

Why Should the Security Council Be Accountable?

Seeking why the Council should be accountable under international law has at least two broad routes to an answer—one based on a legal analysis of what the Council is required to do (or to not do), the other based on a wider analysis in which law is a central feature of considerations about what might be wanted from the Council, or what it ought to do towards fulfilling its Functions and realising its raison d'être. It is not a simple matter, however, to segregate what the case is from what it perhaps ought to be. The *Charter* may oblige the Council to pursue certain ends, and afford it broad discretion in determining what is needed to get that job done,[1] but that is not the same as, for example, the ends sought necessarily being of superior importance to the means used. In turn, related questions are not readily resolved: standards for Council conduct could arise from Article 24(2) of the *Charter*, that the Council 'shall act in accordance with the Purposes and Principles of the United Nations', but, as a principal organ, the Council is to interpret *Charter* provisions for itself.[2] Further, how ineffective Council action may be, if asserted to be ultra vires or not entirely lawful in some way,[3] is not knowable without authoritative review—but even if that were possible, it is not apparent just how productive the Council is to begin with.[4]

There are thus concerns about whether the Council is meeting its legal obligations, or if its actions are entirely lawful. These intersect with wider concerns about results from, and consequences of, its exercise of power and discretion

1 That discretion has been exercised widely, as reflected in its agenda, particularly in the post-Cold War period. See, for example—Jose E Alvarez 'The Once and Future Security Council' (1995) 18(2) *Washington Quarterly* 5, 7.

2 Noting that self-review (of the Council by the Council) is, in effect, monologic introspection which does not suffice as accountability (see above Chapter 2, n 59, and below Chapter 3, n 105, and Chapter 7, n 16), and that the *Charter* does not readily empower another organ to review Council conduct, though of course the Council always has the option to seek an advisory opinion from the International Court of Justice—as does the General Assembly.

3 For example, such as variously raised in relation to: peacekeeper misconduct—see discussion later in this Chapter; Resolution 1267—see discussion in Chapter 6.2.2; or the outbreak of cholera in Haiti linked to the presence of peacekeepers—see Pillinger et al, above Chapter 2, n 97.

4 Noting again that the draft articles on responsibility of international organisations may not prove to represent an advance in this area—see above Chapter 2, n 87 to 89 and associated text.

 DOI:10.1163/9789004444300_004

in the use of its *Charter* powers. Together these concerns point to issues about potential abuse, disrepair, or desuetude, of those legally-enabled powers, or even possible neglect of obligations arising on a wider front though still in the legal context of the *Charter* framework. Features behind such concerns are intertwined in the Council's idiosyncratic design to the extent that, in the interests of its productiveness, it seems doubtful the Council could make a sensible account for one without also accounting for the others. That is, the question of whether accountability may be involved, in legal connections of the Council to other actors, may not be meaningfully distinct from the broad question of why accountability could be desirable, given the Council's politico-legal nature and its place at the intersection of geopolitics and the international legal order.

That much said, on the wider question of using (or not using) such power and powers, it is not novel to suggest '[p]ower entails accountability, that is the duty to account for its exercise'.[5] Ruth Grant and Robert Keohane, for example, discuss how accountability may help to address abuses of power in world politics,[6] and, on a similarly broad front, international law scholarship shows related concerns about the Council, such as put in a summary point by Simon Chesterman:

> [T]he Council's effectiveness as a political actor and its legitimacy as a legal actor are connected: Member States' preparedness to recognize the authority of the Council depends in significant part on how responsible and accountable it is—and is seen to be—in the use of its extraordinary powers.[7]

Pursuing accountability in a narrower legal analysis, others still raise this wider point in relation to powers conferred on the Council under the *Charter*. The nature of a conferral influences specifics of an account—to whom it might be rendered and for what—but the interest in accounting for use of power already arises simply from that conferral. Antonios Tzanakopoulos, for example, says:

> That power must be held to account is a fundamental principle—not necessarily of law, or the 'rule of law' however conceived, or of international law, or of specific national legal orders; it is a fundamental principle of conferral of powers from the entity originally exercising them to

5 International Law Association *Berlin Conference Accountability of International Organisations Final Report* (2004), 5.

6 Grant and Keohane, above Chapter 2, n 61 and associated text.

7 Chesterman, above Chapter 1, n 82, 19 [51].

> another entity. It responds to what could be described as a gut feeling—few people, whether lawyers or not, would be comfortable with an entity exercising power without having to somehow account for that exercise to another entity meant to control such exercise ...[8]

Accountability thus is part of understanding the Council's productiveness—the extent to which it can produce the required results in circumstances that continue to shift, change, and evolve.

From the outset, however, real doubts arise about how productive the Council actually is,[9] and there is not always consensus about ends sought and means used by the Council (among the broader run of states expected to comply with Council decisions, or even Council members).[10] Accordingly, my approach to exploring these issues in this book is to take a (relatively) clear cut case example at the intersection of narrow legal and wider policy concerns, for a perspective on how productive the Council may be from time to time, and then discussion of how accountability may potentially contribute to improving such productiveness.

For this chapter, the case chosen highlights complexities of understanding Council productiveness even when its duty is comparatively clear, as well as the profound ramifications of the Council not carrying out such a duty when there appears to be widespread consensus that it should do so. Further, it illustrates the consequent complexity that transpires when the Council does not modify its conduct, despite various express or implied indications that it should do so to meet a clear legal obligation—which here coincides with what was sought in the wider political interests of the UN membership.

The case example chosen concerns Article 43 of the *Charter*. Article 43 provides that:

1. All members of the United Nations, in order to contribute to the maintenance of international peace and security, undertake to make available to the Security Council, on its call and in accordance with a special agreement or agreements, armed forces, assistance, and facilities, including rights of passage, necessary for the purpose of maintaining international peace and security.
2. Such agreement or agreements shall govern the numbers and types of forces, their degree of readiness and general location, and the nature of the facilities and assistance to be provided.

---

8 Tzanakopoulos, above Chapter 2, n 87, 409.

9 See, for example, discussion in Chapter 2.1.

10 See, for example, further discussion in Chapter 6.2.2.

3. The agreement or agreements shall be negotiated as soon as possible on the initiative of the Security Council. They shall be concluded between the Security Council and Members or between the Security Council and groups of Members and shall be subject to ratification by the signatory states in accordance with their respective constitutional processes.

Thus this requires the Council to negotiate agreements with UN member states to obtain the means for UN enforcement action using armed force, with each step a necessary precondition for states identifying specific forces and then making them ready so as to deliver on their treaty commitment. UN members accept this on becoming part of the UN, and Article 43 is linked to other *Charter* provisions empowering the Council to: take action, by air, sea, or land forces, to maintain or restore international peace and security (Article 42); invite states contributing forces to participate in decisions that would use that state's forces (Article 44); urgently deploy Article 43 air forces (Article 45); and task the Military Staff Committee (Article 46).

Legal obligations arising from Article 43 are taken as sufficiently apparent since it was a treaty provision,[11] and in early Council discussion of Article 43,[12] for example, the USA representative was not challenged after saying:

> Article 43 of the Charter imposes upon the Security Council the responsibility for negotiating "as soon as possible" special agreements [and until] those agreements have been concluded and put into force, the Security Council will be unable to fulfil its responsibilities as the enforcement agency of the United Nations.[13]

A political impasse in the Council stymied the necessary action, so Article 43 instead sat in limbo for five decades before the Council consigned the matter to history in 1996.[14]

Accordingly, this case example is opened to explore questions about why Council accountability may be wanted, including that there is a range of possibilities between too much accountability and close to none. Even though modern notions of accountability were barely on the horizon in 1945,[15] the

11 Given the maxim *pacta sunt servanda* enjoys general acceptance, to suggest otherwise would make a nonsense of the *Charter* as a treaty.

12 UN SCOR, 138th mtg, UN Doc S/PV.138 (4 June 1947) (Item 163).

13 Ibid, 953.

14 By removing it from the list of matters of which the Council is seized—see below Chapter 5, n 31 and associated text.

15 See above Chapter 2, n 48 and also above Chapter 1, n 53.

case of Article 43 engages with the undoubted intention of the drafters that the *Charter* become a reality, which is not negated, nor even noticeably offset, by their thin attention to accountability measures (consistent with a contemporaneous understanding of that term).

The case further shows that over the course of years, there was unrealised opportunity to add to those arrangements so as to enhance the prospects for realising the substantive elements in Article 43 and associated provisions, in the interests of the *Charter* design and maintaining or restoring international peace and security as the Council remains charged to do (notwithstanding any and all imperfections in the *Charter* design).

When the moderating concern is the potential to find ways to better equip the Council, so as to maintain or improve its productiveness by being accountable, consequences of not implementing Article 43 also go to illustrate that the Council remaining silent, or failing to take action to modify its related conduct, does not necessarily signal the end of interest in such a matter by those with a stake in the work of the Council.

3.1 Case Example: Implementing Article 43

On 25 January 1946, at just its second meeting, the Council adopted what is now on record as its first resolution,[16] agreeing a two stage directive: to the P5 to appoint their representatives for the Military Staff Committee, so that the Committee could be constituted, and then for that Committee 'as its first task, to draw up proposals for its organization [and] procedure, and to submit these proposals to the Security Council.'[17]

Discussion of how best to implement Article 43 of the *Charter* was also on the agenda that day, but deferred so the Military Staff Committee could provide necessary advice. A few weeks later, the Council noted receipt of Committee proposals for its organization and procedure, and agreed a directive to the Committee 'to examine from the military point of view the provisions contained in Article 43', with recommendations to be made to the Council in due course.[18]

16 The practice of numbering resolutions was not commenced until 1964, when a retrofitting exercise by the Secretariat numbered substantive decisions of the Council. See the historical note at Dag Hammarskjöld Library *UN Documentation: Security Council* <http://research.un.org/en/docs/sc/resolutions>.

17 UN SCOR, 23rd mtg, UN Doc S/PV.23 (16 February 1946), 369 (Item 90); SC Res 1, UN SCOR, 23rd mtg, UN Doc S/Res/1 (23 January 1946).

18 Ibid: these outcomes are on record as decided, but not then or later noted as resolutions.

Despite urging from the Assembly, making clear its interest in seeing this aspect of the *Charter* realised,[19] implementation of Article 43 was not then addressed for over a year. The Council was advised in April 1947 that 'the Military Staff Committee's report has been received, a report which has long been awaited not only by the Council but by the general public'.[20]

After nearly a dozen meetings, the Council's last recorded attention to this project was in July 1947.[21] No resolution had eventuated, and the discussion adjourned then was never reconvened.[22]

Discussion at the time centred on how to create the forces called for in the substantive advice of the Military Staff Committee.[23] It had attempted to address what might be the purpose of such forces, their composition, strength, employment, general location, strategic direction/command and degree of readiness, as well as the contribution from individual states of forces, logistics, and other support (such as rights of passage through that state's territory or territorial waters). The report put forward 'recommendations agreed upon by all Delegations represented on the Military Staff Committee and the proposals of individual Delegations on which unanimous decision has not been achieved'.[24] Of 41 articles proffered, 25 were agreed unanimously by the Committee.[25]

---

19 For example, see paragraph 7 in *Principles governing the general regulation and reduction of Armaments* GA Res 41(1), UN GAOR, 1st sess, 63rd plen mtg, UN Doc A/Res/41 (1) (14 December 1946), discussed by the Security Council as UN Doc S/231 (30 December 1946) in January 1947—see UN SCOR, 90th mtg, UN Doc S/PV.90 (9 January 1947).

20 UN SCOR, 132nd mtg, UN Doc S/PV.132 (30 April 1947), 822 (President).

21 UN SCOR, 139th mtg, UN Doc S/PV.139 (6 June 1947); UN SCOR, 140th mtg, UN Doc S/PV.140 (10 June 1947); UN SCOR, 141st mtg, UN Doc S/PV.141 (16 June 1947); UN SCOR, 142nd mtg, UN Doc S/PV.142 (18 June 1947); UN SCOR, 143rd mtg, UN Doc S/PV.143 (20 June 1947); UN SCOR, 145th mtg, UN Doc S/PV.145 (24 June 1947); UN SCOR, 146th mtg, UN Doc S/PV.146 (25 June 1947); UN SCOR, 149th mtg, UN Doc S/PV.149 (30 June 1947); UN SCOR, 154th mtg, UN Doc S/PV.154 (10 July 1947); UN SCOR, 157th mtg, UN Doc S/PV.157 (15 July 1947).

22 Inspection of verbatim records, for more than 50 meetings during the remainder of 1947, revealed no mention of this returning to the agenda—this was my confirmatory exercise in view of meetings then being rather less formulaic.

23 *Letter from the Chairman of the Military Staff Committee to the Secretary-General Dated 30 April 1947 and Enclosed Report on General Principles Governing the Organization of the Armed Forces Made Available to the Security Council by Member Nations of the United Nations* UN Doc S/336 (30 April 1947).

24 Noting again that the Committee is limited to representatives of the Council's permanent members under Article 47(2) of the *Charter*—see above n 17 and associated text.

25 See above n 23, covering letter from the Chairman of the Military Staff Committee. See also the overview in Chapter 2 of D W Bowett *United Nations Forces: A Legal Study* (Frederick A Praeger, New York, 1964).

For its part, the Council first addressed articles on which the Committee was unanimous, then the rest, intending to return to the document to consider the whole as amended. The idea was that, if adopted, the whole (however amended) would have provided a set of principles on which planning and development of Article 43 agreements could then proceed. Verbatim meeting transcripts suggest that, besides concerns over locating the forces, linked to post-war anxieties about deployed forces generally,[26] the significant sticking points related to force size and composition.

It is important to note that there was little to suggest states were unwilling to provide troops as called for in the *Charter*, but *apportioning* P5 contributions was at issue.[27] Four P5 members accepted that equivalent or comparable contributions would suffice, without nominating a basis for assessment, while the USSR put equal contributions as 'indispensable as a guarantee to the world that the international forces would not be used to consolidate the domination of any one of the permanent members over the others'.[28]

The overall tenor of debate can be read from concerns of non-permanent members, then the E6, that 'nothing we say or do is going to alter' an article agreed in the Military Staff Committee.[29] They nonetheless made the effort to demur on (proposed) Article 5, for example, which said the 'moral weight and the potential power behind any decision to employ the Armed Forces [will] be very great, and this fact will directly influence the size of the Armed Forces required'. They debated the meaning and relevance of this, including whether

---

26 For example: complaints from the USSR about British forces in Greece—see UN SCOR, 7th mtg, UN Doc S/PV.7 (4 February 1946) and variously about Allied forces in the territory of aligned states; Iran's complaint about USSR forces remaining on its territory—see UN SCOR, 25th mtg, UN Doc S/PV.25 (26 March 1946); several meetings were devoted to Ukraine's complaints about Greek troops in the border regions and whether forces from war-time Allies were involved—such as UN SCOR, 71st mtg, UN Doc S/PV.71 (23 September 1946); see also comments by China in UN SCOR, 140th mtg, UN Doc S/PV.140 (10 June 1947), 999.

27 For example, see UN SCOR, 146th mtg, UN Doc S/PV.146 (25 June 1947); see also UN SCOR, 154th mtg, UN Doc S/PV.154 (10 July 1947), 1267 (letter from Chairman of the Military Staff Committee). See also generally *Report of the Security Council to the General Assembly: Covering the period from 16 July 1946 to 15 July 1947* UN GAOR, 2nd sess, Supp No 2, UN Doc A/366 (vers 3/366 September 1950), [901–1029].

28 As summarised by the representative of France, and not disputed by the representative of the USSR—see UN SCOR, 154th mtg, UN Doc S/PV.154 (10 July 1947), 1271. See also, for example, UN SCOR, 139th mtg, UN Doc S/PV.139 (6 June 1947), 965 (USSR).

29 UN SCOR, 142nd mtg, UN Doc S/PV.142 (18 June 1947), 1029 (Australia). See also above Chapter 1, n 85 and associated text re E6 and E10.

it was reasonably regarded as a 'principle',[30] and the representative of Syria went as far as to say:

> I do not consider this article to be a factor which can serve as a basis of measurement for the size of the armed forces to be put at the disposal of the Security Council.[31]

E6 members also sought 'a political decision which [the] non-permanent members, and probably the entire press of the world await. ... Is the total force to be used against any of the permanent members?'[32] This highlights the range of issues hinging on the outcome of this debate, both:

(a) geopolitical questions, such as whether a P5 member could even be challenged as contravening the *Charter*, particularly in Chapter VII terms; and

(b) pragmatic questions, such as the necessary size of the UN forces, where, if to be deployed against a P5 member, UN armed forces would be the poorer without a contribution from that 'great power', even while they would very likely need to be much larger to stand effectively against it.

Other strategic problems that seem to have been crowded out by the political debate include, for example, the number of concurrent engagements advisedly to be allowed for in planning—where two or more smaller actions may have been more taxing than a single deployment of equivalent size, not least as multiple concurrent logistics support functions would be necessitated.

With such questions still hanging in the air, the Council sought further counsel from the Military Staff Committee, on a force size thought to be advisable from the military perspective. In terms of advancing intentions embodied in the *Charter*, instead this served more to underscore challenges of planning military operations without having some known threat, or even one that was reasonably knowable. Meeting transcripts reveal nothing the Council (or the Committee) saw as a likely threat, or perhaps an unlikely but credible contingency (despite the question being asked).[33] If instructing governments held

30 This article was addressed in multiple meetings, some of which are mentioned below.

31 UN SCOR, 142nd mtg, UN Doc S/PV.142 (18 June 1947), 1026.

32 UN SCOR, 146th mtg, UN Doc S/PV.146 (25 June 1947), 1112 (Australia).

33 See, for example, UN SCOR, 149th mtg, UN Doc S/PV.149 (30 June 1947), 1175 (Syria, in relation to 'the rival'). In that vein, Derek Bowett observed that the Committee's work 'indicates a general conclusion [that] obstacles in the way [are] not, fundamentally, military or strategic ones but rather political ones'—see Bowett, above n 25, 18.

a relevant view, it was not advanced in Council meetings: available records say nothing about the likely size of the opposing forces, geography, and so on, that might have shaped planning in the way typically engaged in a military perspective—not least, for example, to determine the break up of land, sea and air forces.

That 'planning never survives the first battle' is a truism for good reason, and, in any case, military and/or security threats not infrequently arise without being anticipated in planning. Nevertheless, as a practical matter a plan needs an objective, here to provide a basis for formulating agreements which were essential to delivering on the Council's *Charter* obligations, and to facilitate member states delivering on theirs. Its debates reveal that the Council did not agree on such an objective, bearing in mind this was an era of comparatively colourful and textured debate in formal Council sessions—in contrast to the post-Cold War era habit of formularised official meetings held after off-the-record negotiations, consultations, and so on.[34]

In sum, it adopted 25 out of 41 articles put forward by the Committee, some with amendments, but, as noted by Derek Bowett, the Council never reached the stage of considering the document as a whole, or, indeed, discussing many practical issues such as financing of operations and 'the problems of privileges and immunities (and jurisdictional control generally)'.[35]

The fate of Article 43 thus illustrates ways in which Council productiveness engages with notions of accountability. First, accounting for conduct is one method to suitably inform consideration of the need for change, towards both obtaining salutary outcomes and then, over time, continuing to do so while also continuing to respond to non-static circumstances. This calls for better understanding Council productiveness, in which an account of conduct could usefully address contributions to, and detractions from, the purposes for which the entity was created. Although this will always be a non-trivial challenge to ascertain in the Council's peculiar circumstances, Council silence and inaction on Article 43 closed off the option for dialogue in that general vein, and left the matter unresolved. Then, results associated with the Council depend on states each playing their part in maintaining or restoring international peace and security, in particular by acting on the Council's decisions towards such ends. In turn, explaining decisions is one component of bolstering states' willingness to comply.

34 See, for example, below Chapter 5, n 112 and 113, and associated text.

35 Bowett, above n 25, 28. A synopsis of all Council business dates last discussion on the record as being at the 157th meeting, on 15 July 1947—see *Summary Statement*, UN Doc S/7382 (5 July 1966), 11.

Crucially, this all relies on the Council first having made a decision, which it did not do on Article 43.

Overarchingly, the case of Article 43 also points to how accounting for conduct is differentiated from reporting on activities—particularly because, to be informative in understanding productiveness, an account of conduct must go further than just documenting what was done. The question is not the *extent* of information given so much as whether information is appropriately *explanatory*. These points are discussed further in the following sections.

3.2 Understanding Productiveness

The fate of Article 43 shows that not all Council tasks will prove to be feasible, which is not much of a surprise in the UN's geopolitical context, but taking Article 43's inclusion to demonstrate that the *Charter* drafters believed it was feasible to implement, the episode suggests that the Council was not as productive as it might have been if Article 43 had been implemented. Of course, the Article 43 design was not the first project that proved unworkable in the history of 'international organisation', let alone the longer course of related human endeavour. Much more importantly, nor is it the last, even just in the Council's realm: it is by no means the only unfinished business to live long on the Council's agenda, then or since.[36]

The enduring concern is that Council productiveness is no simple matter to evaluate in more detail.

In isolation, the Council's lapse on Article 43 could, for example, be taken as an excusable result—an unprecedented undertaking hamstrung by geopolitical intractabilities of the then-nascent Cold War. Indeed, it is not implausible to suggest the matter was so politically fraught that, at that specific moment in time, the Council may have been more productive by leaving it lie. Equally, the value of asserting narrow legal accountability is not evident, as a legal remedy seems unlikely.[37] Even now it is a stretch to suggest that the draft articles on

36 See discussion in Chapter 5.1.

37 See, for example, the comprehensive discussion in Tzanakopoulos, above Chapter 2, n 85. As an outgrowth of their sui generis nature, in general enforcing performance on an international organisation remains challenging—for example, international law has yet to acquire a concept for seeking to force performance of an 'official' duty, such as by emulating *mandamus* in common law—see generally William M Carter Jr 'Treaties as Law and the Rule of Law: the Judicial Power to Compel Domestic Treaty Implementation' (2010) 69(2) *Maryland Law Review* 344.

responsibility of international organisations would have any real impact.[38] It is also worth noting that although states showed clear willingness to contribute forces at the time, if push had come to shove they may not have actually done so: even with Article 43 agreements in place, if a decision to take Chapter VII enforcement action had proved to be politically possible, for a variety of political and practical reasons it is quite conceivable that the hoped-for mode of enforcement may still not then have materialised in response.

These points all go to highlight that the vagaries of its political context will very often determine Council practice. On the other hand, just as much as *omitting* a mechanism for authoritative review of Council conduct, it was no oversight or accident that Article 43 was *included* in the *Charter* after much deliberation and debate at UNCIO in 1945.[39] Stumbling blocks encountered on Article 43 thus should not be taken as unsolvable just because the Council did not find its own way forward. Moreover, it is a major departure from the *Charter* design (as imperfect as that is), but, whether on Article 43 or on an alternative solution providing an equivalent or corresponding capacity, a larger point stands nonetheless: the Council's capacity to do what it is there to do depends upon its ability to deal productively with such issues that inevitably arise in the course of performing its Functions.

Put simply, answering such questions or resolving practical problems is a basic part of the Council pursuing its role, but one where its demonstrated capacity is rather unclear.

The overarching point thus concerns the UN's organisational capacity to address the Purposes for which it exists, in light of unfinished Council business that is also unexplained: that the Council could not progress on Article 43 in the way set out in the *Charter* is one thing, but another, more enduring concern is that it neither changed its conduct of its own volition, nor explained the problem sufficiently to move deliberately in an alternative direction.

This applies no less across various issues affecting how productive the Council can be, including those that were not addressed, or addressed rather imperfectly, in the *Charter* design. Some of these may constitute obligations for the Council, but all such issues have potential to be persistent, and have wider implications for the Council being productive—and where it is not productive, for there to be less than salutary impacts on international peace and security.

To illustrate further, other developments relatable to Article 43 show, inter alia, that even procedural matters are of concern in this way, and, on substantive

38 See above Chapter 2, n 92 and 93, and associated text.

39 See above Chapter 1, n 30 to 41, and associated text; see also below n 128 and associated text.

matters, that if others chop wood when the Council does not, chips fall where they might for quite some time afterwards—for good or ill in impacts on the Council's authority and perceptions of its legitimacy.

For a procedural example, the Military Staff Committee is a component of the Council's capacity for doing its work. It was created by Article 47 of the *Charter* to 'advise and assist' the Council, and the Council is entitled to its advice under Article 46. The line connecting results from the Committee to Council productiveness thus is comparatively short and straight.

A year after being tasked to examine the provisions of Article 43,[40] but with 'no report at all to the Council',[41] the Council put a deadline on a renewed call for recommendations on 'basic principles which should govern the organisation of the United Nations Armed Force'.[42]

This much was eventually done, but it was a subset of the Committee's remit—the earlier directive having been neither withdrawn nor subsequently completed.

Facing results that others saw as less than effective,[43] no consequences were imposed upon the Committee by the Council. One such incident may not have a profound effect, but left dangling it does not bode well for the Council being as productive as it might be when matters of a military nature are a routine feature of maintaining or restoring international peace and security.

Again, some difficulty arises by the Council's own hand: in the first year, the Council referred the Committee's draft statute and rules of procedure to a Committee of Experts, which then considered the text at 27 meetings and duly reported to the Council.[44] After two decades, in 1966 that report had 'not so far been discussed by the Council';[45] after three more, in 1996, it was dropped from Council business, signified by being removed from the *Summary Statement*.[46]

---

40 See above n 17.

41 UN SCOR, 105th mtg, UN Doc S/PV.105 (13 February 1947), 269 (United Kingdom).

42 Ibid, 273.

43 See below n 95, and associated text, which suggests, inter alia, that states wanted the Committee to be (more) effective.

44 See *Report of the Security Council to the General Assembly: Covering the period from 16 July 1946 to 15 July 1947* UN GAOR, 2nd sess, Supp No 2, UN Doc A/366 (vers 3/366, September 1950), 103.

45 See *Summary Statement*, UN Doc S/7382 (5 July 1966), 12.

46 *Note by the President of the Security Council*, UN Doc S/1996/55 (24 January 1996). Note also that the report from this Committee of Experts, UN Doc S/421, remains restricted—that is, not available to the public—as per email advice to the author from Dag Hammarskjöld Library, 15 February 2016. This was re-confirmed in December 2018, the library officer noting 'there is no indication from the issuing office that it will be derestricted anytime soon'.

That was not the end of the matter, however, as the action was later picked up by others: after urging from the broad UN membership via the outcome of the 2005 World Summit,[47] the Military Staff Committee has since further considered its 'composition, mandate and working methods', changed work practice to include discussion of current UN activities, expanded its comments in the Council's annual report,[48] and now contributes a correspondingly extended section to that report.[49] Even if simply a procedural matter, and though it was quite a while between drinks, this shows that while the Council did not appear to develop capacity to elicit productive help from the Committee, others still pursued possibilities for a more open and/or active Committee. This has rendered a more engaged Military Staff Committee and potential future benefits for UN capacity or capabilities that this may bring.[50]

On a substantive question, the possibility of using armed force was seen as a necessary option, but not the only means of enforcement contemplated under the *Charter*: others are economic sanctions, for example, and the full gamut of diplomatic measures. Then, as things transpired in the UN's early decades, the Council did not call for contributions of forces under Article 43, and what is known now as peacekeeping was 'born of necessity as a largely improvised response to the times'.[51] The impetus came when the Council reached an impasse in the crisis over the Suez Canal in late 1956. After months of deteriorating relations and armed raids by Egypt and Israel into each others territory, access to the Suez Canal was seriously at issue and subject to negotiations in September 1956. Then, in late October 'Israel, in cooperation with the British

47 *2005 World Summit Outcome* GA Res 60/1, UN GAOR, 60th sess, 8th plen mtg, Agenda Items 46 and 120, UN Doc A/Res/60/1 (24 October 2005). The World Summit was informed by Kofi Annan's report and omnibus reform package—see *In larger freedom: towards development, security and human rights for all—Report of the Secretary-General* 59th sess, Agenda Items 45 and 55, UN Doc A/59/2005 (21 March 2005). The event was attended by a significant majority of the UN members: see United Nations Conferences, Meeting and Events *2005 World Summit* (14–16 September 2005, UN Headquarters New York) <http://www.un.org/en/events/pastevents/worldsummit_2005.shtml>.

48 See *Report of the Security Council: 1 August 2005–31 July 2006* UN GAOR, 61st sess, Supp No 2, UN Doc A/61/2 (2006), 191; cf *Report of the Security Council: 1 August 2015–31 July 2015* UN GAOR, 70th sess, Supp No 2, UN Doc A/70/2 (20 October 2015), 191.

49 See, for example, *Report of the Security Council: 1 August 2015–31 December 2016* UN GAOR, 71st sess, Supp No 2, UN Doc A/71/2 (29 August 2017), 249; *Report of the Security Council for 2017* UN GAOR, 72nd sess, Supp No 2, UN Doc A/72/2 (2018), 198; *Report of the Security Council for 2018* UN GAOR, 73rd sess, Supp No 2, UN Doc A/73/2 (2019), 185.

50 See also *In Hindsight: Military Staff Committee* (January 2015) Security Council Report <https://www.securitycouncilreport.org/monthly_forecast/2015-01>.

51 United Nations *The Blue Helmets: A Review of United Nations Peace-keeping* (3rd ed, 1996), 3.

and French Governments, launched an all-out attack on Egypt'.[52] Proposals were put forward in the Council that Israel withdraw, but these failed and the matter was referred to the General Assembly.[53]

An Assembly resolution was adopted,[54] pursuant to its earlier *Uniting for Peace* resolution.[55] The result was that the UN's first major deployment proceeded not at the Council's behest, but based on in an approach architected by the UN Secretary-General of the day, Dag Hammarskjöld, and Lester Pearson, Canada's then-Secretary for External Affairs. This 'improvised response' overcame the paralysis caused by an impasse in the Council, to find the means to enable an initiative not instead of Article 43 enforcement action, but in the absence of that capability.[56]

Moreover, separate to any test of states' support for Chapter VII enforcement action,[57] this still left in abeyance the due governance of such deployments: in terms of accountability for all concerned, the 'improvised response' of peacekeeping lacked a means of governing what was to be done by such armed forces, in whatever way Article 43 agreements would have done if they had been completed. In effect, this is a question that still appears insufficiently answered.[58]

The UN's peacekeeping model has coalesced over the course of decades and many operations.[59] There is plenty to admire in this, but still much to improve.

52 Ibid, 36.

53 SC Res 119, UN SCOR, 751st mtg, UN Doc S/Res/119 (31 October 1956).

54 See Paul F Diehl 'First United Nations Emergency Force (UNEF I)' in Joachim A Koops, Thierry Tardy, Norrie MacQueen, and Paul D Williams (eds) *The Oxford Handbook of United Nations Peacekeeping Operations* (Oxford, 2015). Before this, the UN had mounted two modest observer missions in the 1940s—see Andrew Theobald 'The United Nations Truce Supervision Organization (UNTSO)' in Joachim A Koops, Thierry Tardy, Norrie MacQueen, and Paul D Williams (eds) *The Oxford Handbook of United Nations Peacekeeping Operations* (Oxford, 2015); Christy Shucksmith and Nigel D White 'United Nations Military Observer Group in India and Pakistan (UNMOGIP)' in Joachim A Koops, Thierry Tardy, Norrie MacQueen, and Paul D Williams (eds) *The Oxford Handbook of United Nations Peacekeeping Operations* (Oxford, 2015).

55 See below n 94 and associated text.

56 See discussion in The Editors 'Introduction—Early Experiences: 1948–1963' in Joachim A Koops, Thierry Tardy, Norrie MacQueen, and Paul D Williams (eds) *The Oxford Handbook of United Nations Peacekeeping Operations* (Oxford, 2015), noting observer missions had also been initiated, namely UNTSO and UNMOGIP (see above n 54).

57 A not inconsequential question as shown in many debates then and since.

58 See below n 75 to 78 inclusive, and associated text.

59 For a comprehensive coverage of operations launched up until 2013, including a progressive analysis of how the model evolved, see generally Joachim A Koops, Thierry Tardy, Norrie MacQueen, and Paul D Williams (eds) *The Oxford Handbook of United*

Distinct from persistent issues about the efficacy of mandates and the operating results that follow, there continues to be serious issues in terms of governance and regulation of the use of force, and governance and regulation of those who remain capable of using armed force even if not tasked by the Council to do so.[60]

Importantly, this has now come full circle in two key respects: a call for enforcement by armed forces has (re-)emerged as an important feature of peacekeeping missions, and operations have reached the scale of deployment anticipated in Council discussions of Article 43. These realities are being faced without the governance structure anticipated in the *Charter*, and also in considerably more complicated operational arrangements because of the extensive military and police force elements involved.[61]

In more detail: enforcement was not initially part of the peacekeeping remit—cardinal features were long taken to be the non-use of force, host state consent, and UN impartiality,[62] though how well specific missions have conformed to those features is not uncontested.[63] More recently, 'peace enforcement' mandates include the use of force,[64] but related issues are still much contested.[65] Similarly, in relation to scale, in 1947 the Council entertained

Nations Peacekeeping Operations (Oxford, 2015). See also generally Doyle and Sambanis, below n 62.

60 See for example, the report enclosed with *Identical letters dated 17 June 2015 from the Secretary-General addressed to the President of the General Assembly and the President of the Security Council* UN Doc A/70/95-S/2015/446 (17 June 2015); *The future of United Nations peace operations: implementation of the recommendations of the High-level Independent Panel on Peace Operations—Report of the Secretary-General* UN Doc A/70/357-S/2015/682 (2 September 2015). See also the report enclosed with *Identical letters dated 21 August 2000 from the Secretary-General to the President of the General Assembly and the President of the Security Council* UN Doc A/55/305-S/2000/809 (21 August 2000).

61 See Figures 5 and 6 and associated discussion in Chapter 5.

62 See, for example, Michael W Doyle and Nicholas Sambanis *Making War and Building Peace: United Nations Peace Operations* (Princeton, 2006); William J Durch (ed) *Twenty-First-Century Peace Operations* (United States Institute of Peace, 2006).

63 See, for example, mission-by-mission evaluations in Koops et al, above n 59.

64 See, for example, Lise Morjé Howard 'Peacekeeping, Peace Enforcement, and UN Reform' (2015) 16(2) *Georgetown Journal of International Affairs* 6; John Karlsrud 'The UN at war: examining the consequences of peace-enforcement mandates for the UN peacekeeping operations in the CAR, the DRC and Mali' (2015) 36(1) *Third World Quarterly* 40; Lars Müller 'The Force Intervention Brigade—United Nations Forces beyond the Fine Line Between Peacekeeping and Peace Enforcement' (2015) 20(3) *Journal of Conflict & Security Law* 359; James Sloan *Militarisation of Peacekeeping in the Twenty-First Century* (Hart, 2011).

65 See, for example, above Chapter 2, n 96 to 98 inclusive, and below n 75 to 78 inclusive; see also, for example, Dan Bilefsky and Marlise Simons 'Netherlands Held Liable

estimates that multiple divisions would deploy on its orders.[66] A division is an army formation of 10,000 plus troops,[67] and estimates ranged from 8 to 12 divisions (UK, endorsed by China), up to 20 divisions (USA).[68] This summed to a quantum of ground troops broadly comparable to the first wave seaborne landing for Operation Overlord, World War II's 'D-Day' offensive in Normandy (circa 150,000).[69] A subdued operational tempo for the UN prevailed for much of the Cold War era, but the total uniformed personnel in the field has ranged well north of 100,000 in recent years,[70] matching the scale mooted in relation to Article 43.

In that light, the *Charter* scheme is noteworthy for being designed by statesmen fresh from such wartime experiences: planning (including to surmount institutional and legal complexities) was unfolding even as the *Charter* was being polished at UNCIO.

Crucially, in contrast to the contemplated Article 43 forces, peacekeeping troops now come from many more contributing states, and deploy in very significantly more concurrent operations.[71] This comes with a full measure of the associated complexities and complications but uses a miscellany of legal and institutional practice accumulated over the course of some 60 years.[72] In stark contrast, in 1947 operations on a commensurate scale, but less fragmented and diverse forces, were thought to require treaty-status legal agreements to

for 300 Deaths in Srebrenica Massacre' *New York Times* (online), 16 July 2014 <https://www.nytimes.com/2014/07/17/world/europe/court-finds-netherlands-responsible-for-srebrenica-deaths.html?_r=0>.

66 UN SCOR, 149th mtg, UN Doc S/PV.149 (30 June 1947).

67 As noted in Security Council discussions in June-July 1947, and still the assumption in planning—a division can also be up to around 20,000 troops, depending on its specific function.

68 *Letter dated 26 June 1947 from the President of the Security Council addressed to the Chairmen of the Military Staff Committee and reply dated 30 June 1947* UN Doc S/394 (30 June 1947), tabled and discussed at the 149th meeting and annexed to the verbatim transcript record of that meeting (see above n 66). Commensurate naval and air forces were put at dozens of capital ships and hundreds of aircraft.

69 See A Axelrod and J A Kingston *Encyclopedia of World War II* (Facts on File Inc, New York, 2007), 605.

70 'Uniformed' being armed forces and police—see Figure 5 below.

71 See Figures 5 and 6 and associated discussion in Chapter 5—the total troops deployed has dropped recently, but the point stands.

72 However imperfect Article 43 agreements may have proven to be, and noting that in more recent years, the Secretariat has built up various memoranda of understanding with some troop-contributing states, and some UN 'doctrine' on operations: see United Nations Peacekeeping *Policy and Guidance* <https://peacekeeping.un.org/en/policy-and-guidance>.

provide appropriate parameters for governance and for 'putting into motion [an] existing practical scheme which would have ensured an effective and efficient United Nations Force'.[73]

By no means the least issue involved applies as much or more so today: the pragmatic need for orders to survive intact after transmission in a lengthy command chain, without being made ineffective or unproductive from error, omission, or delay.[74]

Of course, had Article 43 agreements been negotiated, they may have proven to be less than perfect in terms of governing the UN Armed Forces that were thereby created. That would, however, simply indicate another case of the Council standing to benefit from an accountability mechanism by which to evaluate progress, and identify change that might be needed, so providing a coherent basis for moving forward.

Suffice it to say that, despite all of its achievements and positive results, the UN model of peacekeeping and governance of operations has parallel complexities and difficulties, but without a commonly-shared legal starting point. So it should come as no surprise that related issues are much mooted by scholars, publicists, and practitioners, in discourse expressing concerns about, for example:

- the routine and persistent nature of such problems;[75]
- characterising misconduct so as to address it effectively;[76]

---

73 Bowett, above n 25, 28.

74 There is an apocryphal tale of the challenges for military command even in a single nation contingent—often told in officer training, alongside the truism that planning rarely survives the first battle: a World War I British general, said to be commanding the battle front, messaged back to headquarters saying "send reinforcements, we are going to advance"; relayed from one messenger to the next, it comes out as "send three and fourpence, we are going to a dance". There are various equivalents—for example Harold Baldwin *Holding the Line* (A C McClurg & Co, Chicago, 1918), 128; for a contemporary example regarding the Israeli Army, see Ben Rooney 'Send Three and Fourpence, We Are Going to a Dance' *Wall Street Journal* (online) <http://blogs.wsj.com/tech-europe/2011/06/01/send-three-and-fourpence-we-are-going-to-a-dance/>.

75 For the headlines, see, for example, Chris McGreal 'What's the point of peacekeepers when they don't keep the peace?' *The Guardian* (online) 17 September 2015 <http://www.theguardian.com/world/2015/sep/17/un-united-nations-peacekeepers-rwanda-bosnia>; for the UN perspective, see above n 60; for more on each mission, see the specific chapters in Koops et al, above n 59. See also Chapter 5 herein.

76 Such as it being a discipline question (for that national armed force), a matter of ordinary criminality (to be pursued in the host state or in the home state), or an incident between the sovereign nations involved. For example, see Security Council Report, above Chapter 2, n 84; the long series of reports responding to sexual exploitation and abuse in peacekeeping operations, such as *Special measures for protection from sexual exploitation and sexual abuse: Report of the Secretary-General* UN GAOR, 73rd sess, Agenda Item 132

- the challenges of even investigating relevant matters;[77] and
- responding in an effective legal and institutional approach, including to elicit reporting that at least goes towards prevention.[78]

On the whole, the Council's unproductive treatment of Article 43 is not an operational molehill turned into mountain by Cold War politics, but one response to a genuinely challenging task, which would not necessarily have had a productive outcome even if the Council had delivered on its own portion of the obligations created by Article 43. When a pressing need arose in the Suez Crisis, the Council at least admitted its inability to progress at that time, and it should certainly be said again that there is much to laud in what the UN has achieved in peacekeeping. However, not accounting for Article 43 as an unfinished and/or infeasible Council project nonetheless has had multiple profound impacts on the larger *Charter* design and key elements of the UN's legal and institutional Purposes. Some of their governance aspects have been relevant in peacekeeping all along (even if the more so as operations in the field collectively approached a similar scale of deployment), and others are again made fresh and urgent by inclusion of enforcement mandates.

In common with other elements of international organisation,[79] the *Charter* creates 'a regime [that] is designed with an accountability deficit in place',[80] meaning that there is no suggesting that simply following its design would necessarily have led to all being well in UN operations. Nevertheless, it remains

---

and 150, UN Doc A/73/744 (14 February 2019); on legal issues, see Gill, above Chapter 2, n 84; on jurisdictional issues see Kihara-Hunt, above Chapter 2, n 98.

77 See, for example, the report entitled *A comprehensive strategy to eliminate future sexual exploitation and abuse in United Nations peacekeeping operations attached to Letter dated 24 March 2005 from the Secretary-General to the President of the General Assembly* UN GAOR, 59th sess, Agenda Item 77, UN Doc A/59/710 (24 March 2005)—often known as the Zeid Report after HRH Prince Zeid Ra'ad Zeid Al-Hussein of Jordan, responsible for producing the report as Advisor on Sexual Exploitation and Abuse to then Secretary-General Kofi Annan.

78 See, for example, Ed Vulliamy 'Has the UN learned lessons of Bosnian sex slavery revealed in Rachel Weisz film?' *The Guardian* (online) 15 January 2012 <https://www.theguardian.com/world/2012/jan/15/bosnia-sex-trafficking-whistleblower>; Roger Hamilton-Martin 'Ostracised, sacked … and even arrested: the fate of whistleblowers at the UN' *The Guardian* (online) 14 September 2015 <http://www.theguardian.com/world/2015/sep/14/un-united-nations-ostracised-sacked-arrested-whistleblowers>; Sandra Laville 'UN whistleblower who exposed sexual abuse by peacekeepers is exonerated' *The Guardian* (online) 18 January 2016 <https://www.theguardian.com/world/2016/jan/18/un-whistleblower-who-exposed-sexual-abuse-by-peacekeepers-is-exonerated>.

79 Of course, international organisation is by no means alone in this.

80 Simon Chesterman 'Globalization Rules: Accountability, Power, and the Prospects for Global Administrative Law' (2008) 14(1) *Global Governance* 39, 42.

open that more may have been possible towards that design, if not all of its specificities, had conundrums been articulated, investigated, analysed, and so on. Instead, Council inaction has left Article 43 and related provisions to subside into seeming desuetude.

Beyond the immediate gap left in Council capability in the *Charter* design, not explaining to a relevant audience means forgoing an opportunity for organisational learning and development that could well inform enhancement of legal and institutional arrangements surrounding the Council's work. This reinforces the idea that a key reason accountability may help productiveness arises from the nature of accountability. Dialogue involved should be enough to contribute to organisational learning and finding options to solve problems—towards resolving any roadblock in relation to Article 43, or, alternatively, roadblocks to what the Council may have decided to do instead of Article 43, or, otherwise simply governing what the Assembly did in the absence of an operative Council decision to deliver the outcome required by the *Charter*.

Who would have a right to be involved in such a dialogue can be left aside for now,[81] to mark clearly that where accountability can assist in progressing such issues, then a relevant means, mechanism, or process, has potential to improve Council productiveness. In seeking to improve the Council's capacity for obtaining salutary outcomes, that means of accountability would need to consider productive results towards maintaining or restoring international peace and security, balanced against the less productive effects of Council conduct—where its conduct is, for example, said to be ultra vires (or is otherwise contested), or where Council decisions, action, or inaction, in effect somehow work against, for example, 'conditions under which justice and respect for the obligations arising from treaties and other sources of international law can be maintained'.[82]

As an uncontested obligation of the Council, Article 43 thus provides an example of unfinished business that might have been dealt with rather more productively, and, in more recent times, the reform debate would seem to confirm the need for change on a wider front—where even Council members have said the Council 'has to succeed, not just try hard'.[83]

---

81 Noting that it is plausible that any and all members of the UN, who would be affected by how development of the agreements might proceed or not, may well assert an interest in such a discussion based on Article 31 the *Charter*—which provides for UN Members to 'participate, without vote, in the discussion of any question brought before the Security Council [if] the interests of that Member are specially affected'. See generally Chapter 4.

82 *Charter*, third preambular paragraph.

83 *Letter dated 26 May 2016 from the Permanent Representative of Finland to the United Nations addressed to the President of the Security Council* S/2016/506 (2 June 2016), 34

As discussed in the next section, the accumulation of similar cases, duly reported in the Council's annual report on its work, highlights the array of openings where being accountable may help.

3.3 Accountability v Reporting

Article 43 remains an unconsummated element of the *Charter* design, but this did not go unreported or unremarked.

In terms of reporting, Article 15(1) of the *Charter* requires the Council to give 'an account of the measures that the Security Council has decided upon or taken to maintain international peace and security',[84] and, to that end, the Council provides an annual report to the Assembly. With action on Article 43 stalling literally on the cusp of reporting periods, the report to July 1947 includes a synopsis of action thus far,[85] and the next notes Council examination of the Military Staff Committee report is pending.[86] Similar entries appear in the following year's report,[87] and no more in the 1950 report: Article 43 is mentioned in relation to the Commission for Conventional Armaments,[88] and implicitly in noting that from August 1948 'the Military Staff Committee has continued to hold its regular meetings but without further progress on matters of substance'—in which matters Article 43 could safely be assumed to be included.[89]

The Council thus provided an account to the Assembly in the sense of reporting on its activities to satisfy the letter of Article 15(1),[90] but nothing more: this could not be said to 'explain or justify' what it had done so as to meet a 'bare bones' notion of accountability as now understood. The Council

(comment from an unnamed member among the 'outgoing and continuing members' of the Council).

84 To which Article 24(3) is usually taken as equivalent though the wording is different.

85 *Report of the Security Council to the General Assembly: Covering the period from 16 July 1946 to 15 July 1947* UN GAOR, 2nd sess, Supp No 2, UN Doc A/366 (vers 3/366, September 1950), 78.

86 *Report of the Security Council to the General Assembly: Covering the period from 16 July 1947 to 15 July 1948* UN GAOR, 3rd sess, Supp No 2, UN Doc A/620 (September 1948), 139.

87 *Report of the Security Council to the General Assembly: Covering the period from 16 July 1948 to 15 July 1949* UN GAOR, 4th sess, Supp No 2, UN Doc A/945 (August 1949), 95.

88 *Report of the Security Council to the General Assembly: Covering the period from 16 July 1949 to 15 July 1950* UN GAOR, 5th sess, Supp No 2, UN Doc A/1361 (1950), 36.

89 Ibid, 62.

90 And perhaps the way 'account' was understood in those times, though it was was not a term much conceptualised then—see above Chapter 1, n 53, and Chapter 2, n 48.

was silent on what the hold-up was, plus either what plans it had for moving ahead or why it had concluded it was not able to move ahead with fulfilling its Article 43 obligation.

In terms of why accountability may be wanted, this illustrates, by its absence, a crucial distinction.

Accounting for one's conduct is differentiated from merely reporting one's activities: if there are no 'consequences' (or even that possibility) for an account that is somehow lacking, what is done constitutes only a 'non-committal' transmission of information.[91] If, as the case was here, it is not enough of an accountability mechanism to elicit change in the related Council conduct, then, even if the Article 15(1) mechanism works much as the *Charter* drafters envisaged, it does not function to assist Council productiveness. Whatever is done comes to the same if there is no mechanism, means, or other effective capacity,[92] to compel a response to questions or issues remarked upon or raised otherwise.[93]

As it happened, the Assembly remarked on the situation at the time, and then continued to show interest in progressing the matter as time marched on with Article 43 still lying fallow. For example, the omnibus *Uniting for Peace* resolution notes, inter alia, that:

> [The] initiative in negotiating the agreements for armed forces provided for in Article 43 … belongs to [the Council and] failure of the Security Council to discharge its responsibilities [does not relieve] the United Nations of its responsibility under the Charter to maintain international peace and security …[94]

Recording that this had been sent to the Council, the Council's next annual report (to July 1951) notes the point, but it is included in the section listing matters brought to the attention of the Council that were not discussed, in these terms:

---

91 See above Chapter 2, n 62 and associated text.

92 Or, similarly, when preventative 'checks and balances' are not sufficient to change conduct—which would also seem to be the case in relation to the Council (see, for example, Klabbers, above Chapter 1, n 52).

93 Even if a right exists—such as Article 11(3) provides, for the Assembly to bring matters to the Council's attention where it judges them relevant to international peace and security—the actor raising the question is no better served if there is no duty to answer and no means to compel that.

94 *Uniting for Peace* GA Res 377(V), UN GAOR, 5th sess, 302nd plen mtg, UN Doc A/Res/377 (V)A-C (3 November 1950), preamble.

> [The General Assembly Resolution] recommended that the Council should devise measures for the earliest application of Articles 43, 45, 46, and 47 of the United Nations Charter regarding the placing of armed forces at the disposal of the Security Council by the States Members of the United Nations and the effective functioning of the Military Staff Committee.[95]

Indicating Article 43 was not elsewhere receiving substantive attention, perhaps en route to further Council consideration, the report also says that the 'Military Staff Committee has been functioning continuously under its draft rules of procedure during the period under review, in the course of which it held a total of twenty-seven meetings, but without making further progress on matters of substance'.[96] The following year has an almost identical comment,[97] and similarly in 1953,[98] 1954,[99] and 1955.[100] Even if this pattern of conduct met the *Charter* drafters' mark for an 'account', and what the Council considered to be its reporting obligation, that is not the end of it. As Anne Peters notes, effectiveness deficits may stem from legal design,[101] and the example of Article 43 shows one very important situation in which the legal design does not appear to serve the purposes at hand: it did not ensure that the Council was productive in creating the thing that those same drafters saw as an essential enforcement capability—that is, sufficiently essential to include multiple related provisions in an international treaty.[102]

As with the annual reporting process, the interest of the Assembly in this case illustrates a pivotal characteristic of accounting for conduct, in that

---

95 *Report of the Security Council to the General Assembly: Covering the period from 16 July 1950 to 15 July 1951* UN GAOR, 6th sess, Supp No 2, UN Doc A/1873 (1951), 93.

96 Ibid, 88.

97 *Report of the Security Council to the General Assembly: Covering the period from 16 July 1951 to 15 July 1952* UN GAOR, 7th sess, Supp No 2, UN Doc A/2167 (1952), 54.

98 *Report of the Security Council to the General Assembly: Covering the period from 16 July 1952 to 15 July 1953* UN GAOR, 8th sess, Supp No 2, UN Doc A/2437 (1953), 26.

99 *Report of the Security Council to the General Assembly: Covering the period from 16 July 1953 to 15 July 1954* UN GAOR, 9th sess, Supp No 2, UN Doc A/2712 (1954), 55.

100 *Report of the Security Council to the General Assembly: Covering the period from 16 July 1954 to 15 July 1955* UN GAOR, 10th sess, Supp No 2, UN Doc A/2935 (1955), 26.

101 Peters, above Chapter 2, n 16 and associated text.

102 Where actually deploying that capability is another distinct substantive matter, and a step which the history of the UN indicates is not readily agreed to by states—rightly so, one would suggest. The political difficulty was highlighted from the beginning—see generally, for example, mission-by-mission discussion in Koops et al, above n 59, and particularly about mounting UNEF I in Diehl, above n 54. Be that as it may, creating the capability was seen as necessary, but, in the end, not done for want of Council action.

neither interchange is effectively dialogic. Here the Council did not explain in its account, nor respond further to Assembly prompts,[103] but the much more pervasive issue is that the Assembly does not have formally-given expectations of a response, or the means to compel an answer. That is, though the Assembly is not without influence over what the Council does, these processes are not inherently dialogic.[104] In a widely-embracing perspective, Assembly questions being met by Council silence might be taken as some form of dialogue, but in a contemporary context much more is expected in an accountability process.[105] For example, as described by Andreas Schedler this is to ensure debate and avoid either 'mute power' or 'speechless controls of power'.[106]

Overall, this shows that providing all possible information short of actual explanation does not constitute an accountability measure, especially if the process is effectively coterminous with report submission. The actor reported to cannot assert a view of the report, or have questions answered, to show conduct involved has been explained or justified to their satisfaction.[107]

This explanatory value is the pivot point for organisational learning and development to enhance productiveness, and thereby to bolster organisational capacity in its circumstances *and as those circumstances evolve over time*. The Council's 'documentary compendium',[108] though exhaustive, thus remains merely a report. Then, as much as this highlights differences between reporting on activities and accounting for conduct, the fate of Article 43 also points to the question of how much accountability is enough to answer the reasons for which it was sought. The Council was unproductive on its legal obligations created by Article 43, but there is more to accountability just than finding fault,[109] and one such result on a knotty, high stakes geopolitical issue need not necessarily reflect poorly on the Council. The real issue is what it means

103 Noting that extensive trawling of Council records located no discussion of responding, where, in the style of the day, planning to respond would very likely have been remarked in session.

104 For an overview, see generally Klabbers, above Chapter 1, n 52.

105 Though perhaps not unreasonable as an approach at the UN's inception, it is now well wide of the mark in a contemporary understanding of what it means to 'provide an account'—see further discussion later in this chapter. See also below Chapter 7, n 16, on what is *not* 'dialogue'.

106 Schedler, above Chapter 2, n 59.

107 Noting that the Council's report is routinely discussed in a General Assembly session, and the President of the Security Council may attend in that capacity, but there appears to be no obligation on the Council or its members to speak to the report or answer questions that members of the Assembly raise.

108 Tzanakopoulos, above Chapter 2, n 87, 413.

109 See Bovens, above Chapter 2, n 63 and associated text.

when the litany of such cases develops, to the point of (potentially) becoming a cause célèbre in its own right.

What this case thus further illustrates is tensions in finding a suitable form for accountability, to inform an understanding of productiveness but without pursuing accountability for its own sake by 'embracing too many rules and too much accountability [where] the cost of greater accountability [is to] the capacity of the Security Council to respond to a crisis suffered'.[110] Council reports are, I suggest, quite far from that: consistent with what is now long-standing practice, on Article 43 the annual report served only to record what had been done and then not done. This indicates open space in which to be suitably accountable: doing something more than just pro forma reporting, so as to provide for analysis, investigation, and resolution, but doing that systematically, to detect an emerging adverse litany, as well as selectively, to stop short of some free-for-all contest over what happened using miscellaneous 'assumptions that are themselves questionable'.[111]

Debate on Article 43 may have been aired behind the scenes. If the Council engaged in such monologic introspection, then the problem clearly was still not solved. Be that as it may, that is not the point here: whatever was done, and however productive Council members may have perceived their collective work to be, the action for which the Council was obliged by the *Charter* was not completed and the Council did not (openly at least) decide on action towards an alternative way ahead.

Moreover, there is still no saying that the blockage could not have been solved if the Council had engaged with being accountable, in some form of dialogue with an external actor(s). The first choice for this role would likely be the Assembly as the collective of states each with some right to be interested in the Council's work,[112] but the identity of that other actor is less important, for the moment, than that there be one. This is an existential element of what it means for accountability to be real.

Though certainly no panacea for complicated situations such as the Council often faces, and always subject to the quality of investigation and analysis that

---

110 Chesterman, above n 80, 46.

111 Hurd, above Chapter 2, n 43 and associated text.

112 Article 31 provides for states to 'participate, without vote, in the discussion of any question brought before the Security Council whenever the latter considers that the interests of that Member are specially affected'. While it is the Council's judgement as to whom is 'specially affected', application to date is not entirely conclusive (see Simma et al, above Chapter 1, n 29, 1057). On the other hand, this may open up scope to connect UN members to the work of the Council in quite a variety of ways.

is possible within the vagaries of its political circumstances (and, of course, in the context of the *Charter*), the backdrop provided by the case example of Article 43 highlights the purpose of being accountable: *to test whether the Council has done what it can, used the powers that it has, deployed tools within its grasp, and explored other options or alternative approaches to produce the results for which it was granted powers.*

3.4 Accounting for Productiveness

Council productiveness is subject to countervailing forces, some adding to Council outcomes and others detracting from them. Such influences arise from the Council and all those connected to the situation, including states that may or may not heed Council authority in the matters at hand.

In the high stakes realm of international peace and security, the pattern of how such forces work over time is itself of concern, but it would likely be better that what the Council does is not then undone (or even significantly offset) by unproductive elements of, or outgrowths from, its own conduct. That is, the balance of forces from the Council's own conduct should not, on the whole, work against realising its purposes. Progress in a complex and hard-won resolution could well be undone by lack of compliance, arising from, for example:

- the nature of the Council's decision—where it over-reaches its powers, or does not explain the reach of its powers sufficiently to be compelling; or
- the way in which a decision was made—without, for example, engaging, or being seen to engage, sufficiently with relevant states, including those who can make a credible claim to being 'specially affected' under Article 31; or
- implications in practical terms—such as that implementation by states may be unenforceable in their domestic jurisdiction, or involve means that are not acceptable even if the ends are laudable.

Ensuring that the Council's own conduct does not diminish its productiveness involves, for example, the Council avoiding decisions, actions, or inactions, that are perceived as somehow not entirely lawful, or giving directions not able to be implemented (entirely) lawfully by states.[113] More generally, the Council

113 Where even the appearance of being unlawful may not be helpful, and so dilute Council productiveness—see discussion of Resolution 1267 in Chapter 6.2.2. The Council's well-known penchant for less than precise language may be well-intended but still go either way—for example, see below Chapter 6, n 188 and 189, in relation to Resolution 2249.

might address feasibility of its projects, to show that action proposed is accepted as being within its *Charter* ambit, realisable from decisions that it is empowered to make, and that are able to come to fruition in implementation by other actors—for example, by states being willing and able to do so within the strictures of their domestic political and legal circumstances.[114]

In such endeavours, the Council has the capacity to manage its ambit, although whether it does from time to time could be in doubt given a long and undiminished agenda for its work.[115] The Council's decisions to date also show just how expansive its capacity for decision-making can be when the Council so chooses, although its choices are certainly not unremarked.[116]

For why it should be accountable, the pressing point is that Council results inherently depend on states recognising Council authority,[117] and then playing their part to shoulder obligations or make needed contributions towards international peace and security. In effect, this makes compliance with Council decisions by other actors fundamental to its productiveness: after having done what it can do by determining action others should take, the Council must still obtain implementation, by states' compliance (with its decision) or conformity (with other recommendations, and so on), in order to produce a result.[118]

The working assumption in 1945 was that states would be legally obliged to do so, and ought to feel compelled to obey Council directives. This is observable in UNCIO records, which signalled the complexity of the undertaking, the energy with which amendments were proposed to nuance the draft text that became the *Charter*, and how carefully delegates weighed up issues of international law and international relations.[119] This sense of the occasion in San

---

114 Again, see discussion of Resolution 1267 in Chapter 6.2.2.

115 Despite culling by the Council from time to time—see further discussion in Chapter 5.1.

116 See discussion in Chapter 5.2.

117 See, for example, discussion of Indonesia not heeding Council authority in Chapter 6.1.

118 As again noted recently to confirm the freshness of the problem—for example, the need 'to safeguard the stature of the Council by fully and faithfully implementing its decisions'—see *Letter dated 14 February 2019 from the Permanent Representative of Finland to the United Nations addressed to the President of the Security Council* S/2019/144 (15 February 2019), 4. See also *Letter dated 26 May 2016 from the Permanent Representative of Finland to the United Nations addressed to the President of the Security Council* S/2016/506 (2 June 2016), 11: 'the real impact that the Council made on the ground was the best metric, and that would entail making sure that its decisions were followed through.' However, an unnamed Council member noted that 'the Council had frequently failed to live up to its mandate under the Charter' (ibid, at 12). See also below Chapter 6, n 115.

119 Noting the 'strongest circumstantial evidence for the sense of an obligation to comply with treaties is the care that states take in negotiating and entering into them'—Chayes and Chayes, above Chapter 2, n 76, 186.

Francisco is further conveyed by, for example, the 'current affairs' perspective from then Deputy Prime Minister of Australia and Minister for External Affairs Herbert V Evatt,[120] in three lectures he delivered during 1948 while the Holmes Lecturer at Harvard Law School.[121] Evatt's narrative evokes the intensity of the negotiating process, hinging on the belief that states would have to deliver on their promises. His assessment found a clear contribution from other nations to improve the draft put forward by the 'great powers',[122] in which he included change to make powers of the General Assembly plenary rather than limited, create the Trusteeship Council, elevate the Economic and Social Council to the status of 'principal organ' and broaden its powers, along with modifications to regional arrangements. On the document that became the *Charter*, his assessment is not unfair.[123]

Viewing the same event as history rather than current affairs,[124] Ian Hurd portrays it as an exercise in legitimising the plan brought to UNCIO as the 'great powers' preferred way of ordering things.[125] In contrast to Evatt, he sees that objections of other nations achieved nothing significant for all the energy and time that was expended on them.[126] Informed by seeing how the organisation has worked in practice, Hurd's assessment is also not unfair.[127]

---

120 The Dean of Harvard Law School, Erwin Griswold, may have been particularly kind to say that there was 'no one who has played a more intimate part in the foundation and development of the United Nations' (Evatt, above Chapter 1, n 37, Preface). With a distinguished legal career and no small success in domestic politics by then already to his credit, Evatt might at least be allowed a unique insight as he was the third President of the General Assembly, and was also the first President of the Atomic Energy Commission.

121 On the UN's formation, workings, and future, published together as Evatt, above Chapter 1, n 37.

122 Being the UK and the USA, with either the USSR or China which, even then, would not attend the same Dumbarton Oakes meetings together—into which group France was included by the early days of the San Francisco Conference (see Hurd, above Chapter 1, n 25, 85 n 6).

123 See Evatt, above Chapter 1, n 37, 16.

124 For a novel insight with something of both perspectives, see Inis L Claude 'A Scholar's Beginnings: A Study of the San Francisco Charter' (2000) 40(2) *Virginia Journal of International Law* 311. As an eminent scholar of international organisation, Claude brought to light a piece analysing the *Charter* that he drafted before the *Charter* even came into force.

125 Although status as 'great powers' rested on premises that may not survive detailed examination—see above Chapter 1, n 90 and associated text.

126 Hurd, above Chapter 1, n 25, 95 and Chapter 4 therein generally.

127 Hurd also notes the importance of an agent such as Evatt—see Hurd, above Chapter 1, n 25, 94.

What endures is the gist of the *Charter* design for the Council: for the UN to become a reality called for tipping the scales towards a collective purpose despite the concomitant intrusions onto state sovereignty. This came partly—even principally—from favouring the 'great powers', but the draft *Charter* was also a dead letter without subscription from the global hoi polloi, then some four dozen states.[128] After the UN's design was extensively explained and justified at UNCIO (despite 'no go' areas for the 'great powers', including the veto power bestowed on the P5), for those other states the scales were tipped partly—and perhaps largely—by the idea that the Council could feasibly maintain international peace and security, or restore it when the need arose. Self-evidently, implementing Article 43 was to be a pivotal feature of this capacity.

This is the nub of a conundrum of international organisation, inherent in the UN and especially in the Council: to advance their purposes, powerful nations often must obtain the cooperation of those that are less so, with legitimacy—'an actor's normative belief that a rule or institution ought to be obeyed'[129]—cast as an active ingredient in achieving the requisite support.[130] Of course, that is now all the more challenging to achieve in a third millennium world of around 200 states and other entities that assert their statehood.

So, beyond a significant portion of the *Charter* being unfulfilled,[131] desuetude of Article 43 flags a dilemma in implementing Council projects: for success now, the Council relies on formal authority combined with its legitimacy as perceived by states, but success in its present projects is also needed so the Council 'banks' legitimacy as an aid to its future projects. Put another way, the Council must have compliance today to see its projects come to fruition, but also as an ingredient in engendering respect for its authority and, thus, compliance tomorrow. When the Council was called upon to respond to Tunisia's

---

128 Fifty nations were present (obviously, without then 'enemy states')—this included two constituent republics of the USSR (now Belarus and Ukraine) which became 'original members'. Poland was invited but unable to attend as its government was in process of being composed, although it did also become an 'original member'. See United Nations *1945: The San Francisco Conference* <http://www.un.org/en/sections/history-united-nations-charter/1945-san-francisco-conference/index.html>.

129 Hurd, above Chapter 1, n 25, 7.

130 For example, Thomas Franck identifies the 'compliance pull' of legitimacy—Franck (1988), above Chapter 2, n 76; Thomas M Franck *The Power of Legitimacy Among Nations* (Oxford, 1990). See also generally Allen Buchanan and Robert O Keohane 'The Legitimacy of Global Governance Institutions' (2006) 20(4) *Ethics & International Affairs* 405.

131 See above n 11 and associated text about other provisions that are, in effect, inoperative without Article 43.

complaint of aggression by France in 1961, including the resulting devastation of Bizerta, the issue was put thus by an E6 member:

> I should be afraid of desecrating the ruins and dead of Bizerta if I said that non-compliance with a decision of the Security Council, whatever it might be, was more serious than the dispute itself, and even than the aggression with its tragic consequences. That would be a good topic for a dissertation on the value of our institutions and the authority of their decisions. ... The big nations should set the small an example of respect to an institution in which they bear the weightiest responsibilities. The Council will not be entitled in future to impose on small States decisions which it could not impose on large. It is essential, therefore, to secure compliance ...[132]

Thus a legal obligation for implementation of Council directions may well arise from the standing of the *Charter* in the international legal order, but, with due pragmatism, the open question about Council productiveness is the likelihood of compliance or conformity by states. Of course, national interests obviously come into play here, but compliance still relies significantly on the Council's authority and legitimacy, where garnering legitimacy is all the more prudent in the essentially voluntaristic process and system of international organisation.

Though the Council seems no more likely to cease operations than the world is to find ubiquitous and enduring peace and security, evidence for Council productiveness thus is not encouraging so far, as already noted in the views of scholars and practitioners—and, indeed members of the Council.[133] Without substantive change (as opposed to an occasional concession),[134] the future is quite possibly no more so. Ian Hurd, for example, forecasts that:

> The future of the Council looks a lot like its past: long periods of irrelevance punctuated by interventions of "governance" on behalf of the strongest states. The periodization between these is determined by the

132 UN SCOR, 964th mtg, UN Doc S/PV.964 (28 July 1961), 26 [142]-[143] (United Arab Republic).

133 Where a participant in the annual workshop for newly elected Council members 'lamented that there was a prevailing image of the Security Council as an organ that was becoming less effective and less influential over time'—see *Letter dated 14 February 2019 from the Permanent Representative of Finland to the United Nations addressed to the President of the Security Council* S/2019/144 (15 February 2019), 3. See also discussion in Chapter 2.1, for example, including Chapter 2, n 15 and n 18 to 20 inclusive, and associated text.

134 See, for example, later discussion of Resolution 1267 in Chapter 6.2.2.

> interests of the Great Powers—it comes into action when the Great Powers find it useful for their own purposes and it fades when they disagree.[135]

If accountability of the Council is understood only in the sense of ex post facto legal accountability, then the case example of Article 43 could appear just a quaint instance of fallout from the *Realpolitik* of the Cold War. Without an overt decision, construing the Council's action as a wrongful act that triggers legal responsibility is quite challenging even with hindsight. In that light, it could be tempting to simply write off Council missteps, errors, and failures, as 'just politics'—casting lack of an accountability mechanism as a foible of the *Charter* system, along with the Council's 'notorious selectiveness'[136] in engaging with matters raised for its attention.[137]

On the other hand, this discussion highlights Article 43 as an important element of the *Charter*, arguably on par with construction of the Council in the *Charter* design, but one that has been allowed to subside into desuetude by Council inaction. More importantly, Article 43 is but one item in quite an array of unfinished Council business—recommendations, determinations, and decisions—not implemented over the course of decades. The sum of that is quite a glaring shortfall in what the Council might have accomplished.[138]

A particular complexity for the Council is that unfinished business may be so for sound reasons, but if it is also unexplained then that soundness remains unknown and challengeable—and the more so in an era likely to be defined by the impact of social media. This brings associated implications for Council legitimacy: as well as undermining its own ability to learn and adapt to change, a habit of leaving unfinished business also unaccounted is unlikely to bolster its legitimacy.

These aspects of Council productiveness thus are interconnected in complex ways with notions of accountability, so fraught and inconclusive debate over Council reform seems rather unsurprising. Moreover, since associated

---

135 Ian Hurd 'UN Security Council: Future Prospects for a Compromised Hegemon' on *E-International Relations* (8 November 2016) <http://www.e-ir.info/2016/11/08/un-security-council-future-prospects-for-a-compromised-hegemon/>.

136 Martii Koskenniemi 'The Place of Law in Collective Security' (1996) 17(2) *Michigan Journal of International Law* 455, 460.

137 Where such a mechanism might, at least, answer questions noted by José Alvarez, such as 'why the Council chose to act in some cases falling short of manifest interstate aggression but not in other cases of arguable violation of the Charter' (Alvarez, above n 1, 15). See also discussion in Chapter 6.1 as to the Council's interest in conflicts possibly impacting upon international peace and security.

138 See discussions of what it has done in Chapter 2.1, and the Council agenda in Chapter 5.1.

ramifications of Council conduct may play out over decades, impetus for reform appears—at least in retrospect—to face a very steep mountain to climb, one perhaps better approached progressively by accountability being part and parcel of Council working methods, for example. In the Council's idiosyncratic case, this shows that an overarching reason why one would seek a measure of Council accountability is the potential for accountability to contribute to having and sustaining a well-functioning Council, one whose productiveness is rather more in evidence.[139]

Accordingly, to enhance legal and institutional arrangements surrounding the Council and its work calls for going beyond merely reporting its activities, or ad hoc concessions on what it does or how it acts.[140]

The need is to *systematically* articulate, investigate, and analyse, relevant issues, and then respond in a *systemic* frame. Thus the pervasive point is to address promptly, learn from progressively, and respond coherently, in relation to:

(a) unfinished business, which may create doubts about Council productiveness but also has the potential to leave Council obligations unfulfilled or Council duties unattended;
(b) deleterious effects arising from conduct that is contested, which may prove to be ineffective, unproductive, or counter-productive;[141]
(c) effectiveness in obtaining due compliance with Council decisions, along with conformity to its recommendations, where respect for Council authority and its legally-empowered directions underpins all its results; and
(d) the productiveness of Council conduct (beyond just compliance), to be seen in the actual impact of Council decisions or recommendations on the purposes they were said to serve.

Who that may need to engage in dialogue is the next dilemma, as the audience for each of these things may differ: unfinished business affects many others

139 And so also stopping well short of pursuing accountability for its own sake alone.

140 Again, noting persistence by the E10 in seeking a Council response to objections about implementing Resolution 1267 for example—see discussion in Chapter 6.2.2.

141 Where even potentially being unlawful can delay or dilute implementation of what appears necessary in the interests of international peace and security—ibid. Moreover, as, for example, Stephen Holmes puts it—a 'government that is not compelled to give reasons for its actions may soon have no plausible reasons for its actions'—see Stephen Holmes *The Matador's Cape: America's Reckless Response to Terror* (Cambridge University Press, 2007), 6. That is: like other decision-makers (including governments but also various other power-wielders), the Council is still susceptible to acquiring unhelpful habits when not pressed to explain itself in line with relevant standards, to those others to whom it is connected via rules that provide such standards. See also discussion in Chapter 4.3.

besides UN members with a direct interest in the work of the Council; there may be negative effects even if Council conduct is taken as lawful; compliance issues may connect the Council directly to states but engage others as well; and purposes the Council is to serve under the *Charter* are, in any case, not a simple collection of duties readily observable as they are carried out.

As discussed in turn in Chapter 4, responses to such issues are complicated by two aspects of the Council being a unique politico-legal actor: firstly, it is under no compulsion to adopt a particular political style (such as democratic), but the Council remains dependent on many others to make its directions come to fruition; secondly, the Council similarly may choose its own style within the international legal order (not necessarily mimicking the law-making parts of government), but that will be for little benefit if the approach that it takes does not produce appropriate results.

CHAPTER 4

To Whom Should the Security Council Be Accountable?

To whom the Council might account for its conduct is a profound question not merely because the Council has an unparalleled place in the world. Legal arrangements by which the Council exists, and the work that it does, connect it to a veritable constellation of actors, and do so in sundry ways. These are, however, largely not stipulated in the *Charter* or specified elsewhere.

To begin with, Article 7 assigns a province to each principal organ of the UN: the General Assembly, the Security Council, the Economic and Social Council, the Trusteeship Council,[1] the International Court of Justice, and the Secretariat. Many of their practical connections are not mentioned in the *Charter*, and, insofar as they are, the description is thin.[2] This means, inter alia, that as a starting point for answering to whom the Council might account for its conduct, there is no (relatively) straightforward connection to another involving accountability which emanates from the *Charter*, nor is there collection of duties in, or arising directly from, the *Charter*, that could serve to indicate an audience for dialogue on Council productiveness.

With today's concepts of accountability barely on the horizon,[3] such questions very likely did not occupy the drafters in 1945. In any case, they deliberately left these organs to resolve questions of *Charter* interpretation in their own work, which was not then necessarily unusual in a treaty. The result is that the principal organs thus may have cause to interact, and their work towards UN Purposes intersects anyhow, but there is no saying, for example, that such activity will be as productive as it might be with other legal or institutional arrangements.

In a functionalist conception of international organisations, this situation is not that remarkable: functionalism gives scant attention to other links needed for, or consequent upon, international cooperation, beyond those with an

1 Noting that: 'The Trusteeship Council suspended its operations on 1 November 1994, a month after the independence of Palau, the last remaining United Nations trust territory.' See United Nations *Trusteeship Council* <https://www.un.org/en/sections/about-un/trusteeship-council/index.html>.

2 For example, see generally Klabbers, above Chapter 1, n 52.

3 See above Chapter 1, n 53.

 DOI:10.1163/9789004444300_005

institution's member states.[4] Moreover, legality of, and/or benefits from, the actions of international organisations went largely unquestioned quite for some time.[5]

A wider perspective shows, however, that the Council potentially interacts with a range of other actors in the course of its work,[6] and all have some capacity to help or to hinder its productiveness. For example, the Council is linked to the International Court of Justice by its right to request an advisory opinion by Article 96 of the *Charter*;[7] the Court has an obligation to answer by Article 65 of the *Statute of the International Court of Justice*.[8] Such arrangements stand to aid the Council's productiveness—though, in the words of Judge Higgins, the Council 'has failed to make use of this provision for many years'.[9]

As the work of the UN has developed, the picture is, in any case, observably more diverse and complex: an array of other actors outside the walls of the UN can, and very often do, impact upon the outcomes of Council activities and, thereby, the Council's capacity to do what it is there to do. As well as those actors addressed in the *Charter*, a variety of others may feature significantly from time to time in relation to international peace and security—ranging from those intending to somehow facilitate, support, or augment, Council work (for example, non-government organisations which draw attention to states' conduct that potentially engages international law including the *Charter*),[10] through to actors potentially impeding international peace and security (including those whose malice is armed by modern technology which can be deployed to interfere in international relations).

---

4 See above Chapter 2, n 55 and 56.

5 See above Chapter 2, n 11 to n 13 inclusive.

6 See above Chapter 2, n 10 to 16 inclusive.

7 As is the Assembly, noting only states may be parties in cases before the Court—see *Statute of the International Court of Justice*, opened for signature 26 June 1945, 1 UNTS XVI (entered into force 24 October 1945), Article 34.

8 Noting that 'the Court is not bound to give an opinion, but may decline to do so if it considers that course appropriate [though it] has never in fact done so'—see Hugh Thirlway 'The International Court of Justice' in Malcolm D Evans (ed) *International Law* (Oxford, 4th ed, 2014), 612. One comparable possibility of refusal has arisen in a contentious case (at 601). Note also that the Court has not the capacity to instigate a substantive matter with the Council—advising that new judges are needed from time to time being taken as procedural.

9 UN SCOR, 5474th mtg, UN Doc S/PV.5474 (22 June 2006), 8 (Judge Rosalyn Higgins). Speaking as President of the International Court of Justice, Judge Higgins was addressing themes on the rule of law, strengthening international law, and maintenance of international peace and security.

10 For example, see below Chapter 6, n 108, 109, and 111; see also below n 95.

Leaving aside that wider circle of interactions for the moment, the potential for impacts upon productiveness of UN organs can readily be observed in the work of the Security Council and the General Assembly.

The *Charter* does not specify an accountability relationship between these chambers, nor does it define an authoritative mechanism to unravel related contentions.[11] Nevertheless, one need not look far to see that a productive outcome from both is required on some matters in order to achieve a single result for or by the UN. For example, some require action by both, such as appointing a Secretary-General under Article 97, while Article 24(1) allows for Assembly interest in international peace and security despite primary responsibility for maintaining or restoring it being given to the Council. Further, the Assembly may shape the Council agenda under Article 11(3), by referring a matter to the Council, although the Council does not always respond;[12] the Council does shape the Assembly agenda by notifying matters being dealt with by the Council under Article 12(2), on which Assembly consideration must, and almost always does, then pend until the Council has concluded its deliberations.[13]

Taking together the noted roles of the International Court of Justice and the General Assembly, to depict relationships around the Council one might begin with interactions of these three principal organs in matters conceivably impacting upon international peace and security.[14]

As illustrated in Figure 1, their respective agendas show that between the Council and the Assembly there is a constant possibility of interaction, which either may instigate (shown by a continuous, two way arrow). In contrast, both the Council and Assembly interact with the Court on substantive matters only

11 See above Chapter 1, n 47 and associated text; see also Klabbers, above Chapter 1, n 52.

12 For examples discussed herein that involve Assembly requests under Article 11, see Chapter 3.1 discussion of unanswered questions about Article 43 implementation, or similarly Chapter 6.1 in relation to Timor.

13 Noting that Council stalemates have tested this procedure—most notably in the events leading up to the Assembly's resolution, *Uniting for Peace*—see above Chapter 3, n 94. See also the brief points in Simma et al, above Chapter 1, n 29, 504 [MN 39].

14 Limited to these three organs for clarity of the diagram—obviously, the Secretariat plays a crucial role in, for example, mounting peacekeeping operations, and even the Economic and Social Council may contribute over the longer term by, for example, addressing sources of friction that are said to engender resort to force or other disturbances of international peace and security. A similar case might be made, albeit in more negotiable terms, for the interactions that either has with other organs of the UN. See also above n 1 in relation to the Trusteeship Council.

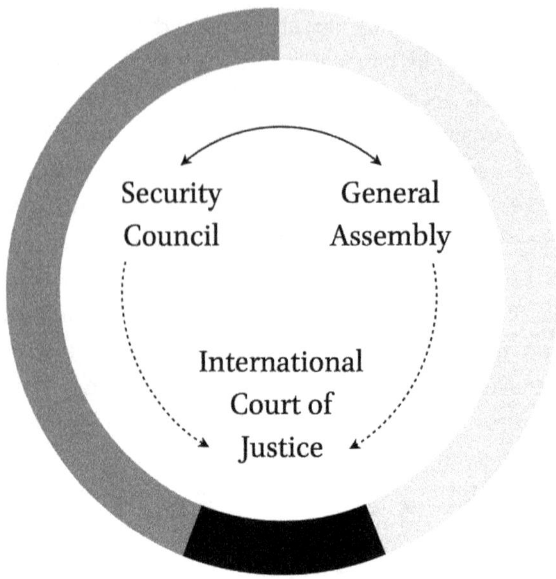

FIGURE 1 Interactions of three principal organs of the UN

occasionally, contact which they may instigate but the Court cannot (as shown by a broken, one way arrow).[15]

One issue for accountability is that this may be the extent, more or less, of their legally-stipulated interactions, but, as becomes evident in a closer look at how the links work in practice, it is not exhaustive of the ways in which one may impact upon the ability and capacity of the other to pursue its Functions and thus its productiveness towards *Charter* Purposes. This is seen, for example, where the Council and the Assembly have a conjoint *Charter* role to deal with applications for membership of the UN under Article 4: in response to a formal application, Article 4(2) means that acquiring new members involves both the Council (to make recommendations) and the Assembly (to decide). This connection can be activated at any time, though it is done less frequently now than in the UN's early years, the decolonisation era, or the surge of UN membership growth after the breakup of the USSR.

15 Of course, the International Court of Justice makes an approach to the Council and the Assembly to make new appointments when serving judges die or retire, but this is taken as being a procedural connection.

Though membership is a substantive question,[16] the Council's post-Cold War approach could appear pro forma: once on the Council agenda, the question is, in effect, usually resolved in the Council's Committee on the Admission of New Members,[17] with just the formality then dealt with at an official meeting of the Council.[18]

In 1990, for example, the Council resolved to recommend Namibia's application be accepted,[19] with Council members plus several UN member states present. Formal proceedings ran for over two hours,[20] but the resolution was adopted unanimously by a show of hands in the first few minutes: speeches marking this moment in Namibia's emergence as a sovereign nation took up the balance of the meeting, though the Assembly had yet to consider the application. Apropos the newest UN member, South Sudan's application was considered in 2011: the Council recorded its decision with just Council members and the Secretary-General present, the resolution was adopted 'without vote' (here meaning without a show of hands),[21] and the meeting lasted five minutes—including time for the President to greet this in a congratulatory message that was barely distinguishable from dozens preceding it, for all the states the Council has recommended since Namibia.[22]

With some political gloss the latter results might be put as 'prompt' or 'efficient', and they certainly appear to have been productive actions by the Council. That is, for states admitted to membership during this period, no (legal) challenge has subsequently been raised: the Council was exercising powers under the *Charter*, and appears to have acted within the law; its decisions appear consistent with the organisation's aspiration for universal

16 Confirmed as a matter of substance in practice, by the applicability of the P5 veto to such decisions—see veto references in the next section.

17 The Committee is comprised of all Council members.

18 The Committee's records are not public and reports in the post Cold War period are uniformly bland. For example, cf *Report of the Committee on the Admission of New Members Concerning the Application of the Republic of Namibia for Admission to Membership in the United Nations* UN Doc S/21251 (17 April 1990); *Report of the Committee on the Admission of New Members concerning the application of the Republic of South Sudan for admission to membership in the United Nations* UN Doc S/2011/420 (11 July 2011)—each runs to less than a page and there are no material differences.

19 SC Res 652, UN SCOR, 2918th mtg, UN Doc S/Res/652 (17 April 1990).

20 UN SCOR, 2918th mtg, UN Doc S/PV.2918 (17 April 1990).

21 Consistent with recent Council usage, but this has varied over time. See, for example, below Chapter 5, n 79 and associated text.

22 UN SCOR, 6582nd mtg, UN Doc S/PV.6582 (13 July 2011). However, see also discussion on Palestine later in this chapter.

membership as an aid to the Purposes for which the UN was created.[23] So, what reason might there be to seek explanation or justification of what the Council has done?

If the post-Cold War process appears anodyne, one reason to look past the surface of this legally-framed task is that, under a veneer of political civility, the same approach is not accorded to all aspirants. Some cases rival Cold War era contests, when membership of Albania and others was delayed for years; others recall post-colonial wrangling over Bangladesh, where qualifications for membership were used as respectable clothes for partiality in blocking that application.[24]

Without being especially numerous, exceptions show that not all membership aspirants can even get on the Council agenda, and some that do then sit there, unproductively bogged down by weight of political baggage. That there are exceptions thus suggests that probing the Council's approach may reveal what is in play, beyond conduct which the thin official record could suggest has become a little cavalier.

One potential issue is that the Court has long since advised that *Charter* requirements are exhaustive of the qualifications for UN membership,[25] so other considerations being pursued would raise implications relevant to accountability—on closer scrutiny being somehow ultra vires, for example, or otherwise not entirely encompassed within the boundaries of law and policy as expressed in the *Charter*. Another potential issue is that Council conduct may, in effect, hold back the UN policy of aiming for universal membership, because even if individual members are influential in Council decision making, the culmination of that process is a collective outcome of the Council: it functions as an entity, distinct from its constituent members, and such states are engaged in Article 4 decisions only by virtue of their Council membership.[26] So UN Purposes may or may not be better served by overt articulation of provisions found in Article 4, but, either way, the pivot point here is *who* may expect their questions to be answered about what transpires on question of UN membership—only the applicant state or entity, or other states supporting or opposing the applicant as well?

23 See discussion in Chapter 1.1; see also discussion in Simma et al, above Chapter 1, n 29, 342.

24 On both points, see discussion in the next section.

25 *Conditions of Admission of a State to Membership in the United Nations (Article 4 of the Charter) (Advisory Opinion)* [1948] ICJ Reports 57.

26 Thus not here suggesting that the institutional veil between the Council and its members be pierced—see generally Catherine Brölmann *The Institutional Veil in Public International Law* (Hart, 2007).

Perhaps even the Assembly as a whole, as the collective awaiting any recommendation from the Council? Even if the Council in not legally obliged to do so, might answers usefully be proffered in the interests of furthering 'conditions under which justice and respect for the obligations arising from treaties'?[27]

Though framed in terms of membership questions, such concerns are indicative of those raised in many Council interactions with others, ranging widely on geopolitically fraught and legally intricate matters of international peace and security.[28] In probing to whom the Council might account for its decisions, membership questions thus are illustrative as matters of substance, but are a step less contestable than many others on the Council's agenda: its right to make recommendations is given by the *Charter*, so reviewing such matters keeps focus on the purposes of this discussion.

Accordingly, Council conduct on dealing with membership is explored to highlight conundrums in finding to whom the Council might account for its conduct.

4.1 Case Example: UN Membership

Over its first decade, growth in the UN's membership was quite sparse, being beset by various challenges—not least, but not only, Cold War roadblocks that largely stalled the Council on making recommendations to the Assembly.[29]

Albania, for example, was the inaugural membership applicant considered by the Council, after being introduced at its third meeting.[30] Promoted by the USSR, Albania's application was twice delayed for 'further study',[31] and twice unable to attract enough affirmative votes.[32] The official record of Council discussions shows that the question was linked to geopolitical machinations then on foot, such as those connected to the Corfu Channel incidents between the UK

27 *Charter*, third preambular paragraph.

28 See discussion in Chapter 2, on how the Council's role is seen, and Chapter 4.2 on relationships engaged by the Council's work.

29 Conventionally interpreted as an affirmative recommendation—see Simma et al, above Chapter 1, n 29, 350 [MN 27 and 28].

30 UN SCOR, 3rd mtg, UN Doc S/PV.3 (28 January 1946).

31 Ibid; UN SCOR, 18th mtg, UN Doc S/PV.18 (13 February 1946).

32 UN SCOR, 57th mtg, UN Doc S/PV.57 (29 August 1946), 136; UN SCOR, 186th mtg, UN Doc S/PV.186 (18 August 1947), 2037.

and Albania,[33] and other disharmony between Albania, Yugoslavia, Bulgaria and Greece.[34]

Albania's application remained pending for a decade until late 1955, when the Council was (again) exhorted by 'the formally expressed desire of [the Assembly to] "consider, in the light of the general opinion in favour of the widest possible membership of the United Nations, the pending applications of all those eighteen countries about which no problem of unification arises".'[35] This prompted debate of epic proportions over five formal meetings, leading to word-by-word voting on proposals and amendments.[36] For example, in voting on one draft resolution,[37] put forward by Brazil and New Zealand late in the fourth meeting:

- One amendment, proposed by China,[38] to include the Republic of Korea and the Republic of Viet-Nam, was dealt with in two votes, each time a majority favouring recommendation being vetoed by the USSR.
- China similarly vetoed inclusion of the People's Republic of Mongolia.
- The USSR vetoed, in turn, Jordan, Ireland, Portugal, Italy, Austria, Finland, Ceylon, Nepal, Libya, Cambodia, Japan, Laos, and Spain.
- The much-amended proposal recommended only Albania, Hungary, Romania, and Bulgaria.[39]
- So much denuded, it failed, supported by the USSR alone.[40]

---

33 See UN SCOR, 114th mtg, UN Doc S/PV.114 (27 February 1947); see also *Corfu Channel (Merits)* [1949] ICJ Reports 4.

34 Addressed under various headings—see, for example, UN SCOR, 70th mtg, UN Doc S/PV.70 (20 September 1946), Item 63; UN SCOR, 82nd mtg, UN Doc S/PV.82 (10 December 1946), Item 94.

35 UN SCOR, 701st mtg, UN Doc S/PV.701 (10 December 1955), 2 (President). The President was quoting from what is now on record as *Admission of new Members to the United Nations* GA Res 918(X), UN GAOR, 10th sess, 552nd plen mtg, UN Doc A/Res/918 (X) (8 December 1955), where Vietnam and Korea were omitted by the Assembly due to the issues of unification (prompting some debate as to the extent to which the Council should be guided by the Assembly's request). This followed up on earlier exhortations such as *Admission of new Members to the United Nations* GA Res 817(IX), UN GAOR, 9th sess, 501st plen mtg, UN Doc A/Res/817 (IX) (23 November 1954).

36 UN SCOR, 701st mtg, UN Doc S/PV.701 (10 December 1955); UN SCOR, 702nd mtg, UN Doc S/PV.702 (10 December 1955); UN SCOR, 703rd mtg, UN Doc S/PV.703 (13 December 1955); UN SCOR, 704th mtg, UN Doc S/PV.704 (13 December 1955); UN SCOR, 705th mtg, UN Doc S/PV.705 (14 December 1955). There may well have been commensurate out-of-session 'negotiations' as well, but these are not—then or now—officially recorded.

37 *Admission of New Members—Brazil and New Zealand: draft resolution* UN Doc S/3502 (10 December 1955).

38 China was then represented by the nationalist, Republic of China regime based in Taiwan.

39 See UN SCOR, 704th mtg, UN Doc S/PV.704 (13 December 1955), 9–15.

40 Ibid, 14.

Advice from the International Court of Justice was already to hand confirming that requirements given in the *Charter* are exhaustive of qualifications for UN membership. The applicant must '(1) be a State; (2) be peace-loving; (3) accept the obligations of the Charter; (4) be able to carry out these obligations; and (5) be willing to do so'.[41] Meeting transcripts show, however, a haphazard array of national political views being aired that went beyond Article 4 to varying degrees.

Deliberations were also weighed down by debate on procedure that, arguably, had a substantive impact upon the matter at hand. For example, in relation to the sequential order for considering the applications: inconclusive discussion, on following the letter of the *Provisional Rules of Procedure*,[42] was circumvented by considering all applications as a group—meaning, in effect, acceptance of one application became conditional upon acceptance of all.[43] Thus a substantive effect arose from procedure, in an arguably dubious approach to doing what the *Charter* empowers the Council to do.[44]

Against that backdrop, these tortuous deliberations in 1955 did culminate in a decisive vote to recommend 16 of the 18 countries put on the table by the Assembly. Hard on the heels of four tense sessions, nugatory when the Brazil-New Zealand 'draft resolution as a whole falls to the ground',[45] the fifth meeting opened with a momentary détente. Somewhat surprisingly, the Soviet ambassador tabled another draft, omitting only Mongolia and Japan among those already supported in the Assembly.[46] The proposal was adopted, New

41 *Conditions of Admission of a State to Membership in the United Nations (Article 4 of the Charter) (Advisory Opinion)* [1948] ICJ Reports 57, 62.

42 *Provisional Rules of Procedure* UN Doc S/96/Rev.4 (29 July 1952).

43 A feature of a tranche of meetings in mid-1949—for example, see UN SCOR, 429th mtg, UN Doc S/PV.429 (24 June 1949); UN SCOR, 430th mtg, UN Doc S/PV.430 (11 July 1949); UN SCOR, 439th mtg, UN Doc S/PV.439 (7 September 1949), (especially Egypt, cross-referring to this point). This was not unrelated to the USSR's desire to redress the balance of voting power in the Assembly, which made its vetoing of membership applications infamous long before the last of 32 such cases (in 1961)—to this time in 1955, of 57 proposals vetoed by the USSR, 26 were on admission of UN members.

44 Ultimately, offset to a degree by voting on each inclusion—see Simma et al, above Chapter 1, n 29, 344 [MN 8].

45 UN SCOR, 704th mtg, UN Doc S/PV.704 (13 December 1955), 15 (President).

46 UN SCOR, 705th mtg, UN Doc S/PV.705 (14 December 1955), [7–8]; see also above n 35. To that point in the process, the USSR had enthusiastically supported Mongolia, as did western powers, but China had vetoed its inclusion; equally, while the west favoured Japan, the USSR did not. This approach appeared to seek political balance and, in particular, obviated the possibility of a further veto of Mongolia by China.

Zealand's representative saying the decision 'remedies an injustice done to many well-qualified applicants'.[47]

So here the Council did answer the Assembly's requests, if rather belatedly, but it is not clear how much of the related contention—over the course of a decade—could credibly be cast in terms of Article 4 qualifications for UN membership.

The Council's conduct since the passing of the Cold War remains notable for the occasional exceptions. The point of interest is not the conduct of states individually, but what that sums to collectively in Council decisions—showing routine, bland treatment is not afforded to all, and, in turn, that the Council's power to decide such things, conferred on it by states through the *Charter*, carries with it the capacity to affect diverse others.

Then and, perhaps more importantly, since, the substance of the question hardly features.[48] Even where argumentation is asserted in light of the *Charter*, it reads often as rhetorical, not infrequently as partisan, and occasionally as becoming, or heading towards, polemical.

Membership applications were, for example, last vetoed in 1976: the USA blocked Angola, though 13 Council members were in favour,[49] and (newly reunified) Vietnam, in the face of an otherwise unanimous Council.[50] On these cases, argument from the USA reads largely as rhetorical, especially if discounted by likely political implications of their formal names—being the People's Republic of Angola and the Socialist Republic of Vietnam. Shortly thereafter Angola was recommended for membership, when the USA abstained from voting.[51] The USA continued its stance on Vietnam, without swaying fellow Council members. Those 14 states appear to have been voicing the view of the UN's collective membership, because when Vietnam's membership was again proposed, in mid-1977, dozens of member states attended the Council meeting, without the right to vote, to announce their views in favour. A recommendation in favour was then 'adopted by consensus'—on this occasion meaning

47 UN SCOR, 705th mtg, UN Doc S/PV.705 (14 December 1955), 10.

48 See, for example, below n 92.

49 UN SCOR, 1932nd mtg, UN Doc S/PV.1932 (23 June 1976), 24. China did not participate in the voting—not unusual in the first decade of China being represented by the People's Republic of China (from late 1971, see below n 64).

50 See UN SCOR, 1972nd mtg, UN Doc S/PV.1972 (15 November 1976), 13. The USA had also twice previously vetoed applications from both the Democratic Republic of Viet-Nam and the Republic of South Viet-Nam—see UN SCOR, 1836th mtg, UN Doc S/PV.1836 (11 August 1975); UN SCOR, 1846th mtg, UN Doc S/PV.1846 (30 September 1975).

51 UN SCOR, 1974th mtg, UN Doc S/PV.1974 (22 November 1976). The recommendation was made by 13 votes to none, with the USA abstaining and China not participating in voting.

in the absence of overt objections,[52] but also without a show of hands and so having the effect of circumnavigating a further USA veto.[53]

China had earlier vetoed a positive recommendation on the application from Bangladesh in 1971.[54] Objections from China included the assertion that Bangladesh had 'violated the principles of the Charter and the relevant resolutions and is therefore not qualified at all to be admitted into the United Nations',[55] though precisely how so was not detailed. A credible contrary perspective is that China's objections had more to do with serving its partisan political interests by supporting the positioning of an ally, Pakistan, in post-war negotiations with India.[56]

In either case, the actual reasons for votes by the USA and China very likely included what amounted to a stratum of additional conditions,[57] something that a member of the Council is not entitled to impose.[58] These frustrated collective action (as vetoes on Article 4 applications had done during the impasses of the Cold War), but beyond the direct impact upon applicants, they were not without indirect impacts on, for example, those residing in the places affected. Rather than such political rhetoric and partisan consideration passing into history along with the Cold War, views nearing polemical feature in departures from the pattern of contemporary conduct.

To illustrate further: after Namibia's application engaged it just briefly, later in 1990 the Council recommended Liechtenstein without so much speechifying, in a Council meeting of less than an hour though taking time for a show of hands.[59] The following year, three Council meetings together took about

52 Where evolving Council practice on this point is one of the many details of Council work that seem carved in stone but in fact have changed non-trivially over the years, and continue to do so—see, for example, below Chapter 5, n 78.

53 UN SCOR, 2024th mtg, UN Doc S/PV.2024 (19 July 1977); UN SCOR, 2025th mtg, UN Doc S/PV.2025 (20 July 1977), [90].

54 See the report on the application from Bangladesh and associated competing proposals—*Report of the Committee on the Admission of New Members* UN Doc S/10773 (23 August 1972); *India, Union of Soviet Socialist Republics, United Kingdom of Great Britain and Northern Ireland and Yugoslavia: draft resolution* UN Doc S/10771 (23 August 1972); *China: draft resolution* UN Doc S/10768 (21 August 1972). Open contention in the Council at the 1660th meeting led to Bangladesh then being denied membership—see UN SCOR, 1660th mtg, UN Doc S/PV.1660 (25 August 1972).

55 UN SCOR, 1660th mtg, UN Doc S/PV.1660 (25 August 1972), 7.

56 Joel Wuthnow *Beyond the Veto: Chinese Diplomacy in the United Nations Security Council* (PhD Thesis, Columbia University, 2011), 31.

57 *Conditions of Admission of a State to Membership in the United Nations (Article 4 of the Charter) (Advisory Opinion)* [1948] ICJ Reports 57, 65.

58 Nor is a member of the Assembly, when the application reaches that chamber—ibid.

59 UN SCOR, 2936th mtg, UN Doc S/PV.2936 (14 August 1990).

that time to support the applications from the Democratic People's Republic of Korea and the Republic of Korea, the Federated States of Micronesia, and the Marshall Islands, with no show of hands taken on any of these.[60] Whether perfunctory or instrumental, this pattern of Council conduct is mimicked for over 30 states since recommended to the Assembly, including one whose name was still disputed at the time.[61] In contrast, on two occasions a show of hands was taken: on Nauru in 1999, and on Tuvalu in 2000. China abstained from voting, allowing each proposal to be adopted by 14 votes in favour. Reasoning from China for withholding its support was 'that the most important thing [is] upholding of the principles and purposes of the Charter [and] implementation of General Assembly resolution 2758 (XXVI)'.[62] The principles said to be offended were not, however, set out. Moreover, together Nauru and Tuvalu are home to just around 20,000 people, have less than 50 km^2 of territory all up, and are not (yet) home to significant elements of the global economic framework. So—while meaning no disrespect—these states did not, at the time of their applications being made, indicate significant capacity to affect international peace and security.[63] Further reading suggests that, rather than hinting at

60 UN SCOR, 3001st mtg, UN Doc S/PV.3001 (8 August 1991); UN SCOR, 3002nd mtg, UN Doc S/PV.3002 (9 August 1991); UN SCOR, 3003rd mtg, UN Doc S/PV.3003 (9 August 1991).

61 Being the state then sometimes known as the Former Yugoslav Republic of Macedonia—see UN SCOR, 3196th mtg, UN Doc S/PV.3196 (7 April 1993); *Admission of the State whose application is contained in document A47/876-S/25147 to membership in the United Nations* GA Res 47/225, UN GAOR, 47th sess, Agenda Item 19, 98th plen mtg, UN Doc A/Res/47/225 (27 April 1993). Since February 2019, this state is called North Macedonia—see United Nations *Growth in United Nations membership, 1945-present* <http://www.un.org/en/sections/member-states/growth-united-nations-membership-1945-present/index.html>. For further background see Niki Kitsantonis 'Macedonia and Greece Sign Historic Deal on Name Change' *The New York Times* (online) 17 June 2018 <https://www.nytimes.com/2018/06/17/world/europe/greece-macedonia-name-dispute.html>; Aristotle Tziampiris 'The Macedonian name dispute and European accession' (2012) 12(1) *Southeast European and Black Sea Studies* 153; Francesco Messineo 'Maps of Ephemeral Empires: The ICJ and the Macedonian Name Dispute' (2012) 1(1) *Cambridge Journal of International and Comparative Law* 169.

62 UN SCOR, 4103rd mtg, UN Doc S/PV.4103 (17 February 2000) in relation to Tuvalu; in relation to Nauru see UN SCOR, 4017th mtg, UN Doc S/PV.4017 (25 June 1999).

63 Or, indeed, even a vanishingly slight impediment to China's interests if that were a permissible consideration, and nor was there a suggestion that, for example, these states are home to terrorists or the means of financing their activities. Note also that the question of 'micro-states', an issue from the 1970s, had largely been resolved by the early 1990s. It was overcome by simply accepting such states as members in absence of another solution—see, for example, Simma et al, above Chapter 1, n 29, 347 [MN 15]. For further discussion, see Thomas D Grant *Admission to the United Nations: Charter Article 4 and the Rise of Universal Organization* (Martinus Nijhoff, 2009), 238.

some rogue behaviour or conduct contrary to or contravening the *Charter*, this logic instead screened China's partisan political interests. The cited Assembly resolution concerns 'restoration of the lawful rights of the People's Republic of China', in part that its representatives 'are the only lawful representatives of China' to the UN.[64] This was the instrument by which the (communist) People's Republic of China supplanted the (nationalist) Republic of China in 1971.

Put bluntly, then, it is likely that China did not support the membership applications of Nauru and Tuvalu because those states recognise Taiwan,[65] and China's commentary suggests strong criticism of that choice. By the expedient of dissuading most countries from even recognising (or continuing to recognise) Taiwan,[66] China has also kept Taiwan's UN aspirations off the agenda, despite the latter's active attempts to apply for membership from 1993 to 2007.[67]

Leaving aside, for the moment, politicking over Taiwan's status, it might be said that there was little real harm from China's stance on Nauru and Tuvalu, or even perhaps that China was praiseworthy for showing restraint in not vetoing the applications. However, China's logic potentially impinges on the sovereign right of states to independence in conducting diplomatic relations as that state sees fit: the primacy of state sovereignty in negotiating international treaties means it is unsurprising that the *Charter* does not—and, arguably, could not—require homogeneity among UN members as to recognition of other states, nor does it prohibit diplomatic relations with non-members of the UN. China's

64 *Restoration of the lawful rights of the People's Republic of China in the United Nations* GA Res 2758 (XXVI), UN GAOR, 26th sess, 1976th plen mtg, UN Doc A/Res/2758 (XXVI) (25 October 1971).

65 As does Palau since 1999, but this post-dates approval of its UN membership in 1994—see UN SCOR, 3469th mtg, UN Doc S/PV.3469 (29 November 1994). On states recognising Taiwan, see Shaohua Hu 'Small State Foreign Policy: The Diplomatic Recognition of Taiwan' (2015) 13(2) *China: An International Journal* 1. See Table 1 therein (at 3) on characteristics of Taiwan's diplomatic allies. See also below n 66 and 83.

66 Where China's related initiatives also impact upon other Council decisions: 'When the Council had to renew the mandate of the UN Preventive Deployment Force in 1999, China decided to veto it not because UNPREDEP had failed in its mission, but because Macedonia had established diplomatic relations with the government in Taiwan'—see Kishore Mahbubani 'Council Reform and the Emerging Powers' in Sebastian von Einsiedel, David M Malone and Bruno Stagno Ugarte (eds) *The UN Security Council in the 21st Century* (Lynne Rienner, 2016), 161.

67 On which the Assembly appeared to agree, but rather more doubtful is the right of the Secretary-General to find the application 'unreceivable' as Ban Ki-moon did in 2007—see United Nations General Assembly 'General Assembly Adopts Work Programme for Sixty-Second Session, Rejects Bid to Include Agenda Item on Taiwan' (United Nations General Assembly Meetings Coverage and Press Releases, UNGA/10617, 21 September 2007).

abstentions, and reasons given for them, however, could be seen to go in that direction.

Action by China was suffered to shape Council conduct, but, in contrast to vetoes in earlier times, membership aspirations of Nauru and Tuvalu were not impeded. More worrying exceptions arise, however, where candidates struggle to even get a hearing and, when they do, they remain bogged down by the weight of not dissimilar political baggage that attends the collective decision of the Council: Taiwan is one example, as already mentioned, and Palestine is another.

Palestine is recognised by states amounting to two thirds of UN members, and has applied for membership as recently as 2011.[68] In response, the Council's Committee on the Admission of New Members was unable to formulate a recommendation to the Council after several formal meetings plus however many more informal sessions.[69] The Committee's report appears no further advanced by the Council, nor revised by the Committee.[70]

With substantive discussion kept off the agenda by the prospect of a veto by the USA, the larger point is that this cause is taken up from time to time in the Council anyhow, thus highlighting how matters of membership are less prosaic for being interconnected to wider, more intricate issues of international peace and security. For example, in December 2014 Jordan tabled an omnibus proposal for an agenda item entitled 'The situation in the Middle East, including the Palestine question'. The proposal included a proposition that the Council anticipate 'welcoming Palestine as a full Member State of the United Nations within the timeframe defined'.[71] Jordan succeeded in mustering another seven votes in favour from both P5 and E10 members, despite the USA being quite vocally against it.[72]

For its part, the Assembly continues to express disapproval of the Council's stance on the question of membership for Palestine. Years of escalating

68 *Application of Palestine for admission to membership in the United Nations: Note by the Secretary-General* A/66/371-S/2011/592 (23 September 2011).

69 Recalling that the Committee is comprised of all members of the Council, but its meetings are not on the public record.

70 See *Report of the Security Council: 1 August 2011–31 July 2012* UN GAOR, 67th sess, Supp No 2, UN Doc A/67/2 (8 November 2012), 53—in relation to *Report of the Committee on the Admission of New Members concerning the application of Palestine for admission to membership in the United Nations* S/2011/705 (11 November 2011).

71 *Jordan: draft resolution* S/2014/916 (30 December 2014) [5].

72 Where the USA's vote against this resolution was not a veto as those in favour fell one short of the minimum needed for a Council decision—see UN SCOR, 7354th mtg, UN Doc S/PV.7354 (30 December 2014).

Assembly measures have progressed Palestine to a footing in UN activities tantamount to having UN membership anyhow.[73] This is demonstrated, for example, by the Assembly:

- in 1974, inviting the Palestine Liberation Organization 'to participate in the sessions and the work of the General Assembly in the capacity of observer [and] in the sessions and the work of all international conferences convened under the auspices of the General Assembly';[74]
- since 1975, operating a responsible committee and devoting a notable part of the UN's Division of Political Affairs to the human rights of the Palestinian people;[75]
- after the Council left the case hanging in 2011, choosing to accord Palestine 'non-member observer status' in 2012, and express 'the hope that the Security Council will consider favourably' Palestine's application;[76] and
- in 2015, after the Council had denied Palestine consideration by its treatment of Jordan's initiative in 2014, deciding to fly flags of non-member observer states alongside those of members—something that affects only Palestine and the Holy See.[77]

Not without irony, this last proposal was sponsored in the Assembly by the 'State of Palestine' and 20 members. It was also co-sponsored in session by another 34 members, and ultimately adopted by 119 votes to 8 (with 45 abstentions).[78] Thus, a quarter of UN members were overt supporters of the proposal, and more than 60 per cent were at least willing to go on record in favour of a scheme architected by an entity whose standing is very much at issue in the Council.

In short, Assembly action runs counter to Council decisions withholding or avoiding an affirmative recommendation on Palestine's standing, or the question being kept off the agenda by influence of the USA (which occurs also,

---

73 Though without, of course, the capacity to seek election to the Council. See also discussion in Alvarez, above Chapter 2, n 71, 186.

74 *Observer status for the Palestine Liberation Organization* GA Res 3237 (XXIX), UN GAOR, 29th sess, 2296th plen mtg, UN Doc A/Res/3237 (XXIX) (22 November 1974).

75 *Invitation to the Palestine Liberation Organization to participate in the efforts for peace in the Middle East* GA Res 3375(XXX), UN GAOR, 30th sess, 2399th plen mtg, UN Doc A/Res/3375 (XXX) (10 November 1975). See also below n 95.

76 *Status of Palestine in the United Nations* GA Res 67/19, UN GAOR, 67th sess, Agenda Item 37, 44th plen mtg, UN Doc A/Res/67/19 (4 December 2012) (emphasis omitted). The resolution was adopted by 138 in favour and 9 against, with 41 abstentions.

77 *Raising the flags of non-member observer States at the United Nations* GA Res 69/320, UN GAOR, 69th sess, Agenda Item 120, 102nd plen mtg, UN Doc A/Res/69/320 (15 September 2015).

78 UN GAOR, 69th sess, 102nd plen mtg, UN Doc A/69/PV.102 (10 September 2015), 20.

presumably, with the collective acquiescence of Council members—at least for the most part, where, for example, the initiative from Jordan mentioned above could be an exception).

A key point to note is the impact upon productiveness of Council action arising from concerted effort by states.[79] In effect, this has been able to undo or circumvent much of what seems to be the intention of the Council's Article 4 deliberations and determinations on Palestine—importantly, before even engaging the question of states' compliance with Council decisions,[80] which is crucial in matters of international peace and security.[81]

On another tack, this shows that chamber-to-chamber links between UN organs may be relevant for Council productiveness, but here 'signalling' via the Assembly is significant more as a bellwether of support for Council initiatives from the broad run of member states. The Assembly is a venue in which to gauge the collective view of states as according with the Council, and so suggesting support for implementing its decisions, or at odds with it, and so suggesting otherwise—as the case has been in relation to Palestine.[82]

These more recent examples suggest that the Council's capacity to resolve issues on membership applications is not noticeably improved since 1955, and not materially more governed or regulated to such ends. Far from subsiding, unlamented, into the mists of time, such issues remain germane to international peace and security—China continues to assert territorial claims on Taiwan by direct and indirect means,[83] and to extend them in other

79 Concerted effort as demonstrated by the results in the Assembly, but the venue is not the point—it is that sufficient concerted effort was collected.

80 And noting that compliance is by no means a foregone conclusion despite the legal framing of the Council's powers: see discussion in Chapter 6.1, especially Chapter 6, n 66 and 74, and associated text, and see generally discussion in Chapter 6.2.2.

81 On the other hand, concerted effort may also be seen to arise in inaction—when action is lacking due to collective acquiescence in bowing to P5 views, for example.

82 Where, in parallel, what collective acquiescence may mean in this case is the also open to debate.

83 This goes beyond events in Hong Kong running through much of 2019 and into 2020—see, for example, Alexandra Stevenson ' Will the U.S. Soon Treat Hong Kong Like China? Much Is at Stake' *The New York Times* (28 May 2020) <https://www.nytimes.com/2020/05/28/business/hong-kong-special-status-explained.html>. On Taiwan itself, see for example Katie Hunt 'China's ramping up pressure on Taiwan' *CNN* (online) 29 May 2018 <https://edition.cnn.com/2018/05/28/asia/taiwan-china-explainer-intl/index.html>; Ed Bryan 'Taiwan: how airlines are being dragged into China's bitter dispute over the island's sovereignty' on *The Conversation* (6 August 2018) <https://theconversation.com/taiwan-how-airlines-are-being-dragged-into-chinas-bitter-dispute-over-the-islands-sovereignty-100932>; 'Japanese airlines rename "Taiwan" as "China Taiwan" on websites'

places,[84] for example. Beyond that, pervasive implications arise which may be shown, in part, by returning to a diagram of relationships between three of the UN's principal organs. As with the general sweep of issues that potentially affect international peace and security, membership questions engage the Council and the Assembly as a matter of course, and the International Court of Justice stands ready to provide advice when called upon by either. First, however, for these organs to play their part on membership (or other questions), they must be constituted by due operation of the *Charter*.

Emplacing E10 members implicitly creates a transient group of 'candidate states' until that election is duly resolved, conceivable as sitting in the intersecting organisational space between the Council and the Assembly.[85] Similarly, the Assembly and the Council elect judges under Articles 4(1) and 8 of the *Statute of the International Court of Justice*. Neither the Council nor the Assembly has adopted rules sufficient to set out what states may, must, or might, consider in casting their votes, and it is not self-evident that the obligations of states would bear a resemblance to their obligations in any other UN decision-making process. Thus, among many political subtleties of how the arrangements work, obligations on states voting in these processes are not more fully specified than those of states voting in Council decisions on UN membership applications. In turn, long before international peace and security situations arise, the Council must interact with states in these prosaic processes, and do so without enough rules to establish uncontested duties or obligations for the Council or for these states.

The Guardian (online) 19 June 2018 <https://www.theguardian.com/world/2018/jun/19/japanese-airlines-rename-taiwan-as-china-taiwan-on-websites>.

84 See, for example, 'China keeps building infrastructure on disputed islands in South China Sea' *Deutsche Welle* (online) 15 December 2017 <http://www.dw.com/en/china-keeps-building-infrastructure-on-disputed-islands-in-south-china-sea/a-41805980>.

85 Where that process, like membership questions, can be more than passingly brief—for example, in October 2006, a result was stalemated when 47 rounds of voting could not obtain a definitive result, and the impasse was resolved only by a fresh, compromise candidate. See 'Panama wins new UN council seat' *BBC News* (online) 7 November 2006 <http://news.bbc.co.uk/2/hi/americas/6125730.stm>. More recently, see Security Council Report 'Security Council Elections: Italy and the Netherlands Agree to a Split Term' on *What's in Blue* (29 June 2016) <http://www.whatsinblue.org>; for additional background see Security Council Report *Security Council Elections 2006* (Special Research Report No. 4/2006, Security Council Report, 14 August 2006), 7. While this latter case was politically expedient, and shows a laudable spirit of compromise in one sense, the price may be paid in how effective each state is able to be in a foreshortened term—see below Chapter 5 n 26 and 27, for example. See also below Chapter 7, n 50).

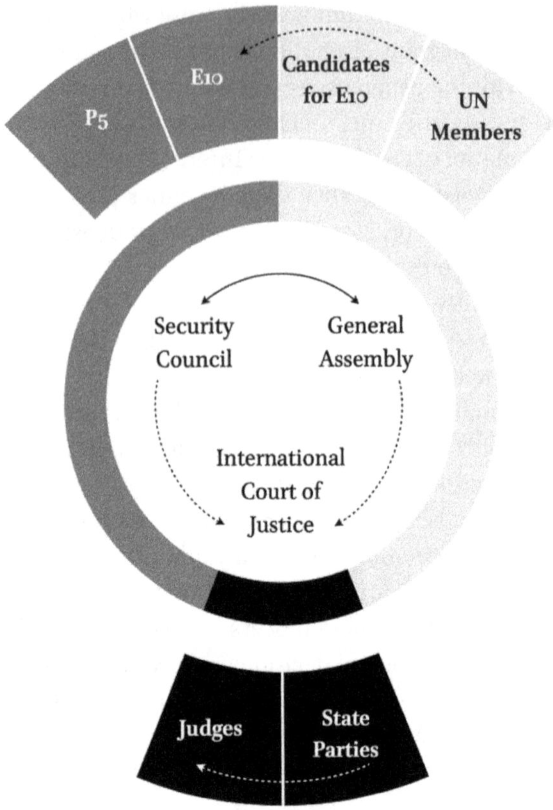

FIGURE 2 Composing three principal organs of the UN

Building on Figure 1, Figure 2 illustrates these points.

A broken, one way arrow shows workings needed for election of Council members by the Assembly; another reflects practical effects of provisions (mainly in Chapter I of the *Statute of the International Court of Justice*) that see judges elected by combined efforts of the Assembly and the Council, and obliges them to be nationals of a UN member state (which has, perforce, become party to the *Statute of the International Court of Justice*).[86]

One consequence is that without agreed rules, and standards that they express or imply, the conduct of states is particularly challenging to evaluate. In turn, another is that if the conduct of individual states is not sufficiently

86 A theoretical argument might be made about the potential revocation of their citizenship while a judge, but the likelihood of this argument having practical affect seems remote.

governed by such rules, then whatever outcome they are part of the Council achieving remains prey to doubts on legitimacy of that conduct—even without somehow removing, lifting, or piercing, the institutional veil drawn between the Council and its constituent members.

The *Charter* provides some boundaries around Council decisions, to which the Council's *Provisional Rules of Procedure* also adds something, and, as noted earlier, the *Charter* drafters expected contentions would be dealt with in the course of business.[87] Practice shows, however, at least two pervasive issues: even together, the *Charter* and the Council's *Provisional Rules of Procedure* do not appear to sum to a sufficient guide to circumscribe rightful and/or productive conduct for the Council, and, in any case, practical issues still arise—as demonstrated by the decisions on membership questions outlined in the case example.

On the whole, membership questions are, I suggest, a reasonable gauge for the broad run of Council decision-making conduct and highlight a fundamental issue: in this interest-laden geopolitical arena, legal and political dimensions of its decisions are inextricably intertwined, and, in effect, also largely ungoverned for want of an evidently shared understanding of duties or obligations for the Council or its constituent members. A key consequence is that, even if provided with mechanisms for reviewing Council conduct, a review would struggle to find conduct standards to apply. Moreover, earlier discussion suggests standards are unlikely to be agreed by the Council and the Assembly: prolonged reform debate has not (yet) produced agreement on governing key elements of its decision-making (such as using the veto), or addressed the issue of 'representativeness' in its composition, or characterised what Council members are there to do or what they must, may, or might, consider in doing whatever that may be.[88] Obviously, beyond UN membership questions the consequences will be all the more fraught in parallel to the complexity and seriousness of the matter at hand.

Whether the Council's conduct is ungovernable, just because the basis for governance is contested, is, however, a rather different question. As discussed in the next section, the question of whether the Council's conduct is acceptable is relatable to who may help or hinder Council productiveness, and thus to whom it perhaps should be accountable.

---

87 See above Chapter 1, n 47.

88 See discussion in Chapter 2.2.

4.2 Source of Powers and Those Affected

The case example of UN membership highlights some ways in which actors relate to the Council, and thereby impact upon its productiveness through their interaction. This unfolds largely in the absence of a scheme for organising pragmatic detail of its political and legal relationships. That is:

(i) links to actors with capacity to impact on the Council's work are, to begin with, as sui generis as the Council itself; but

(ii) Article 4 questions highlight that there is more to the Council's relationships to states than a functionalist paradigm would suggest by characterising them in formalist, legally-based terms; and

(iii) in any case, the Council has more, and more diverse, links to others—such as UN organs and non-state actors (including entities whose statehood may be at issue, or those whose conduct indicates malign intent towards international peace and security)—and they may affect Council productiveness towards its Functions or other contributions to UN Purposes; moreover

(iv) to date, the Council has largely eschewed rules for governing these idiosyncratic circumstances to assist its 'flexibility',[89] which does have an impact upon its productiveness—but, it must be said, by no means always for the better.

The question thus is whether a measure of accountability for such things would contribute to maintaining or enhancing Council productiveness. If this would flow from meeting expectations of actors with capacity to help or hinder Council work, in order to engender their respect for its authority and thereby their compliance with its directions,[90] this begs a further question: who would those actors be?

Recalling that, as a legal construct, the Council exists only because of the *Charter*, links to other actors in the first instance emanate from it being empowered by the *Charter*. This means that, inter alia, Article 4 decisions signify the tip of an iceberg of issues on respecting its authority and complying with its decisions—and this is essential in order for the Council to get much done at all. In turn, actors relevant to such matters signify the range of actors that may at least need to be acknowledged, if not engaged, in a process of the Council explaining or justifying its conduct in aid of enhancing its productiveness.

---

89 On 'flexibility' as mentioned in relation to the Council, see below n 114 and 115, and associated text.

90 Where the Assembly largely getting its way on Palestine's membership, for example, speaks to the contrary.

To begin with, UN member states collectively empower the Council through the medium of the *Charter*, and presumably are concerned both that powers conferred are duly exercised, and such use is intra vires. Beyond the precise nature of that conferral,[91] pressing the point on legality suggests an important possibility that could undermine Council productiveness: some Council decisions may be flawed, or otherwise fall short of the legal mark, *which arises whether or not they can be reviewed judicially*.

As one example, Article 4 decisions are legally-framed and aided by International Court of Justice advice, and (at least in essence) less fraught than questions on the use of force in international relations. Even so, no set formula can weigh up the extent to which a candidate may meet Article 4, with its qualitatively-expressed requirements, and what may constitute a 'peace-loving' state offers especial challenges.[92] Even politics aside, this means that it is not out of the question that the Council could interpret and apply such factors in a way that would not stand up to judicial scrutiny. Pivotally, states may resist these decisions as legally dubious, or not entirely legitimate because of how they were made. Concerted efforts on Palestine, for example, show how the Council's outputs become less than fully productive in the face of such resistance (or even silent 'non-support') and this arises whether or not a legal determination is ever made.

Beyond that, even if not so much as a quibble arose on this score, questions of membership still show material and (potentially) far-reaching effects from the Council's use of its powers. States' interests may be affected by active Council decisions, but this may apply on a wider front than direct interests, and impact upon quite a diversity of other actors when the result of its approach is that the Council passively 'decides not to decide'. For example, this may arise if those interests intersect with states or entities not afforded UN membership. All who reside there may well be affected, much as the situation impacted upon the people of Trieste as a result of the Council's inability to appoint a Governor after World War II.[93] The result of the Council not making

91 For example, in his comprehensive analysis of characterising the conferral of powers on international organisations by states, Dan Sarooshi identifies a spectrum of agency relationships, delegations and transfers and a related typology—see Dan Sarooshi *International Organizations and their Exercise of Sovereign Powers* (Oxford, 2005).

92 Though noting that framing the Council's decision by using those words is exceptional. Rare cases are membership resolutions on Israel and Indonesia—see, respectively, SC Res 69, UN SCOR, 414th mtg, UN Doc S/Res/69 (4 March 1949); SC Res 86, UN SCOR, 503rd mtg, UN Doc S/Res/86 (26 September 1950).

93 The Council was assigned the responsibility by treaty, but this became another Cold War impasse—see above Chapter 2, n 107 and 111.

an overt decision occluded Trieste's status and, consequently, the status at law of its people—even as the UN was forging the *Universal Declaration of Human Rights* and all that has emanated from it.[94] There were direct consequences for the people of Trieste, but this Council lapse also affected all states surrounding Trieste—in comparatively mundane matters of simply policing of their borders, for example, and seeking to deal properly with people from Trieste who wished to cross them.

Where current membership cases may end is not yet knowable, but:

- there are comparable impacts upon the status of the people of Palestine, seen in work of the UN Committee on the Exercise of the Inalienable Rights of the Palestinian People, and its network of support involving over 1,000 civil society organizations from around the world;[95] and
- the same holds on, for example, Taiwan (even without an active conflict), where the legal status of residents remains under a cloud, and this is specifically and actively at issue in current geopolitics.[96]

UN members could, in some fashion, view this as having an indirect impact on their interests—at least in part motivating Jordan and others to attempt to progress the aspirations of Palestine, as mentioned earlier, or to some degree influencing Saudi Arabia to decline to take up membership of the Council when elected.[97] This reflects a distinction made in scholarship suggesting those who wield power may owe an explanation or justification to various other actors. In this, it is not novel to differentiate models hinging on delegation

94 *Universal Declaration on Human Rights* GA Res 217A (III), UN GAOR, 3rd sess, 183rd plen mtg, UN Doc A/Res/217A (III) (10 December 1948). See also below Chapter 6, n 9.

95 Distinct from what may arise from the ongoing conflict in the region—for further details see United Nations *The Question of Palestine* <https://www.un.org/unispal/committee/>, the section on civil society notes that 'a network of more than 1,000 civil society organizations from all regions of the world, active on the question of Palestine, has been established over the years. National and international non-governmental organizations (NGOs), organizations involved in political and humanitarian work, NGOs promoting human rights or economic and social development, solidarity-, charity- or action-oriented groups, churches, academic institutions, trade unions and professional associations, and organizations that focus on women, children, refugees and detainees, are all part of the network'.

96 See above n 62 to 65 inclusive, and associated text.

97 Elected for 2014–2015, Saudi Arabia later announced 'its apology for not accepting membership in the Security Council until the Council is reformed and enabled, effectively and practically, to carry out its duties and responsibilities'—see *Letter dated 12 November 2013 from the Permanent Representative of Saudi Arabia to the United Nations addressed to the Secretary-General* UN GAOR, 68th sess, Agenda Item 114(a), UN Doc A/68/599 (14 November 2013).

or on participation,[98] and actors to whom the powerful should be accountable on those bases.[99] In delegation, it is those entrusting the power-wielder with relevant capacity; in participation, it is those affected by the power-wielder's decisions or their consequences. Both models may coexist around an actor from relationships that attend their use of power, but they lead to 'different strategies and mechanisms for accountability, because they are grounded in different notions of legitimacy' as perceived by the other actors in those relationships.[100] The importance of this distinction is that the functionalist paradigm is set to prioritise states, in their capacity as those empowering the Council, but a wider institutional and legal perspective on Council activities shows that this is not the only consideration, even in relation to UN member states. That is, Council outcomes from implementation of its decisions call for states to perceive Council action as legitimate, and so feel compelled to heed its legal authority and decisions that it makes, but this may be swayed by who the Council's decisions affect—or not, if it fails to make a decision that could somehow have had a beneficial effect. What shapes the view of a UN member is not necessarily limited to its presumed interests as a state, or those concerns ascribed to its citizens—it may embrace the many and various indirect connections that the Council has from its work.

Figure 3 highlights this by incorporating sample links as an extension of Figure 2. For example, one such link might be drawn from the Council to peacekeepers,[101] then on to persons in states where peacekeeping operations (PKO) take place (which is sometimes referred to as 'hosting' PKO). Similarly, courts and tribunals created by the Council may cast a very wide net on indirect but still associated consequences: accused who appeared in the International Criminal Tribunal for the Former Yugoslavia,[102] or the International Criminal Tribunal for Rwanda,[103] are linked indirectly to the Council,

98 Admittedly often connected to discussion of democracy and its variations, but that is, again, not to suggest that being democratic is a priority or that it should be. See above Chapter 2, n 65 and associated text.

99 See, for example, the discussion of this (and associated references) in Grant and Keohane, above Chapter 2, n 61.

100 Grant and Keohane, above Chapter 2, n 61, 32. Democratic political models of various hues fall under the participation heading, for example, delegation encompasses 'principal-agent' and 'trustee' relationships.

101 Recalling that contributing troops to peacekeeping missions is *not* an obligation stipulated under the *Charter*, taking place in lieu of, but not as a direct substitute for, implementation of Article 43.

102 Created by SC Res 827, UN SCOR, 3217th mtg, UN Doc S/Res/827 (25 May 1993).

103 Created by SC Res 955, UN SCOR, 3453rd mtg, UN Doc S/Res/955 (8 November 1994).

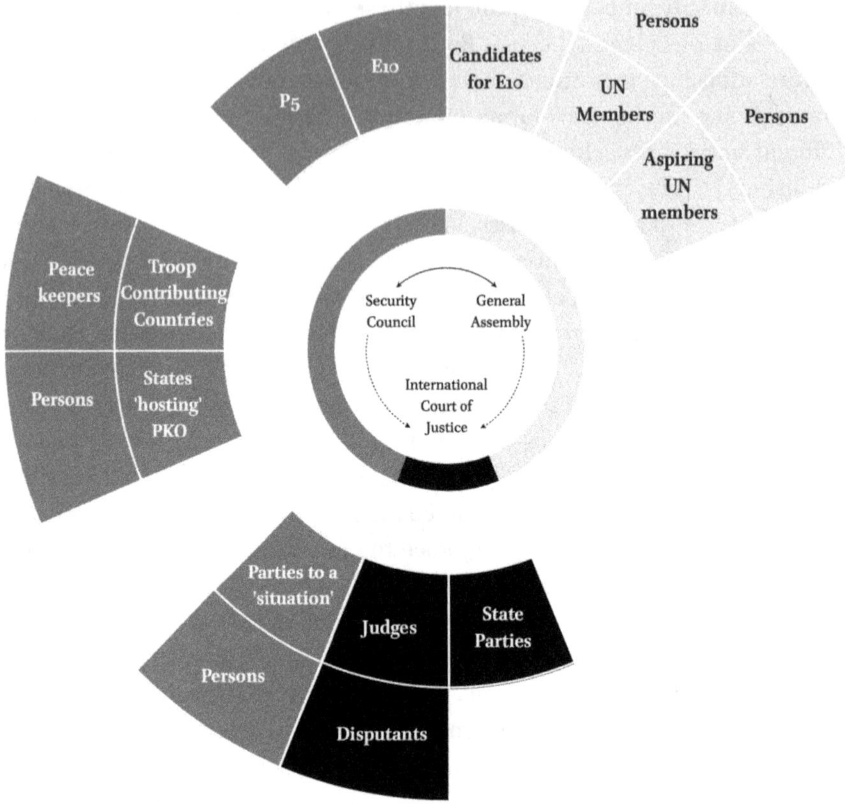

FIGURE 3 Links from the Council to 'those affected'

and also connect the Council to (alleged) victims and other witnesses in the case.[104]

Where such a tribunal (or court) is not established and advisedly could have been, it might be argued the Council has a similar, if hazier, connection to those it passively failed to serve—a link that is a degree less definitive than that to the people of Trieste (where at least there was a legal instrument obliging the Council in the matter), or to those who reside in a place aspiring to UN membership (where the *Charter* and associated advice from the International Court of Justice provide a legal framework for the link). Similarly, other such

104 The same point might be advanced on a more direct logic in relation to consequences of Council decision-making in situations involving the use of force—see for example above Chapter 2, n 98.

'persons affected' may be created via the International Criminal Court, when the Council directs states to 'cooperate fully' in the arrest and surrender of an individual: for officials involved in border and immigration control, the link to the Council involves at least their agency, its state, and that Court, but could affect those allegedly harmed by an individual not apprehended if a Council resolution is not implemented.[105]

Momentarily leaving to one side the issue of who may be affected, a question also arises about how this may flow from Council decisions and actions: as with applicants who prove to be exceptions to the Council's routine approach to Article 4 matters, indirect connections highlight that a de facto Council result still arises when the Council does not engage actively, or does so without deciding the issue one way or the other. In effect, the Council decides passively, because by its lack of a result it 'decides not to decide'.

Such lapses—or passive decisions—are not, however, free from ramifications: the Council avoiding an issue does not, necessarily or entirely, negate potential impacts upon Council productiveness. Passive decisions can still create significant bow waves, as is observable in relation to, for example, Taiwan and Palestine,[106] and this arises before the Council's approach is apprehended as either ultra vires or otherwise somehow not entirely within relevant law.[107]

On this point, it is worth just briefly revisiting China's 1971 veto on Bangladesh.[108] Though China did not substantiate its case, it is not—just on face value—unreasonable to say that violating principles of the *Charter* could be sufficient grounds for objecting to a proposed member. However, if those are sufficient grounds, the dormancy of Article 6 appears as something of a mystery. It provides for expulsion if a state has 'persistently violated' *Charter* principles, and making recommendations on this again falls to the Council. The utter absence of expulsions, and only one related Council debate in the life of the UN,[109] cannot credibly be taken to suggest that each and every UN member

105 See also discussion of Resolution 1267 in Chapter 6.2.2.

106 And a more complex but plausible case might also be made in relation to the aspirations of, for example, on Tibet (in some views, taken by force in 1950 by China, when China was already a UN member), or Kosovo, (recognised by over half of UN members, but opposed by Russia).

107 Again, such as arose in relation to Resolution 1267—see discussion in Chapter 6.2.2.

108 See above n 54, and associated text.

109 In relation to South Africa during its apartheid era—see 11 Council meetings: UN SCOR, 1796th mtg, UN Doc S/PV.1796 (18 October 1974) to UN SCOR, 1798th mtg, UN Doc S/PV.1798 (22 October 1974); UN SCOR, 1800th mtg, UN Doc S/PV.1800 (24 October 1974) to 1804th mtg, UN Doc S/PV.1804 (28 October 1974); and 1806th mtg, UN Doc S/PV.1806 (29 October 1974) to UN SCOR, 1808th mtg, UN Doc S/PV.1808 (30 October 1974). At the latter

is, and always remains, a 'peace-loving state'.[110] If that gap instead speaks to received wisdom that the UN is seen to be more productive as an institution by retaining members in the orbit of its supposedly moderating influence, that may still not be the end of the legal or policy dimensions to the question. A 'persistent violator' may pose a threat to international peace and security, for example, so such logic leaves dangling important questions about whether some onus remains on the Council to evaluate whether related objectives of the UN may, from time to time, *better* be served otherwise.[111] That is, the Council's obligations for maintaining or restoring international peace and security could include determining whether, and to what extent, UN members must adhere to, and be seen to adhere to, relevant conduct standards—at least those relating to international peace and security, which are said to underpin collective best interests as indicated in the preamble and Article 1 of the *Charter*.

This is no small issue in the light of wars, armed conflicts, and threat or use of force in international relations, a plethora of each being in evidence since 1945. Those empowering the Council may well be interested in an explanation from time to time, but, no doubt, those affected by the actions of a 'persistent violator' would very probably want it justified in terms of the Council's ambit.

On the whole, multifaceted connections that the Council has to UN member states, their interests beyond those attending their status as members, and the wider range of actors affected by Council decisions and actions, together revert attention to the admixture of authority and legitimacy which is essential to Council decisions becoming a reality. Action by UN member states remains necessary to implementing Council directions, and legitimacy is integral to having such directions heeded. Unaccounted decisions, especially when

meeting, a proposal from Kenya, Mauritania, and Cameroon—see UN Doc S/11543 (24 October 1974)—recommended that the General Assembly expel South Africa. With 10 Council members in favour, it was vetoed by France, the UK and the USA (Austria and Costa Rica abstaining). See also C N Patel 'The politics of state expulsion from the United Nations—South Africa a case in point' (1980) XIII(3) *Comparative and International Law Journal of Southern Africa* 310.

110 See generally Thomas D Grant 'International Responsibility and the Admission of States to the United Nations' (2009) 30(4) *Michigan Journal of International Law* 1095; Michael George Zifcak *Termination of Membership in the League of Nations and United Nations: A Study of the Withdrawals and Lone Expulsion* (PhD Thesis, The American University, Washington, 1970). More generally, see Konstantinos D Magliveras *Exclusion From Participation in International Organisations: The Law and Practice Behind Member States' Expulsion and Suspension of Membership* (Kluwer, 1999).

111 The balancing of which was topical in the UN's early years—see, for example, Louis B Sohn 'Expulsion or Forced Withdrawal from an International Organization' (1964) 77(8) *Harvard Law Review* 1381.

perceived as insufficiently governed, are unlikely to be helpful in banking legitimacy with actors whose compliance matters to Council productiveness.

Concern over whether action intended by the Council will come forth via the hands of states is heightened by acknowledging that, in the voluntaristic world of international cooperation, even decisions that are well accepted as within the Council's legally-based authority will not necessarily be respected by states. While perhaps less intricate than matters involving the use of force, for example, membership recommendations serve to illustrate this generally, and specifically in the concerted efforts of states in relation to Palestine.

Beyond that, as the matter at hand becomes more complicated, the circle of those affected by the Council's decisions and actions, or indecision and inaction, widens commensurately: this suggests that those to whom the Council might account goes some way beyond states empowering the Council via the *Charter* as its constituent legal instrument, or even those towards whom an identifiable legal duty or obligation may be found to exist.

While ever the Council does not set rules for itself, and no other body can, such questions must remain contested, and that contest itself tends to detract from legal and institutional arrangements around the Council and, in turn, the Council's productiveness.

4.3 Who Aids Council Productiveness?

Observations in this chapter show that being cast as a 'member state' of the UN cannot encompass all possible interactions that a state has or may have with the Council. Council conduct is a more complicated matter than signified in the *Charter* as a treaty between states, and correspondingly creates relationships on a wider and deeper basis:

(a) wider by engaging with myriad actors capable of impacting upon what the Council is able to do (including other principal organs of the UN and actors such as aspirants to UN membership) and by engaging UN member states in ways not expressed in the *Charter*; and

(b) deeper by working beyond activities or responsibilities explicit in the *Charter*, a sometimes unavoidable necessity in evolving circumstances but one which has consequences reaching all corners of the planet and persisting to affect future generations.[112]

---

112 Although, for the discussion at hand, presumed to be staying within the purposes and principles of the *Charter*.

Some such relationships the Council chooses by its own decisions and actions, others are thrust upon it by circumstances or the actions of others, but all have implications: in particular, discussion in this chapter points to the many places in which other actors may help or hinder the outcomes sought by decisions or actions of the Council, especially from consequences for its authority and legitimacy that may hinge on those outcomes.

Without exhausting the possibilities arising from Council activities, Figure 4 shows that beyond being empowered by states as UN members, the Council connects to states in multifaceted ways, and is linked to something of a constellation of actors that are affected by its work. Of course, such complicated circumstances do not themselves bar the Council from pursuing its Functions and UN Purposes productively, and some of these more diverse connections may even facilitate that. The greater question is whether the relatively ungoverned nature of this set up allows the Council to be as productive as it might be with other legal and institutional arrangements under which to pursue its contribution. Were an added measure of governance to be in prospect as an alteration of those arrangements, discussion so far indicates that one should ask who aids Council productiveness such that being accountable to them would be a step in the right direction. The logic for reform and observations in this discussion align to suggest that states hold the key, since, in effect, no result can follow a Council decision without due implementation by states. Moreover, UN member states do not seem to accept that the Council should be unconstrained in its actions, if the reform rhetoric is any guide at all. How far one would promote reaching beyond that depends on how much weight one might ascribe to states' concern for other actors affected by Council decisions, perhaps offset by the extent of one's tolerance of the idea that ends sought may justify any and all means used.

That much said, this point may better be answered by the Council speaking for itself: it has options to do so—by, for example, expanding what is covered by the *Provisional Rules of Procedure,* to further shape how the Council relates to other actors involved in maintaining or restoring international peace and security. Signifying an open task for governance of the Council, these have yet to lose their label as 'provisional',[113] despite very longstanding use and very largely

113 Where, as has been noted at the annual workshop for newly elected Council members, they 'could not be considered provisional forever'—see *Letter dated 14 February 2019 from the Permanent Representative of Finland to the United Nations addressed to the President of the Security Council* S/2019/144 (15 February 2019), 11. Predictably, this was again raised in the 2019 workshop—see *Letter dated 11 February 2020 from the Permanent Representative of Finland to the United Nations addressed to the President of the Security Council* S/2020/116 (11 February 2020). (See below Chapter 5, n 108 in relation to the workshop itself.)

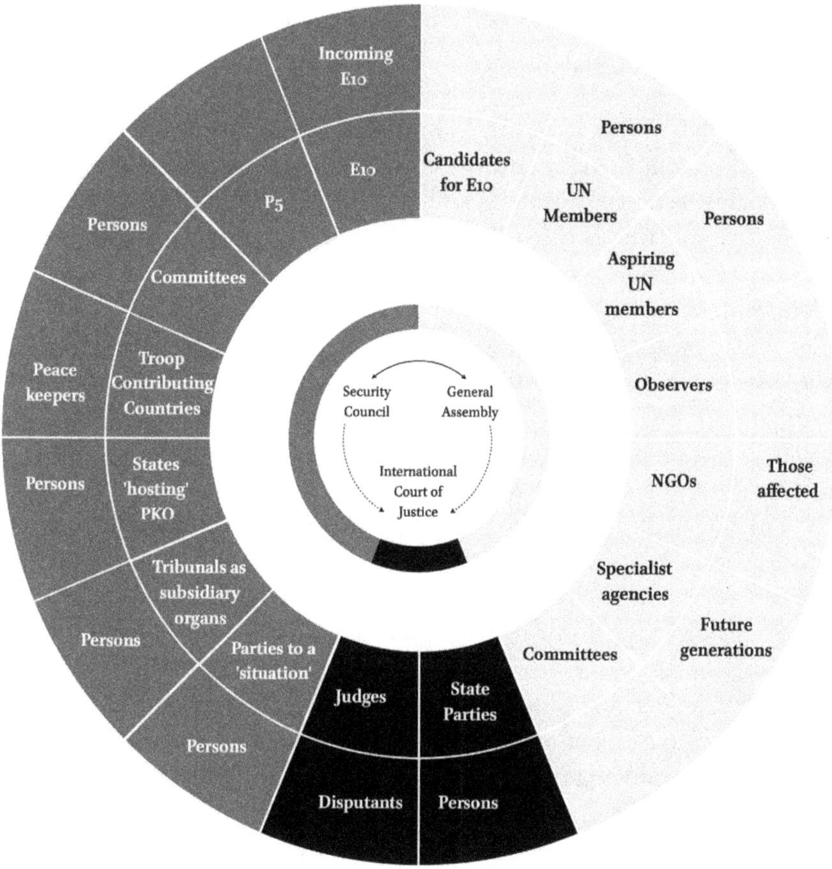

FIGURE 4 The Council's 'constellation'

undisturbed content. The Council's disinclination to change this is ascribed by some to a preference for 'flexibility':

> Some diplomats and observers have pointed out that there are pragmatic reasons to keep the rules in their provisional form: it gives the Council more flexibility and allows it to adapt better and faster to the changing international environment. Others have noted that the lack of formally

However, as Kishore Mahbubani notes: 'The P-5 have steadfastly refused all effort to remove the "provisional" label'—see Mahbubani, above Chapter 1, n 74, 259. See also below Chapter 6, n 125 to 127 inclusive, in relation to the 'preliminary question' and the 'double veto'.

> binding procedures creates doubt, leaving everyone [except the P5] on an uncertain footing.[114]

One does not, however, need to be a hardened cynic to contest whether such 'flexibility' actually delivers on that score, thereby providing a real benefit to Council effectiveness.[115] Secondly, and more generally, it is also fair to say that rules can capture the essence of tears spilled in hard experiences: they are distilled over time and experience to become a guide for behaviour in a given relationship between actors, in the context of the subject matter of their relationship. Indeed, the process of negotiating and refining such rules is itself evidence of the capability for resolving issues productively. Rules thus have capacity to help, not just hinder, particularly in expressing important parameters of the interaction between those actors. As Stephen Holmes puts it:

> Rules do not function always and exclusively as disabling restraints [but] also serve as steadying guidelines, focusing our aim, and reminding us of long-term objectives and collateral dangers that might otherwise slip from view in the flurry of an unfolding crisis.[116]

Used well, rules become a bulwark in support of UN Purposes and/or Council Functions which could otherwise be subordinated to the partisan interests of certain states—such that the Council is less productive than it could be, and than the broader sweep of states empowering it want the Council to be from time to time. If the reason for having rules is respected as much as the rules per se, they instead offer a prospect of benefitting from experience and avoiding the need to re-learn such lessons. Here the specific content of rules is not significant so much as the overarching function that rules could serve: to structure interaction with those carrying out tasks at its behest, as a basis for their accountability to the Council, or for explanation of those actions to others—both to states as those empowering the Council, via the *Charter*, as well as to state and non-state actors taking an interest in who may be affected by the Council's decisions.

---

114 Security Council Report *Security Council Working Methods: Provisional Progress* (Research Report No. 1/2018, Security Council Report, 22 January 2018), 3.

115 The state of the agenda, for example, could be taken to rather suggest otherwise—see Chapter 5.1.

116 Stephen Holmes 'In Case of Emergency: Misunderstanding Tradeoffs in the War on Terror' (2009) 97(2) *California Law Review* 301, 303. See also above Chapter 3, n 141 and associated text.

In recent times, applicability of such ideas has been animated in Council circles by both those involved in empowering the Council, *and* those whom it affects by its decisions. For example, some member states have made concerted efforts to emplace Council 'working methods' as tantamount to rules,[117] including when in the E10 (that is, as part of what they do while elected for a term as a constituent member of the Council).[118] By such efforts, in effect these states seek a greater means of governing Council decision making, even if there are still blockages to updating the *Provisional Rules of Procedure* and duly amending their label to confirm what practice shows—to recognise that they are, in effect, no longer 'provisional', if that label even had a material impact on their relevance beyond the very early years of the UN's operation.

For another example, external actors enjoined UN members to foist their interest on the Council: in late 2014, a group of non-government organisations launched a civil society campaign entitled '1 for 7 Billion', where the basic idea was to prevent the Council from entirely holding sway over the appointee to follow then Secretary-General Ban Ki-moon, and the manner of finding a replacement ahead of his term expiring at the end of 2016.

A launch letter encapsulated what the campaign intended to press on the Council. It was sent to all member states of the UN, saying, in part:

> It is imperative that the selection process [is] changed to meet the higher standards that the UN General Assembly, UN experts and civil society have persistently called for. A more open and inclusive selection process engaging all UN Member States will also help to revitalize the UN and enhance its global authority. [Proposals include] publication of formal selection criteria, a call for nominations and a clear timetable for the selection process that enables adequate assessment of candidates, including

---

117 For an overview, see *In Hindsight: Note 507* (28 September 2017) Security Council Report <https://www.securitycouncilreport.org/monthly_forecast/2017-10>; *Security Council Working Methods* (31 January 2018) Security Council Report <https://www.securitycouncilreport.org/monthly_forecast/2018-02>. See also discussion in Simma et al, above Chapter 1, n 29, 1033.

118 Ibid, and also noting that Colin Keating observes 'Progress in developing and expanding the content of Note 507 has been very slow and painful. It has suffered from constant pushback by the P5. But the achievements that have been made are largely a credit to the efforts by Japan to sustain momentum over two separate terms on the Council.' See Colin Keating 'Power Dynamics Between Permanent and Elected Members' in Sebastian von Einsiedel, David M Malone and Bruno Stagno Ugarte (eds) *The UN Security Council in the 21st Century* (Lynne Rienner, 2016), 151.

> through an official list of candidates and the submission of candidate vision statements.[119]

The campaign gathered momentum and supporters through 2015, and then in 2016 recorded the involvement of 750 organisations said to reach some 170 million people worldwide.[120] Related consequences are quite evident: unprecedented steps were taken along the way to appointing António Guterres, which also illustrates the currency of calls to be responsive to *both* those that empower the Council and those whom its decisions affect (however indirectly).[121]

Potential to enhance Council productiveness also arises in orchestrating Council interactions with member states contributing (uniformed) personnel for peacekeeping.

As at December 2019, there were 13 subsidiary organs of the Council in the form of peacekeeping missions based on a Council mandate, and these arrangements linked the Council to 117 troop contributing states. Each link is, however, specific to a combination of mission and contributing state—at least due to the different circumstances for each mission, but also because of each having specific mandate and operational differences that may apply, even when there are some similarities involved. Thus, again in December 2019, this could be better characterised as 484 links to the Council, being the total *combinations* of missions and countries contributing.[122]

From this angle, at least two significant consequences arise for Council productiveness:

(a) Such arrangements are unlikely to be as productive as they might be, when largely without related rules and standards (that have been promulgated, and are enforceable) by which to govern those links and their consequences. This is, in particular, because some process for agreeing such Council rules—whatever the content may

---

119 1 for 7 Billion *NGO Open letter to Member States of the General Assembly on the Selection Process of the UN Secretary-General* (5 November 2014). On the importance of the legitimating influence of civil society, see Jan Aart Scholte 'Civil Society and the Legitimation of Global Governance' (2007) 3(3) *Journal of Civil Society* 305; also see generally Jan Aart Scholte 'Relations with Civil Society' in Jacob Katz Cogan, Ian Hurd and Ian Johnstone (eds) *The Oxford Handbook of International Organizations* (Oxford, 2016).

120 1 for 7 Billion *Who We are* (at 6 June 2016) <http://www.1for7billion.org/who-we-are/>.

121 There is more to this story that is relevant to Council accountability—see further discussion in Chapter 6.2.3.

122 See Figures 5 and 6, and associated discussion, in Chapter 5, noting revised organisational arrangements for the UN embracing a wider definition of 'UN peace missions'.

eventually be—would afford opportunities for the organisation to learn so as to develop future capacity.

(b) How (productively) flexible a sparsity of governance actually is always remains contestable,[123] but gaps in governance do, inter alia, create uncertainty—and potentially quite significant uncertainty—about the effectiveness of a response when things go otherwise than as planned.

Plans are, of course, wont to go awry, as is abundantly clear in peacekeeping missions which not infrequently (and, to my eye, not surprisingly) face a range of difficulties—both in delivering on their mandate and in managing their interactions with the miscellany of states involved.[124] Moreover, when they do deliver, offsets to beneficial outcomes arise from misconduct by peacekeepers,[125] for example, or other ineffective governance of these Council-authorised activities.[126] In the same vein, effectiveness of Council exhortations to remedy such problems again relies on Council authority and legitimacy as perceived by audiences for those decisions. It is not a stretch to suggest this is impinged upon by the Council seeking accountability (here from troop contributing countries with respect to conduct of their troops) which the Council does not offer in relation to its own conduct. Accordingly, these examples show that desire for 'flexibility' may well be getting in the way of, rather than facilitating, what the Council is there to do—and that this may well be the case on a much wider front.

In response, accountability of the Council to those that empower it would by no means be a panacea, even if that also addressed important ways in which Council decisions and actions affect others. The prospects for being accountable in order to enhance legal and institutional arrangements around the Council, and governance of Council-authorised activities, nonetheless give reason to believe that positive dividends are possible for the Council—in being more productive than its record to date would suggest that it has been.

What the Council does to give effect to its Functions, or otherwise contribute towards the UN's Purposes, always remains subject to countervailing forces in the interest-laden realm of geopolitics. These potentially include at least consequences and outgrowths of contested legality of what the Council decides, plus wider assertions of insufficient legitimacy for what others do at its

123 Where keeping all the options open does not necessarily lead to finding the right option when it is needed anyway—see, for example, discussion in Holmes, above n 116.

124 Again, see Chapter 5—Figures 5 and 6, and associated discussion.

125 See above Chapter 3, n 75 to 77 inclusive, and associated text.

126 See above Chapter 3, n 78.

behest. Leaving that unaccounted, by its own hand the Council misses a range of openings to dilute, offset, or avoid, prejudices to its productiveness.

In that light, acknowledging that the Council should account for its conduct, at very least to UN member states collectively, stands to aid Council effectiveness. As discussed in the next chapter, the question is then what would need to be accounted for, to suggest whether change to Council conduct may be needed, and, if so, to inform what specific change may provide, or assist in providing, the desired improvements.

CHAPTER 5

For What Should the Security Council Be Accountable?

Establishing the contours of what the Council may be accountable for could begin with analysing the scope of the Council's legally-enabled responsibilities and associated legal limitations: Article 24(1) assigns the Council primary responsibility for the maintenance of international peace and security, while Article 24(2) requires that the Council 'shall act in accordance with the Purposes and Principles of the United Nations'. Beyond such headlines, however, finding accountabilities that could be assessed is challenging on two broad fronts—first to establish what work is at hand, and second to identify relevant standards to which Council actions (or inactions) might be compared.

First, the scope of the Council's work emanates from a core purpose of the UN—that is, to 'save succeeding generations from the scourge of war'.[1] The Council is tasked by the *Charter* under:

(a) Chapter VI, with investigating and making recommendations in relation to obtaining pacific settlement of disputes;
(b) Chapter VII, in relation to determining the existence of, and responses to, threats to the peace, breaches of the peace, and acts of aggression, including via decisions on provisional measures, and/or measures short of armed force, and/or measures involving armed force;
(c) Chapter VIII, with encouraging development of regional arrangements to such ends, including Article 52(3) in relation to pacific settlement of local disputes, and Article 53(1) empowering the Council to 'utilize such regional arrangements or agencies for enforcement action under its authority'; and
(d) Chapter XII, in relation to the UN's international trusteeship system—though the tasks on this were, in effect, completed in 1994.[2]

1 *Charter*, first preambular paragraph.

2 After the last trust territory, Palau, established its independence and became a member of the UN—see SC Res 956, UN SCOR, 3455th mtg, UN Doc S/Res/956 (10 November 1994). See also above Chapter 4, n 1.

 | DOI:10.1163/9789004444300_006

Setting out such responsibilities in more detail is complicated by the fact that the Council needs to address them in the interest-laden geopolitical environment of international relations. As an actor in that environment, the Council has an inherently political role of its own, and that is intertwined with the legal dimensions and practical realities of its role under the *Charter*.[3] Anticipating such conditions, the drafters left the Council to interpret the *Charter* for itself.[4] Aside from layers of politics, however, interpreting tasks from a legal point of view is quite a challenge—seen in, for example, ongoing debate about what amounts to a Council 'decision', as distinct from a Council 'recommendation' or other outputs from its deliberations.[5]

Second, and similarly, there is also no small debate about boundaries around Council work, and discussion of what the Council should do, or should not do, is caught up in a larger question on what limits the (legal) discretion of international organisations.[6] For example, José Alvarez notes that for 'those for whom institutional practice and the general acceptability of what [international organisations] do provides the ultimate test of legality, there are no inherent legal limitations on [their] powers, apart from the procedural rules clearly established in the underlying charters',[7] but that there are others 'for whom such discretion is incompatible with the limited purposes for which the UN Charter collective security scheme was established, [who] have attempted to find legal limits on what the Council—and other [international organisations]—can do.'[8]

Together this suggests a conventional legal approach, of interpreting and applying the *Charter*, provides but modest help in answering the main

3 Some may even agree with the opinion from the UK's representative: 'Most of the time the Security Council is dealing with decisions of policy, and not responding to an obligation under international law. Having a primary responsibility for peace and security is not an obligation under international law; it is description of a function. … We should be modest in doing good, not only because of the prudent limits to our own strength but because, however much we do, there will be much evil in the world about which we do nothing.' See UN SCOR, 4288th mtg, UN Doc S/PV.4288 (Resumption 1) (7 March 2001), 11.

4 See above Chapter 1, n 47.

5 Simma et al, above Chapter 1, n 29, 792. Outputs now routinely include Presidential statements and media releases (and COVID-19 operating conditions brought on some other adjustments that may or may not persist once the pandemic has passed—see below n 80).

6 For just one example, see discussion in Christopher Michaelsen 'The Competence of the Security Council Under the UN Charter to Adopt Sanctions Targeting Private Individuals' in Andrew Byrnes, Mika Hayashi and Christopher Michaelsen (eds) *International Law in the New Age of Globalization* (Martinus Nijhoff, 2013), 25.

7 Alvarez, above Chapter 2, n 70, 266.

8 Ibid, 267.

question raised here—about what the Council should be accountable for. Put another way, Council effectiveness, or productiveness, and thus opportunities to enhance that through being accountable, turn on a question that actually proves to be deceptive in its simplicity—is the Council doing what it is there to do?

The complexity becomes apparent when probing further, as one does in a typical legal analysis, because this generates rather more questions than it answers. An evergreen reform discourse tends to confirm this on a wide front: many years of wrangling over what an improved Council might look like has not yielded a majoritarian position, or not one sufficient to underpin formal *Charter* change towards improving the legal and institutional arrangements around the Council. In keeping with the intention that the UN's principal organs each interpret such matters for themselves, of course the Council might seek to determine an answer in its own cause: the Council may fare no better, however, because it is not clear that its constituent members would be enough in accord for the Council to form an answer.[9]

A traditional legal analysis thus does not suffice alone, but in various blends of politics and law one might still at least start from the point as put by Bardo Fassbender:

> The functioning of the Council [is] not an end in itself but oriented towards the achievement of certain purposes, the most important of which is the maintenance of international peace and security.[10]

Assessing whether and to what extent the Council is identifying, and responding to, what matters to international peace and security then calls for unpacking what the Council engages with, the means of that engagement, and what gets in the way of it proving to be duly productive.

To begin with, even though political influences are ever-present in Council operations, it remains the Council's choice as to what it will engage with—'situations', topics, themes, or other subject matter. No other actor can, by means of law or policy, force the Council to consider a matter when it chooses not to: in UN circles, for example, the International Court of Justice so far appears not to have a relevant power, and the Assembly is limited to drawing a matter

9 Quite possibly not, if an assessment of Council performance in 2017 by Council members is any guide—see, for example, *Letter dated 30 April 2018 from the Permanent Representative of Finland to the United Nations addressed to the President of the Security Council* S/2018/404 (3 May 2018), 5. See also below n 97 and associated text.

10 Fassbender, above Chapter 1, n 33, 284.

to Council attention,[11] or exerting political pressure towards its preferred outcomes.[12] Nor can another actor formally cause the Council to desist when it does engage: outside the UN, for example, the Council is protected by UN immunities, so while courts or parliaments might impact upon the conduct of those whom the Council directs, and others may influence Council member states, there is little legal or political capacity to direct the Council itself. Then, the means and degree of the Council's engagement are also matters of its choosing, but it is no small issue that to achieve much at all, the Council needs to strike a balance of talk and action. That is, the Council needs to debate and deliberate enough to find a way ahead, but then move on to request or require action, or otherwise conclude the matter, in some output that may, but will not necessarily, be named or styled a 'recommendation' or a 'decision'. On both points it is worth bearing in mind that individual states may be more or less influential in the Council making such calls, in public sessions or behind closed doors, but the prevailing fact is that the Council is a separate entity under the *Charter*.[13] Thus its powers operate accordingly: its constituent members (both permanent and non-permanent) participate in making such choices by virtue of that status, but the choice itself remains an output of the Council, owned collectively by those whose rights come together to deliver that.

Drawing these threads together, the Council's role is to somehow, and to some extent, engage with what impacts upon international peace and security, presumably in order to get productive results that go towards maintaining or restoring it. The Council cannot possibly give its attention to every potentially relevant issue, however, and on those where it does engage, the extent to which it does what it is there to do is a multi-faceted question. Those things on which the Council does choose to engage provide opportunities for the Council to be productive, and what it then does (or does not do) creates outputs associated

11 Though not forgetting the Assembly's *Uniting for Peace* resolution (see above Chapter 3, n 94), this is shown, for example, in cases where the Assembly does this under Article 11(3), such as on Article 43—see Chapter 3.1, or Timor—see Chapter 6.1.

12 Though that is by no means trivial, as shown by José Alvarez in his broader discussion of the impact that the Assembly has had on international law, particularly in relation to the Assembly as an institutional actor engaged with peace and security—for example, see Alvarez, above Chapter 2, n 71, 186. In discussion herein, this was shown in relation to Palestine—see Chapter 4.1, Chapter 4, n 70 to 75 inclusive, and associated text. It also sits in the background to discussion of Syria in Chapter 5.5—such as in urging the Council to take 'appropriate measures' via *The situation in the Syrian Arab Republic* GA Res 66/253(B), UN GAOR, 66th sess, Agenda Item 34, 124th plen mtg, UN Doc A/Res/66/253(B) (7 August 2012) [9].

13 International organisations and their organs being taken here as two types of entities allowed for by international law.

with the Council—but, undoubtedly, it remains that actual results materialise through implementation.

As I see it, the key is that being accountable could add to a picture of the Council's productiveness by explaining what comes of what the Council does (or does not do), plus whether and how that proves to be salutary for the Council's Functions or the UN's Purposes.

Accordingly, the process of doing what the Council does can be set out as a series of openings for explaining or justifying its conduct so as to aid in enhancing the legal and institutional arrangements around the Council and its work. As an analytical approach to such openings, Council work might be seen as occurring in broad phases, to be addressed by correspondingly broad questions:

(a) *Setting the Council's agenda*: Is the Council taking up issues that matter, and matter sufficiently, for it to have reasonable prospects of fulfilling its Functions under the *Charter*? This could be seen in, for example, what is added to its agenda compared to what is otherwise promoted for its attention.

(b) *Deciding what matters*: On those issues where the Council engages, does some mix of talk and action bring its work to a recognisable conclusion—a decision or recommendation that charts a course for action, closes the issue off as needing no further attention, or otherwise concludes Council involvement (including by handing off action to another actor)? This is indicated by the state of its agenda over time, as items progress to some identifiable point of conclusion (by active completion of associated actions, for example), then are removed from the list of the ongoing business of the Council.

(c) *Mattering by results*: Where it sets an agenda to include items that duly matter for international peace and security, and brings agenda items to a conclusion, do Council decisions, determinations, recommendations, and so on, themselves matter, at least prima facie, by being implemented? In the first instance Council results largely arise from what it is able to get other actors to do in compliance or conformity with the Council's decisions, particularly where Article 25 is engaged explicitly. Beyond that, maintaining or restoring international peace and security calls for sustaining productiveness of the Council and its initiatives over the long term, and on wide subject matter, so disregard for the Council's views should not be taken lightly. Amongst other things, this means what is signified by 'implementation' would well-advisedly not separate Article 25 decisions from others by drawing a bright line between them, but instead embrace conformity with Council determinations and recommendations, and showing support for direction set by the Council in other outputs.

In effect, this would establish what Council work is at hand, setting the scene for what accountability may add if relevant standards could be identified—to which Council actions (or inactions) might then be compared. Thus, such an analysis stands to be taken further by:

(d) *Understanding how results matter*: What comes of conclusions reached by the Council? If the Council were to account for what it has done, one aspect is the raw results, or outputs, that it has produced (decisions or recommendations or whatever), and the extent of their implementation, for example. But there is more to Council productiveness than merely being busy (which is already shown by exhaustive documentation). This question instead concerns what actually came of such outputs and how this impacted upon international peace and security: what associated outcomes arose and what standards or qualities are relevant to them potentially being results that actually matter?

(e) *Seeking results that matter more*: Results that matter connect back to the idea that accountability is about changing behaviour to better meet a mark that another actor holds one to. Considering what may get in the way of results in the voluntarist environment of international organisation, persuading others to take action may hinge on how an outcome is to be obtained just much as what that outcome is. Accordingly, one aspect of results that matter is to what extent the ends sought were obtained, but another is what means were used and whether they met the mark that another actor expects.

On that logic, an analytical approach to what the Council might account for here begins from the Council's agenda, in line with the broad questions just noted.

To understand the work at hand, in Chapter 5.1 the case example illustrates how the Council's *agenda* is orchestrated and provides opportunities for it to be productive, while Chapter 5.2 looks at the state of the Council's agenda over time, to detect whether it is deciding *what matters* so as to be basically productive by reaching a conclusion—not least, to finish what it has started by putting the item on the agenda. That may be enough if one equated a busy Council with a productive Council. But *mattering by actual results* is something more, so what comes from Council work is looked at in Chapter 5.3, in terms of the extent to which it matters by Council directions being implemented.

This illustrates a baseline productiveness, as results pivot on whether what the Council wanted others to do was done—at all, not enough, partly, or fully—and if that was then somehow undone, by actions or inactions of national parliaments or decisions of national courts, for example. However, as discussed in Chapter 5.4, understanding *how results matter* also involves what gets in the way of that engagement proving to be duly productive. This means that both ends sought and means used have characteristics that are relevant for realising overall outcomes that matter towards the Council's raison d'être. In the same vein, accountability will not amount to much if conduct does not change for the better, so an accountability process is incomplete without a response from the actor accounted to—being their assessment of what change may be called for. Rounding out this discussion of what the Council should account for, Chapter 5.5 thus turns to what would constitute 'better' Council productiveness and so where to start in order to *seek results that matter more*.

5.1 Case Example: The Security Council's Agenda

For a body empowered to make decisions, an agenda is a basic instrument for orchestrating formal interaction of its members so that, collectively, they may make the decisions falling within that body's purview. Composing an agenda is itself usually cast as a procedural step, but observation readily shows that it is not empty of substantive consequences: as and when a decision-making body accepts carriage of some items and not others, it is conducting, in effect, a continual filtering process of refining the scope of its interests and assignment of related priorities. Agenda-setting thus guards the doorway to the deliberating chamber: the process of admitting some issues to the business list, but not others, has a substantive impact upon, for example, any denied access (as clearly indicated in earlier discussion of membership questions).

Unsurprisingly, given the ambit of the Council's activities, practicalities about its agenda arose from the first. Recalling the era of public administration in which it began, the President had no mean task to order its business when faced with myriad questions of interpretation.[14] For example, what did an item being 'placed on the agenda' mean? Should it be put on the agenda before the Council engaged in substantive discussion? Who had the right to

14 For example, a lengthy discussion on delay in considering Albania's membership application more concerned who had the right to make the matter a higher priority on the agenda—see UN SCOR, 18th mtg, UN Doc S/PV.18 (13 February 1946).

decline to engage on the matter?[15] Did being on the agenda necessarily confirm that the matter fell within Council competence? What role should the merits of the case play? In the Council's idiosyncratic mode of operation for 'functioning continuously', to meet Article 28 of the *Charter*, was 'the agenda' just for a specific meeting, or was there to be some longer, permanent list of business pending for future attention?[16]

Adopting the *Provisional Rules of Procedure,* helped to some degree: by Rule 8 the Secretary-General is required to communicate a provisional meeting agenda, and Rule 9 requires that adoption of the agenda to be the first item of business at a meeting.[17] Seven decades on, having a meeting agenda is somewhat overtaken by events: in contemporary practice, Council meetings frequently deal briefly with a lone agenda item, to express a Council conclusion (a decision in the general sense), which is often largely a product of 'consultations' or other informal sessions (however extensive, or brief, those may be).[18]

Since scheduling is found elsewhere,[19] attention returns to what may stand as the Council's 'permanent agenda', as a way of ordering its workload.

On that score, the inaugural Secretary-General, Trygve Lie, initiated reporting under Rule 11. This stipulates the requirement to 'communicate each week [a] summary statement of matters of which the Security Council is seized and of the stage reached in their consideration',[20] and so the listing was

15 For example, see UN SCOR, 59th mtg, UN Doc S/PV.59 (3 September 1946)—the meeting convened at 3pm, ran until 7.15 pm, and determined only that point 2 of the provisional agenda was adopted by seven votes to two.

16 Egypt's representative, for example, distinguished the 'actual and immediate agenda' from 'a kind of permanent agenda'—see UN SCOR, 3rd mtg, UN Doc S/PV.3 (28 January 1946), 27.

17 Article 99 of the *Charter* also provides that the Secretary-General 'may bring to the attention of the Security Council any matter which in his opinion may threaten the maintenance of international peace and security'. Though not formally invoked that often, there is various relatable practice—for example, see *In Hindsight: Horizon-Scanning Briefings* (1 May 2013) Security Council Report <https://www.security councilreport.org/monthly_forecast/2013-05>.

18 Noting that quite recent practice on Council use of the agenda item 'any other business' is interesting—see *In Hindsight: Making Effective Use of "Any Other Business"* (1 April 2016) Security Council Report <https://www.securitycouncilreport.org/monthly_forecast/2016-04>. There may also be various issues to be explored about the as-yet-unfolding lessons from Council arrangements that have operated through the COVID-19 pandemic—see also below n 80.

19 See, for example, the Council's programme of work and meetings schedule accessible at: United Nations Security Council *Programme of Work* <https://www.un.org/securitycouncil/events/calendar>.

20 *Provisional Rules of Procedure of the Security Council* UN Doc S/35 (10 April 1946).

entitled.[21] That initial edition was four pages, covered six matters, and gave a synopsis of the Council deliberations on each.[22] In effect, this made the *Summary Statement* an aide-memoir of the Council's 'permanent agenda'.[23]

While the Council had 11 members, following editions show that the Council became seized of over 80 distinct matters of substance, a few of which it managed to close off.[24] By July 1966, soon after the Council began operating with 15 members, it was said to be seized of some 70 matters, the *Summary Statement* synopsis of these running to well over 150 pages.[25] Apart from the quantum of seemingly pending work, this raised a rather daunting 'catch up' barrier in front of all non-permanent members elected to the Council. For example, at that time the Netherlands was in its third term, continuing from 1965 with first time members Uruguay and Jordan. Earlier in 1966, they had been joined by Argentina for its third term, and Japan and New Zealand for their second, along with first time members Bulgaria, Mali, Nigeria, and Uganda. In terms of history as a state, national capacity to assist on international peace and security, and experience on the Council, this inaugural E10 thus was certainly a mixed bag of countries—but hardly unusual in the Council then or since. This highlights persistent questions about how soon,[26] and how well,[27] the elected members gain command of all necessary matters and materials,

---

21 *Summary Statement by the Secretary-General of Matters of Which the Security Council is Seized and of the Stage Reached in Their Considerations* UN Doc 45 (23 April 1946). While this series of documents is not otherwise identifiable than in the general sequence of Security Council official documents (shown by the UN symbol 'S/'), perusal of UN Doc S/1 to UN Doc S/44 inclusive confirmed that this was the first Summary Statement.

22 Lamentably, perhaps, after 70 years the list still bears Trygve Lie's bequest of an inordinately long title, though shorter by its ultimate 's' since the second edition in 1946. In the interests of brevity, throughout this book the particular edition of the *Summary Statement* is indicated by including its UN symbol and date of issue: '*Summary Statement* UN Doc [UN symbol and document number] (date)'. For example, see below n 25.

23 Practice for the *Summary Statement* has varied since then, but generally a complete list has been issued at least annually (and sometimes monthly), and weekly addenda give updates and actions along the way.

24 Author's analysis of *Summary Statement* editions up to 31 December 1965.

25 *Summary Statement* UN Doc S/7382 (5 July 1966).

26 The Assembly has helped by deciding to conduct elections much further ahead of when terms commence, widening the opportunity for preparation ahead of taking office—see *Revitalization of the work of the General Assembly* GA Res 68/307, UN GAOR, 68th sess, Agenda Item 122, 108th plen mtg, UN Doc A/Res/68/307 (18 September 2014), [17].

27 Especially given the paucity of collated, well-organised rules for the conduct of Council business that, in Stephen Holmes words, would 'transmit lessons distilled from a multigenerational learning experience with managing complex contingencies'—Holmes, above Chapter 4, n 116, 318.

so they may then participate fully and effectively in the Council's work—and about what the Council collective could or should do as its part in facilitating this, or what consideration the Assembly should duly afford to this in electing the E10.

In the early 1990s, in a climate of heightened activity in comparison to the stalemates of the Cold War, the *Summary Statement* had grown to over 200 matters.[28] The Council began culling the list, closing nearly 80 items in November 1993,[29] another two dozen in July 1994.[30] Laudable as far as it refocussed attention towards active matters, this removed items on which Council deliberation had been suspended inconclusively. Consigned to history was Council business such as negotiating and using Article 43 agreements to create the armed forces for the UN,[31] approving a statute and rules of procedure for the Military Staff Committee,[32] and responding to various disputes or 'situations'—one being the fracas over the Falkland Islands, or Islas Malvinas,[33] which involves Argentina and the UK and which is still unresolved.[34] This may have amounted to not much more than due burial of long dead deliberations, but the reason for their demise is material to understanding the capacity of the Council. Without an explanation, the Council appears largely unproductive on these matters—that is, unable to have the desired impact on international peace and security, and so conclude the matter that way, or to find another

28 *Summary Statement* UN Doc S/25070 (11 January 1993).

29 *Note by the President of the Security Council* UN Doc S/26812 (29 November 1993).

30 *Note by the President of the Security Council* UN Doc S/1994/896 (28 July 1994).

31 *Note by the President of the Security Council: Simplification of the list of matters of which the Security Council is seized (rule 11 of the provisional rules of procedure of the Security Council)* UN Doc S/1996/603 (22 August 1996).

32 *Note by the President of the Security Council* UN Doc S/1996/55 (24 January 1996). See also *Summary Statement* UN Doc S/1997/40 (10 January 1997). See also above Chapter 3, n 17 and associated text.

33 For background see United Nations General Assembly 'Special Committee on Decolonization Approves Draft Resolution Calling for Argentina, United Kingdom to Resume Talks Over Falkland Islands (Malvinas) Dispute' (United Nations General Assembly Meetings Coverage and Press Releases, GA/COL/3314, 23 June 2017). For additional background, see Carlos Escudé 'Argentine Territorial Nationalism' (1988) 20(1) *Journal of Latin American Studies* 139; Samuel Luckhurst 'Argentina's Falklands Banner Threatens To Reignite England Rivalry' *Huffington Post* (online) 9 June 2014 <http://www.huffingtonpost.co.uk/2014/06/09/argentina-falklands-banner_n_5471453.html>.

34 After two resolutions—see UN SCOR, 2350th mtg, UN Doc S/PV.2350 (3 April 1982); UN SCOR, 2368th mtg, UN Doc S/PV.2368 (26 May 1982). For background, see also UN SCOR, 2345th mtg, UN Doc S/PV.2345 (1 April 1982). Regarding removal: see above n 29, this being item number 107, then above n 28, 13.

conclusive pathway, such as by actively transferring further consideration or action to another actor.[35]

At that time, the Council also attempted to institute 'automatic' removal of items that had not been considered for five years.[36] From one perspective, this might be taken as all to the good in owning that no further action was intended by the Council, but, in any case, this process of interment proved less successful. Reaction from some states led the Council to add an exception procedure, based on consent to removal from concerned member states.[37] Several have proven assiduous in ensuring that their items are retained on this 'permanent agenda'.[38]

Such refashioning of the 'permanent agenda' may not have left recent Council members much better served by the *Summary Statement* than those in 1966. If reputable news sources are to be believed, recent years are replete with emerging or escalating matters of international peace and security, but in early 2020 the list included just six items initiated during 2013 to 2019 inclusive,[39] whereas that *Summary Statement* showed more than a dozen matters slated for removal that were subsequently retained at the request of a UN member state, though there is little or no indication of the Council returning its attention to them. Such long-standing matters were listed along with over 50 attended to in the last three years, but without giving a sense of Council priorities among them. In fact, acquiescing to requests from individual UN members, the Council still listed five items dormant for 50 years or more which were faced by the E10's erstwhile colleagues from 1966—perhaps creating some sense of déjà vu for Japan, New Zealand and Uruguay, again members of the Council in 2016, or the Netherlands, again a member of the Council in 2018. In contrast, the Council's most recent annual report once again gave no small list of matters

35 Noting again that the advent of peacekeeping did not satisfy Article 43.

36 See above n 29.

37 See explanation included in *Note by the President of the Security Council: Simplification of the list of matters of which the Security Council is seized (rule 11 of the provisional rules of procedure of the Security Council)* UN Doc S/1996/704 (29 August 1996).

38 See, for example, *Summary Statement* UN Doc S/2018/10/Add.9 (5 March 2018), 4. Items 53 and 54, for example, are at the top of the list of those items slated for deletion but retained at the request of a member state. These concern 'the India-Pakistan question', dating to January 1948 and in abeyance since November 1965, and 'the Hyderabad question' from September 1948 and unactioned since May 1949.

39 Ibid; see also *Summary Statement* UN Doc S/2019/10 (2 January 2020), 3 [51–56]. Of these, only one new item was added during 2018 and another in 2019, but all the long standing items were still retained—see *Summary Statement* UN Doc S/2019/10/Add.9 (4 March 2019), 3 [54] and [56–69]; *Summary Statement* UN Doc S/2020/10/Add.9 (2 March 2020), 3 [56] and [57–69].

that the Council was yet to discuss.[40] Unless it indicates otherwise, these items might be taken as pending aspirants to the agenda, addition of which awaits a Council decision.

On the whole, new or additional issues of international peace and security continue to arise, but the preponderance of items on the Council's list of business appear well-rehearsed, and the laudable, but amorphous,[41] loiter cheek by jowl with the venerable, but recalcitrant.[42] Meanwhile, nothing joins the 'permanent agenda' unless or until a formal meeting is convened on it, even if it takes up significant Council time in informal 'consultations' and so on. This means that myriad items on which the Council passively declines to engage may not be accounted differently from nascent crises of international peace and security.

The case example thus first concerns agenda-setting as an essential capability and capacity for a decision-making body, to make and collate the necessary variety and quantum of such procedural decisions. This is pivotal for ensuring due, and duly prompt, coverage of that body's functions and/or other responsibilities, and thereby creating opportunities for it to be productive towards its raison d'être. Agenda-setting can contribute by orchestrating what a decision-making body such as the Council does—as opposed to, for example, strategic issues being crowded out by routine reports that 'dominated the Council's monthly agenda'.[43]

Second, such assessments are not usually a simple binary question, of inclusion or exclusion, but show relative assignment of time to specific items of business, and then juggling that to ensure the Council makes an active response (one way or the other) to all items put before it as a decision-making body. The case example thus illustrates the importance of the prevailing state of the agenda—showing whether the Council does what matters in organising its business, so it is then well-placed to do what matters for maintaining or restoring international peace and security. If the Council is to be 'action-oriented,

40 *Report of the Security Council for 2018* UN GAOR, 73rd sess, Supp No 2, UN Doc A/73/2 (2019), 189.

41 Such as strengthening the rule of law in the maintenance of international peace and security, or 'women and peace and security', which are 'thematic' discussions in Council parlance.

42 Such as the situation in Cyprus, or the Middle East, both receiving attention for over 50 years but seemingly still some way from a long term solution.

43 *Letter dated 26 May 2016 from the Permanent Representative of Finland to the United Nations addressed to the President of the Security Council* S/2016/506 (2 June 2016), 16; see also below n 108 and 111, and associated text.

not just a debating club',[44] in important part this is gained from agenda-setting as a legal and institutional component of Council capacity.

Third, the Council may serve other purposes than those immediately and directly linked to its *Charter* Functions. By no means least, on a wide front the Council is a venue for diplomatic interchange, for goodwill initiatives towards building friendly international relations as the UN was intended to foster, and for relevant thematic discussions. All these have potential to be salutary influences on conditions supporting international peace and security over the longer term even if there is no immediate issue of that kind. Dealing with these effectively is thus also at issue.

For one such example, in 2014 the Secretary-General wrote to the President of the Security Council with a plan to implement a Council resolution which might be put under the 'goodwill' heading. Responsibility for this had been laid on him as part of that resolution, where the Council had decided to create the 'Captain Mbaye Diagne Medal for Exceptional Courage' to commemorate a Senegalese peacekeeper serving in Rwanda at the time of the 1994 genocide. To that end, the Council had tasked the Secretary-General to propose an implementation plan.[45]

Records show that the Secretary-General's proposal lay dormant until mid-2015,[46] when he wrote again saying in 'the absence of a response [I] have proceeded with the implementation'.[47] Last Council action was in 2015—a neutral, even non-committal, response from the President, to the effect that the Secretary-General's letter had 'been brought to the attention of the members of the Security Council, who take note of the information provided and the intention expressed therein.'[48]

It terms of agenda-setting, how this correspondence was classified in managing Council business is not material. It matters very little—and perhaps not at all—whether it was implicitly 'on the agenda', because it was a follow up item of business, or 'not on the agenda', because it remained undiscussed. From another angle, however, it is not trivial that completing the next step was needed to acquit the Council's role, but it was not re-admitted to the Council's

44 Ibid, 11.

45 SC Res 2154, UN SCOR, 7170th mtg, UN Doc S/Res/2154 (8 May 2014).

46 *Letter dated 16 December 2014 from the Secretary-General addressed to the President of the Security Council* S/2014/946 (24 December 2014).

47 *Letter dated 20 May 2015 from the Secretary-General addressed to the President of the Security Council* S/2015/385 (28 May 2015).

48 *Letter dated 27 May 2015 from the President of the Security Council addressed to the Secretary-General* S/2015/386 (28 May 2015).

business and afforded the small morsel of time needed to endorse, amend, or reject, the plan proffered by the Secretary-General. Either way, dealing with the matter promptly would have demonstrated effective agenda-setting and time management, and fostered goodwill with the states promoting the initiative. Leaving it unactioned brings doubt about what the Council decided, if anything, and whether the matter is concluded, though the relevant annual report suggested not.[49] Moreover, this (non-) handling of the matter might be seen as falling a bit short on showing due regard for those states promoting the scheme's implementation.

Interestingly, potentially unhelpful impacts from lack of a further Council response arose from the manner in which the original decision was framed. In particular, reasonable options for a timely and complete response did not turn on further Council deliberation: after doing what it seems only the Council could, by resolving to institute the award, without further ado the Council could simply have delegated implementation to the Secretary-General.[50]

When that matter first appeared in a previous annual report of the Council, there was another item that signals the diversity of what finds its way into the Council's in-tray. A letter from the Russian delegation requested that a report, prepared by the Ministry of Foreign Affairs of the Russian Federation, be circulated to UN members as a document of the UN.[51] Entitled 'Neo-Nazism: a dangerous challenge to human rights, democracy and the rule of law', the report was indeed circulated.[52] Official UN records suggest the Council is yet to consider it, a passive response to the implicit suggestion that it be put on the Council's agenda.[53] Council silence leaves open whether, for example, this was

---

49 Though the Secretary-General had taken this further in seeking nominations, but the matter was listed as not discussed: *Report of the Security Council: 1 August 2014 to 31 July 2015* UN GAOR, 70th sess, Supp No 2, UN Doc A/70/2 (29 October 2015), 199. Other than to Captain Mbaye Diagne as the inaugural recipient, the medal was not then awarded until May 2019: see United Nations 'Secretary-General to Honour Fallen Malawi Soldier with Captain Mbaye Diagne Medal for Exceptional Courage, at Headquarters, 24 May' (Meetings Coverage and Press Releases, PKO/786, 20 May 2019).

50 The effect of the Secretary-General's handling when lacking Council direction amounted to taking the task as delegated anyhow—while not necessarily or always an acceptable approach, here his initiative seems not unreasonable because he is already responsible for award of the Dag Hammarskjöld Medal to those members of peacekeeping operations who lose their lives.

51 *Letter dated 4 May 2015 from the Permanent Representative of the Russian Federation to the Secretary-General* A/69/891-S/2015/311 (5 May 2015).

52 Albeit only as submitted, in Russian.

53 A related note from the Head of the Delegation of the European Union to the UN, attaching the joint EU response to the Russian report, was also circulated. This points out that the subject report appears 'geographically incomplete' as a 'chapter on the situation in the

a legitimate claim on the Council's attention, but time does not permit consideration of the report, or that it is not, but the Council perhaps lacks the will or the courtesy to say so.[54] If this were the only such example, a case might be made that the Council was sending a purposive message by its silence—but, as highlighted by the hotchpotch of 'undiscussed items' listed in annual reports over decades, the frequency of Council non-response rather belies that suggestion.

The difficulty is not that such things are unimportant for the Council to do. Rather, it is a twofold question of how the Council uses its time.

Firstly, gains from addressing such issues may be outweighed by detriment to productiveness, if dealing with them leaves the Council short of time to duly address, and deal with effectively, active matters of international peace and security—particularly, one would suggest, those relatable to Chapter VII of the *Charter,* where no other institution has comparable powers.

On the other hand, over the longer haul the Council stills needs to be productive by finishing what it starts (even on less pressing matters), or by actively declining to engage on those matters where Council time and attention cannot, or should not, be afforded to them. As something for which the Council could account, the case example already provides cause for concern. This is not so much about the Council's long, unremitting agenda because maintaining international peace and security is unlikely ever to be a simple matter, readily managed. Nor is it primarily that the Council chooses not to respond on some items, such as the report submitted by the Russian Federation, or does so belatedly or rather less than definitively on others, like the Captain Mbaye Diagne commemorative award. It is simply not feasible for the Council to address the entire host of matters over which other actors attempt to claim its attention. The central point is that managing the Council agenda needs to be effective, in order that everything which might flow from it also has an opportunity to be effective: it does not suggest sound results to have doubt about the status of some items on the 'permanent agenda', and others pending with no definitive outcome or otherwise not showing that the Council has finished whatever it started by placing the item on its agenda (especially on relatively

Russian Federation, for example, is missing.' See *Identical letters dated 18 June 2015 from the Secretary-General addressed to the President of the General Assembly and the President of the Security Council* A/69/928-S/2015/457 (19 June 2015), 3.

54 As far as this arises from the collective decisions that the Council, as an entity, takes, does not take, or defaults into by inaction, for example. Not 'receiving' the correspondence was also an alternative—which the Secretary-General has also done, albeit not without contention (see above Chapter 4, n 67).

straightforward matters). Further, in the light of its unparalleled remit under the *Charter*, a particular difficulty is that things that *may* be done by the Council are sometimes done at the expense of what *may only* be done by the Council. While that is the Council's call to make in the present arrangements, it is hard to deny that the Council is then less productive than it might be, particularly on those things where no other actor has a comparable standing to maintain or restore international peace and security.

Of course, there are many and varied approaches to agenda-setting, and judgement exercised by the person presiding in that chamber is an essential ingredient; naturally, genuine emergencies would also rightfully trump a planned order of business. Nonetheless, an account of its conduct would usefully include explaining how the Council has juggled its priorities and arranged its business to meet its *Charter* remit, not least to show that it is not unduly captive to political exigencies of the moment.

5.2 Deciding What Matters

Deliberation is a necessary feature of what a decision-making body needs to do, in order to determine what to engage upon, and how, in the course of conducting its business. Accordingly, the meat of activity for the Council is deliberating—that is, using a manner and means of engagement suited to its agenda items, in order to gather, sift, and debate, information, while also weighing out attention and available resources to matters of unequal urgency, substantive importance, stage of consideration, complexity, and so on.

This culminates in deciding, in the general sense of choosing a course of action—where, of course, the perennial option is to close off the agenda item with no further action.[55] That is, having entered a deliberating chamber by being added to the agenda, and so recognised as something that matters, the item finds an exit point by a further decision. The worry is when something admitted to Council business cannot do so, but instead loiters with little or no prospect of a Council result. This, in all likelihood, makes the Council not as productive as it might be, nor as effective as one would hope in contributing to resolving that item of business (even just to hand it off to another actor better placed to address it, perhaps another UN organ or a regional organisation).

55 Although frequently choosing to do nothing on matters admitted to its work program would not, it must said, speak well to that body's productiveness—no matter what its ambit.

Council deliberations serve a crucial purpose in the political framing of work that is a cooperative and collective endeavour under the *Charter*. The Council's peculiar circumstances could mean that the most important role of talk may be in persuading others to act—especially states. States are, to some extent, legally obliged to heed Council wishes by Article 25, but that provision is not always relevant, and, as is generally known, willing and sufficient implementation of Council directions by states has, in any case, proven to be quite another matter.[56]

Despite its work being framed by an associated treaty, the voluntarist environment of international cooperation provides a serious challenge: to have states comply with Council decisions, or conform to its recommendations, the Council must first be persuasive in the face of time and tide in states' geopolitical positioning and their domestic political considerations. Actual implementation is another question, but explaining, in the way that would otherwise be said to account for a decision, nonetheless is a useful part of deliberating and reaching conclusions, so as to underpin engendering implementation and thus achieving the desired results from Council work.

The reasoning in, and form of, such explanation or justification is shaped by perceptions of how the Council decides on behalf of states.[57] One might advocate for conceiving of this as being delegation, or representation, or some admixture,[58] to be answered by forms of accountability that embrace participation, or demonstration of faithful performance of duties, or both.[59] Whatever the case may be, fidelity to the *Charter* is the common denominator—found in lawfulness from conforming with the *Charter*, at least, even if not with the entirety of the broader corpus of international law. Showing these things might well be done post-operatively, in accounting for decisions, but it stands to help if also done in the decision process.[60]

---

56 For specific examples, see discussion of Indonesia's responses on Timor in Chapter 6.1, or on states responses generally in relation to Resolution 1267 in Chapter 6.2.2.

57 In line with Article 24—see, for example, discussion in Chapter 4.2.

58 See Grant and Keohane, above Chapter 2, n 61.

59 Ibid, noting the view from José Alvarez on 'voice' as participation, in the context of received wisdom that expulsion of states is to be avoided: 'The push to enhance "voice" is so insistent precisely because international lawyers have been relatively successful in discouraging "exit" '—Alvarez, above Chapter 1, n 8, 343.

60 Standing in lieu, for example, of what might elsewhere be called 'checks and balances' in government, but few analogous arrangements are common in international organisation—see Klabbers, above Chapter 1, n 52, and points noted from Selznick—see above Chapter 2, n 86.

The Council thus decides what matters to its work when it exercises its discretion to set its own agenda, but it must also decide what is to be done for that work to matter by obtaining actual results towards its raison d'être. Beyond individual merits of a conclusion that the Council reaches (a decision in the general sense), implementation of every conclusion is connected to these interlinked considerations:

(a) seeing that what the Council decides (again, in the general sense) is put in an acknowledged form, regardless of its content, to know that a decision has been made, and made properly according to the law that enables it (and, if relevant, would be used to enforce it); and
(b) apprehending the decision's content, and this being unambiguous enough for its substance to be sufficiently knowable to underpin states' responses.

Since member states have not entirely mortgaged their sovereignty by acceding to the *Charter*, for Council decisions to matter as a result of what follows relies on these considerations. Together they need to persuade states to pay in sovereignty that is shared or diminished by implementing the Council's decision or conforming to its recommendation. This is discussed further in the next section, after looking a little more at what these considerations may mean in a Council decision.

In terms of showing it has decided, or reached a conclusion, the Council uses several acknowledged forms, some of which comply overtly with *Charter* requirements. Those that do so are self-evidently lawful, at least in so far as how the decision was made,[61] and thus may be less likely to be brought into question on that point. Others are not so evidently lawful and implementation may be avoided by those with concerns, or this used as a convenient basis for it to be ignored by others. These issues are highlighted below by examples from Council practice.

By way of background, when the Council came to decide things early on in 1946, the President asked for those in favour. Finding the minimum of seven members then needed and the P5 all among that number, he declared the proposal adopted without further details. The transcript did not record who participated in the voting and how they cast their vote, to make evident that it was done properly in accordance with law that might be used to enforce it.

When Council practice evolved, enumerated voting overcame such doubts. Variations in practice are seen in 1946,[62] until a tense debate on how the

61 Leaving aside for this discussion secret ballot practice used when voting on appointments of Secretary-General or judges for the International Court of Justice.
62 For example, see UN SCOR, 18th mtg, UN Doc S/PV.18 (13 February 1946).

UN should regard Franco's Spain: Australia's representative pressed for each member's stance to be recorded,[63] and the President (Mexico) repeated the approach for the rest of that Presidency. The next round of substantive decisions came under Poland's Presidency, when closing a series of highly-charged meetings on UN membership: abstentions were not initially counted, bringing an immediate question from the representative of the USA.[64] A recount was taken, enumerating all those in favour, against, and abstaining, a process repeated for the ten applications on the table.

This appeared sufficient to cement the pattern, as this approach was replicated by later Presidents.[65] It still applies to most matters of substance put as a resolution, and is augmented in the verbatim record of Council meetings by note of members not counted in voting due to absence or non-participation. As decision-making practice, this is salutary in providing evidence of a decision being made properly in procedural terms, by removing doubts about who was present, who participated in voting, and what, if any, vote they cast.[66]

The question of what absence of a member might mean in Council decision-making was also an early issue of *Charter* interpretation. The USSR delegate walked out of the 27th meeting, sparking questions over whether a decision could validly be taken with a member(s) not present. He declined to participate in discussion about the presence of Soviet troops in Iran,[67] remained away from the next three meetings, and then absented himself subsequently when that was discussed again.[68] After a separate and impromptu absence,[69]

---

63 UN SCOR, 48th mtg, UN Doc S/PV.48 (24 June 1946), 388.

64 UN SCOR, 57th mtg, UN Doc S/PV.57 (29 August 1946), 136.

65 Generally, although not ubiquitously in the early years. There are also later exceptions as Council practice further evolved in the years 1966 to 1989, and time may show that adjustments made for the COVID-19 pandemic are not entirely transient but do actually persist in ongoing practice (see below n 80).

66 Recalling that an abstention is, literally, not a vote.

67 UN SCOR, 27th mtg, UN Doc S/PV.27 (27 March 1946), 58.

68 UN SCOR, 28th mtg, UN Doc S/PV.28 (29 March 1946); UN SCOR, 29th mtg, UN Doc S/PV.29 (3 April 1946); UN SCOR, 30th mtg, UN Doc S/PV.30 (4 April 1946). See also, for example, UN SCOR, 40th mtg, UN Doc S/PV.40 (8 May 1946).

69 When the Council was meeting in Paris in 1948 (because the Assembly had convened there for its 3rd session), it was re-convened in emergency conditions due to the situation between Indonesia and the Netherlands. The Council did not proceed with substantive discussions in the 387th meeting as the representatives of Colombia, Ukraine and the USSR were absent, having left Paris after the previous meeting for their holiday break—see UN SCOR, 387th mtg, UN Doc S/PV.387 (20 December 1948). Representatives of Colombia and the USSR returned in time for the 388th meeting, but the Ukraine not until the 393rd meeting—see UN SCOR, 388th mtg, UN Doc S/PV.388 (22 December 1948); UN SCOR, 389th mtg, UN Doc S/PV.389 (22 December 1948); UN SCOR, 390th mtg, UN Doc

in 1950 the USSR repeated the performance over the course of months as a way of objecting to China being represented by the nationalist regime of the Republic of China. Although not yet tested judicially, the point is that either the implicit Council quorum is full attendance, so with even one member absent it cannot 'function continuously' as required under Article 28(1) of the *Charter*;[70] or the quorum is something less, and such absence of a member does not impede the Council from functioning and making valid decisions.[71] The latter interpretation is embodied in the Council continuing to adopt decisions, in meetings held during the USSR's absence in 1950,[72] and occasionally since then while having empty seats.[73]

On the first point above—that decisions follow acknowledged and lawful forms—records of Council meetings list attendance,[74] and enumerated voting is widely practiced on matters of substance. Thus together their virtue is evidencing satisfaction of *Charter* requirements,[75] showing each time that Article 27(3) has been met. For procedural matters, practice has evolved to rely

---

S/PV.390 (23 December 1948); UN SCOR, 391st mtg, UN Doc S/PV.391 (23 December 1948); UN SCOR, 392nd mtg UN Doc S/PV.392 (24 December 1948); UN SCOR, 393rd mtg UN Doc S/PV.393 (27 December 1948).

70 No requirement for a quorum is expressed in the *Charter*.

71 A view along such lines was advanced by the UK representative during the earlier Soviet absences—see UN SCOR, 40th mtg, UN Doc S/PV.40 (8 May 1946), 251.

72 If the USSR had been joined by four other members, the Council would have lacked the potential number of affirmative votes to adopt any decision at all—so it could hardly be said to be 'functioning continuously'.

73 The Council functioned with only 11 of 15 members from September to December in 1965—see above Chapter 2, n 26. More recently, when Rwanda was serving on the Council in 1994, at a point in Rwanda's civil war it became unclear who was entitled to represent the country in the UN. The Council functioned with 14 members for some weeks during which decisions were made and resolutions adopted: see, for example, UN SCOR, 3406th mtg, UN Doc S/PV.3406 (19 July 1994); UN SCOR, 3407th mtg UN Doc S/PV.3407 (21 July 1994); UN SCOR, 3409th mtg UN Doc S/PV.3409 (28 July 1994); UN SCOR, 3412th mtg UN Doc S/PV.3412 (29 July 1994); UN SCOR, 3413th mtg UN Doc S/PV.3413 (31 July 1994).

74 But this does not apply to 'consultations', the Council's umbrella term for its off-the-record machinations—on which there has been a major upswing in activity during the COVID-19 pandemic as shown on the relevant parts of the UN web site, with as yet unknown implications for transparency and visibility of what the Council has, or has not, done during that time (see also below n 80).

75 It is the record of that meeting, proposals presented, and votes cast that provides such evidence—if the Council decided out of session, it would need similarly unambiguous records or likely face challenges to process correctness. It is worth noting that nothing in the *Charter* strictly requires Council decisions to be taken on the record in a formal meeting, but that serves as one robust way of evidencing sufficiently what the Council decided, and how the collective will to that purpose was duly constituted by Council members.

more directly on the record of attendance without enumerated voting. Instead, the President calls for objections on the proposal;[76] if none are voiced, members present are taken to vote in the affirmative,[77] and the President declares it successful—in effect, presuming that the meeting record will show those in attendance constituted enough to meet Article 27 and so allow the proposal to be adopted.

Council practice now terms this as deciding 'without vote',[78] but it would, more strictly, be described as deciding 'without a show of hands'. A generic label used elsewhere for this method is voting *viva voce*, or 'voting by the voices'. The import of the distinction lies in the need for some form of a vote to be recorded, as evidence of a Council decision being made that satisfies the *Charter* provisions.[79] Put another way: though not uncontestable, it is a fair summary to say that Council practice signifies that the Council has used a different method for voting to meet *Charter* requirements for a decision, rather than dispensing with Article 27 altogether. Importantly, as part of a formal Council meeting these variations on what might be called a *viva voce* method still appear to afford due opportunity for the exercise of independent agency by Council members—as may be shown in their objection, comment, or voting against the proposal on the record, at least by Council members.

Not dissimilarly, out of session drafting of resolutions for the Council in recent years may be put under a 'silence procedure' to facilitate prompt conclusion of the work: 'consultations' halt to give opportunity for silence to suggest assent, or circulating of amendments or new documents to suggest otherwise.

---

76 Words to this general effect being seen in council meetings in the 1970s. In other chambers, it is often a literal reference, where the person in the presiding chair 'listens' to determine, for example, whether the 'ayes' or the 'nays' are louder (more numerous).

77 While not specifically allowing for abstentions, there is always the opportunity for a member to speak up to that effect as much as for an objection. The qualm that some have over using this approach is the lack of individual accountability for votes cast—such as where constituent members may later assert that they were actually abstaining by their silence.

78 A further step in evolution of the practice—another was when, for a period in the 1970s, this same approach was termed in official records as deciding 'by consensus'. See Sydney D Bailey and Sam Daws *The Procedure of the UN Security Council* (Clarendon Press Oxford, 3rd ed, 1998), 259 (in particular, Table 12); Loraine Sievers and Sam Daws *The Procedure of the UN Security Council* (Oxford, 4th ed, 2014), 335–337.

79 A show of hands is, in effect, the form of a 'division' used for small deliberative assemblies. This practice is in contrast to the 'rising vote' of standing in one's place to cast one's vote, or, in a very large assembly (such as a national parliament), leaving one's place to pass by the nominated teller to register one's vote. The point is to find an unambiguous telling of the result in the particular operating circumstances.

The silence being unbroken, the draft proposal will probably then succeed if put to a vote in session. This approach may bring efficiency in deliberation, and is definitive to the extent that a decision is still taken and recorded in a formal meeting—that is, silence is not being equated to formal assent.[80] Though an aid to Council time management and accommodating necessary political processes, this does raise issues, however, about potential of the practice:

- to infringe independent agency—by members being somehow unduly put upon out of session; or
- to denude substantive decisions of due deliberation—usually obtained from open articulation of a case;[81] or
- to otherwise give short shrift to the opportunity for states' participation in, or the due process of reaching, a conclusion of the Council.

Thus, some methods and forms of Council decision-making evidence clarity—in an unmistakable conclusion set out in a resolution adopted after deliberations on the record, for example. On the other hand, open issues include what it may mean if deliberations are avoided, a determination remains pending, or the content of determinations reached is ambiguous to the point of being legally ineffective and/or practically unproductive—some implications of which are illustrated by briefly returning to decisions on membership.

---

80 Though in some uses, the silence procedure does have strong overtones to the contrary—for example, where P5 states monopolise penholding (see below n 162) and give scant opportunity for other Council members to put forward objections, using that process might be seen to amount to almost daring other members to disagree when the matter goes to a formal Council session. See discussion in Keating, above Chapter 4, n 118, 147. It has also been interesting to see how this was procedure was adapted and deployed in the COVID-19 pandemic. To my eye, in explaining or justifying Council conduct, this would be an obvious choice of an issue to be explored further for the as-yet-unfolding lessons from that experience, particularly if these changes prove *not* to be entirely transient—see, for example, *In Hindsight: Security Council Working Methods in the Time of COVID-19* (30 April 2020) Security Council Report < https://www.securitycouncilreport.org/monthly-forecast/2020-05/in-hindsight-security-council-working-methods-in-the-time-of-covid-19.php>; see also *Letter dated 27 March 2020 from the President of the Security Council addressed to the Permanent Representatives of the members of the Security Council* S/2020/253 (31 March 2020); *Letter dated 2 April 2020 from the President of the Security Council addressed to the Permanent Representatives of the members of the Security Council* S/2020/273 (6 April 2020); *Letter dated 7 May 2020 from the President of the Security Council addressed to the Permanent Representatives of the members of the Security Council* S/2020/372 (7 May 2020).

81 Articulation rather than debate: since Council sessions now are rather orchestrated towards prepared speeches, and do not customarily include the opportunity to question speakers, it could be argued that such formal deliberations are already somewhat minimalist.

As discussed in Chapter 4, when considering membership applications the Council has generally eschewed itemised findings, and, at least since 1990, the decision is expressed using a fairly pro forma text and taken mostly without a show of hands.[82] Still, even if expressed in rather ambiguous terms, this approach shows the Council's decisions being clearly made and sufficiently evidenced, with due visibility of what the Council is concluding.[83]

Less visible is that affirmative recommendations inescapably entail something else: the Council's implicit determination that the applicant meets the criteria for membership. For example, being a 'peace-loving state' is one criterion under Article 4(1)—this means that each and every Council recommendation favouring membership perforce engages this standard as being applied and met. That is, whether or not the Council states its assessment on the record, whatever 'peace-loving' means and however that may be assessed, an affirmative Council recommendation by implication means the applicant is adjudged to be a 'peace-loving state'.[84]

The determination to recommend granting membership thus is accompanied by another—an assessment with respect to the membership provisions of the *Charter*.[85] So far unspecified in all but a couple of cases,[86] that determination still appears to be definitive under the *Charter*.

More generally, this highlights that an active decision may well carry baggage in unvoiced choices on associated questions. For example, faced by egregious conduct of a state, Chapter VII need not necessarily be engaged by the Council, but if it does not do so, nor respond otherwise by escalating political

---

82 See above Chapter 4, n 16 to 21 inclusive, and associated text.

83 Especially as the Council has not, in contemporary practice, stinted on allowing access to relevant formal meetings to any who want it, and, of course, the meeting transcript is freely available. On the point about ambiguity, and how that can be a detriment to productiveness of the Council, see also discussion of Resolution 2249—below Chapter 6, n 188 and 189, and associated text.

84 Or, at least in theory, that the Council is choosing to make an affirmative recommendation while harbouring (collective) reservations about whether the applicant is qualified to be a UN member. No recommendation has been made using words that amount to a qualified recommendation, for example, or formally acknowledging that an applicant's capacity to fulfil the requirements of membership is somehow impinged upon, so the suggestion that silence on this point embodies a reservation is really quite a stretch.

85 That assessment cannot be taken as perennial, which also highlights that such implicit conclusions (on assessments) resurface when the Council does not revisit or repeal its view that a state is 'peace-loving', no matter how egregious that state's subsequent conduct.

86 See above Chapter 4, n 92.

measures under Chapter VI (or even perhaps Article 6 expulsion provisions),[87] the Council chooses to overlook that state's conduct. That is, the effect of the Council's silence is that it decides that the conduct somehow does not matter to international peace and security, or matter enough to enjoin a response. This is no less of a Council result for the decision being made passively, arising as an implication of avoiding formally addressing the conduct.

The need for decisions to have an explanatory account thus embraces the risk that what is said may appear anodyne, but what is not said still may prove noxious.

Such things going unremarked may work to dilute persuasiveness of one determination, but the greater concern is that the appearance of systemic inattention or inaction can have the cumulative effect of eroding legitimacy of *Charter* provisions, including those on which the Council bases its authority. Over time, non-use of powers lets inaction morph into desuetude, repeated practice gradually erecting a barrier to the eventual use of such powers.

This also shows that the first concern noted earlier in this section, to flag that a decision has been made, is not meaningfully separable from the second, to be able to apprehend the content of that decision and reasoning for it. Among other things, this is because:

(a) as much as the decision voiced, what is not said, but necessarily implied, may need explanation to show that it at least accords with the *Charter*; and
(b) ambiguous wording may well dilute, undo, or contradict, clarity gained by voting on the decision, so it is challengeable in national courts or, in any case, not satisfactorily explicable for implementation, in turn undermining having made the decision at all.

Stepping back from Council practice, it is worth recalling that voting was 'a concept alien to the traditional management of international relations',[88] and, prior to the advent of the UN, James Brierly summarised the situation thus:

> The general body of states has no legislature, no machinery, that is to say, which allows a majority to outvote a dissentient minority and to pass measures into law which will then become binding on all, whether they have agreed or not [since] one of the consequences of sovereignty is that a state's legal position cannot be altered without its consent.[89]

87 Though again noting the received wisdom that expulsion may be self-defeating when the UN aspires to universality as a key feature of its capacity to influence states—see, for example, discussion in Alvarez, above Chapter 2, n 70, 149. See also above n 59.

88 Fassbender, above Chapter 1, n 33, 278.

89 J L Brierly *The Outlook for International Law* (Clarendon Press, Oxford, 1944), 99.

Discussing 'the problem of voting', Inis Claude observes the 'history of international organization is the story of efforts to achieve progressive emancipation from the tradition-based rule of equality and unanimity' and 'the steady lifting of the dead hand of the unanimity rule'.[90]

That paradigm shift was advanced by the *Charter* deliberately embracing majority voting to signify decisions—by Article 18(2), for example, which provides for Assembly decisions to be made by a two-thirds majority.

The value of unanimity, or where it should sit in the considerations of the Council, is undefined, but it is noteworthy here that the post-Cold War habit of the Council is the antithesis of practice in its early years. In October 1961, for example, the representative of Turkey was moved to say that the retiring President 'has had the rare privilege of counting two unanimous votes cast in the Council in the same month.'[91] In contrast, of over 1,850 Council resolutions adopted from 1 January 1990 to 31 December 2019, some 90 per cent were unanimous decisions.[92]

Claude correctly observes that 'voting does not solve problems or resolve conflicts',[93] and 'we carry it too far if we assume that the will of the majority of states is necessarily entitled to the ideological prestige which democracy confers upon majority decision'.[94] However, voting does clearly signify active decisions when they are made, and, as a significant number of *Summary Statement* editions attest, issues associated with international peace and security have not infrequently languished (some at considerable length) for lack of an active decision.[95]

Noting a sample observation that a 'debate could have been resolved in 15 minutes had it been put to a vote, but the Council ended up in consultations for 17 hours [to] secure unanimous support for a particular decision',[96] this raises two particular concerns.

---

90 Claude, above Chapter 1, n 8, 120 and 121.

91 UN SCOR, 970th mtg, UN Doc S/PV.970 (2 October 1961), 1.

92 Though what this may signify is very much open to debate and alternative interpretations, as are the results for 2018 and 2019: a higher than usual proportion of Council decisions were not unanimous—about 1 in 5 resolutions in 2019. There was also more than the usual run of vetoes, albeit these came after 2017, in which there were more vetoes than in any other year after the Cold War.

93 Claude, above Chapter 1, n 8, 140.

94 Ibid, 124.

95 Distinct from when a decision is made but not implemented.

96 *Letter dated 1 August 2011 from the Permanent Representative of Finland to the United Nations addressed to the President of the Security Council* S/2011/484 (2 August 2011), 17. Nor is unduly seeking unanimity the only problem—as already noted (see above n 83), ambiguity of wording is itself a distinct issue (for a recent example, see below n 105) even

One is that doubts persist about the Council's ability to work with the speed and on the scale required to acquit its role under the *Charter*, and examples such as this do nothing to dispel those doubts. It is worth noting that Ban Ki-moon, after the experiences of almost 10 years as Secretary-General, is said to have 'cautioned against letting the drive for unanimity block timely and much needed action [and that consensus] should not be equated with unanimity, especially in life or death situations.'[97] The other concern is that a decision may have the acknowledged form, but be rather less clear or compelling after the content has been so much 'negotiated' to obtain unanimity. In contrast, dissenting opinions of judges are unremarkable per se, and occur routinely in many places including the International Court of Justice.

For the Council, prioritising a predilection for unanimous decisions thus hints at a price paid in the quality of substantive deliberations and the clarity of outcomes—and, not to be forgotten, in the timeliness of its work.

Importantly, in persuading states to take action unanimity is not necessarily more compelling than any other decision configuration: no small amount of contention attends resolutions in the post-Cold War era, which coexists with the high propensity for unanimous decisions just noted—it is also quite visible in specific cases.[98]

Concerns, that unanimity 'confers upon the minority of one the procedural competence and moral authority to determine policy in a negative fashion',[99] rightly survive in relation to the P5 veto power. As illustrated here, the quest for 'consensus' (the present Council watchword for unanimity) may, however, be a more pervasive influence that re-engages with practical restrictions the *Charter* was designed to avoid.

Ultimately, if prized above all other qualities in Council decision-making, unanimity again becomes a dead hand. It is of another calibre or character to that of pre-UN days, perhaps, but a dead hand all the same, with unknown ramifications for the legal effectiveness and practical productiveness of the Council's deliberations and determinations.

To better persuade states to pay in sovereignty, which may be diminished or diluted by the effect of implementing Council directions, that dead hand

---

though often connected to negotiations towards unanimity (on which Resolution 2249 provides a further example—see below Chapter 6, n 188 and 189, and associated text.

97 *Letter dated 30 May 2017 from the Permanent Representative of Finland to the United Nations addressed to the President of the Security Council* S/2017/468 (1 June 2017), 5. See also related concerns expressed by global thought leaders—above Chapter 2, n 109.

98 See, for example, discussion in Chapter 6.2.2.

99 Claude, above Chapter 1, n 8, 125.

probably needs to be lifted—in part by adequate and sufficient explanation.[100] This likely has greater value, for countering shortfalls in lawful compliance, than stands to be gained from the political 'hurrah' value of unanimous decisions that fall well short on persuasive rationale and, consequently, practical results.

All of that said, even if the Council set and acquitted a robust agenda duly focussed on its *Charter* responsibilities, concluding each item clearly and lawfully (at least in *Charter* terms), there would still be few, if any, results to show for its efforts.

This is a key issue embroiled in understanding accountability of the Council a decision-making body: what the Council decides is not, itself, action—implementation action by others is what makes a Council decision more than just ink on paper, with potential to matter by the results that eventuate.

5.3 Mattering by Results

Sovereign states volunteer to participate in the UN as an international organisation, the existence and work of which is framed by law but which remains an indubitably political environment. When it comes to Council decisions mattering by the results that they deliver, this means that what states do tends to speak more loudly than what they say. Put another way, as far as what states do flows from what the Council says, approbation will show in a compliant response, disquiet in resistance—however geopolitically polite or diplomatic push-back by states may be. These responses dictate outcomes of Council projects, even those about which no opprobrium is ever expressed. It remains, of course, in the eye of the beholder how much talk in, or by, the Council is enough, or too much.

As discussed in the previous section, that stands to be eased, and results facilitated, by showing clearly that a decision has been made, made properly according to law that enables the decision and would potentially be used to enforce it, and with decision content that is sufficiently unambiguous to be implementable. These things together need to be enough to persuade each state to implement the Council's decisions or conform to its recommendations, because even if the decision is likely to be legally effective, for anything

100 Or, as Ian Johnstone puts it, 'public policy succeeds best when voting and bargaining are accompanied by reasoned argumentation'—see Ian Johnstone 'Legislation and Adjudication in the UN Security Council: Bringing Down the Deliberative Deficit' (2008) 102(2) *American Journal of International Law* 275, 276.

to eventuate from it the question is whether it will be practically productive as a result of implementation.

As decision-making bodies generally do, the Council thus faces puzzles entailed in being charged with making decisions that it (presumably) wants implemented. These arise where legal parameters of a given decision might be at issue, but also include that, in all the miscellany of choices that come the way of the decision-maker:

- voting cannot resolve a problem, but neither does avoiding a vote make that problem go away;
- decisions can be implemented only after they are reached;
- any lack of clarity about what constitutes a decision may impede action that is supposed to come next;
- where a decision was made, unclear content is more challenging to implement for those who are willing, and provides an easy way out for those who are not, but also undermines later assessing what actually came of that decision; and
- if lacking ways and means of being formally held accountable, implementation that remains incomplete, inadequate, or inapt, can signal an account of decision-making which contemporary journalism and social media are ready, willing, and very able, to share with all the world.

Importantly, whichever way the cognoscenti might wish to characterise the role of the Council, and to whom that would suggest it might be accountable (if anyone), the cumulative effect of how well the Council deals with such conundrums surfaces in media coverage. This stands to shape views of the UN and its productiveness, and today is a far cry from 1946, when the Council readily resisted representations from 'the Press' about filming its proceedings 'for posterity'.[101] To mark the 70th anniversary of forming the UN, for example, in September 2015 *The Guardian* newspaper gave an account of UN achievements under the banner 'A world of problems: the United Nations at 70'.[102] This heralded perspectives including an interactive illustration of how UN action may generally have affected individuals given their age, gender, and country,[103]

101 UN SCOR, 3rd mtg, UN Doc S/PV.3 (28 January 1946), from opening remarks by the President suggesting filming might be allowed for 10 to 15 minutes.

102 'A world of problems: the United Nations at 70' *The Guardian* (online) September 2015 <http://www.theguardian.com/world/series/united-nations-70-years>.

103 Mark Rice-Oxley, Andrew Mason, Chris Newell, Daan Louter, Richard Nelsson and Kate Lyons 'What has the United Nations ever done for you?' *The Guardian* (online) 15 September 2015 <http://www.theguardian.com/world/2015/sep/15/united-nations-what-has-it-ever-done-for-you-interactive>.

including giving credit to the World Health Organisation for work to eradicate smallpox, and to the UN High Commissioner for Refugees for efforts to care for and assist refugees and displaced persons. The Council was accorded rather less esteem, where 1994 events in Rwanda were the 'nadir of many lows for UN peacekeeping',[104] and:

> The politics of the UN security council continues to hamstring action over some conflicts, such as Syria and Darfur. Other missions drag on indefinitely, such as in the DRC and Haiti. There is friction between the UN and some governments over who has ultimate command over peacekeeping troops, which has resulted in conflicting orders with disastrous consequences. Then there are spreading conflicts against [armed groups] in central and west Africa.[105]

Views about the Council are now broadcast and retailed into the lives of people everywhere, influencing related opinion-leadership and discourse in civil society. In important part, assessments such as this one can be influential in propagating an overarching notion of what powerful actors ought to be accountable for, largely regardless of the nature of their power: in this example, it is that those with the power to have an impact ought to answer for it, or for *the lack of it*.[106]

---

104 For background from the UN perspective, see United Nations Security Council 'Chairman of Independent Inquiry into United Nations Actions During 1994 Rwanda Genocide Presents Report to Security Council' (Security Council Press Release, SC/6843, 14 April 2000).

105 McGreal, above Chapter 3, n 75. In more recent times, a further illustration on this point is noteworthy and unlovely in equal parts, and so something for which an explanation or justification would be welcomed by many states along with many of those affected by the Council's failure to act—when in March 2020 the Secretary-General called for a global ceasefire in the face of the COVID-19 pandemic, six weeks of Council wrangling was unable to produce a result. That is, in what would have been an almost entirely hortatory resolution anyhow, the Council was still unable to agree wording in support of the Secretary-General's initiative—see United Nations 'Secretary-General Calls for Global Ceasefire, Citing War-Ravaged Health Systems, Populations Most Vulnerable to Novel Coronavirus' (United Nations Secretary-General Statements and Messages, SG/SM/20018, 23 March 2020); Julian Borger 'US blocks vote on UN's bid for global ceasefire over reference to WHO' *The Guardian* (online) 9 May 2020 < https://www.theguardian.com/world/2020/may/08/un-ceasefire-resolution-us-blocks-who>. It was not until July 2020 that the Council was able to find an acceptable form of words: see SC Res 2532, UN SCOR, UN Doc S/Res/2532 (1 July 2020).

106 This is not a new phenomenon even if more accessible with each new generation of technology. For example, in the 1980s and 1990s—the days of print newspapers, TV news being mostly in the evening, and reliance on hard copy reports—Amnesty International

In that light, Council productiveness may be evidenced from public or private sessions of the Council that can be shown to lead to action by others. However, discussion based on formal Council meetings, which occur on the record, so far provides only rather lukewarm evidence of salutary results from items on the Council's 'permanent agenda' being dealt with promptly through well-implemented decisions.

More encouraging evidence might be found in private sessions, 'consultations', and other activities leading up to public meetings, which are almost entirely opaque to view by others. These occur off the record in, for example, the 'infamously secretive Council (side-) chamber'.[107] Something of a window into that chamber is, nonetheless, provided by Council member opinions voiced at an event sometimes entitled 'Hitting the Ground Running'. Sponsored by the Government of Finland, this workshop has been convened each year since 2004, usually timed for shortly prior to E10 terms commencing. The intent is to prepare incoming E10 members for taking up office: attendees also include P5 members and continuing or outgoing E10 members, in sessions on looming strategic issues, the heavy agenda, Council working methods, and so on. Importantly, routine effluxion of Council membership over the years means that the event has now engaged something approaching a third of all UN member states.[108]

Afterwards, a workshop report is sent to the President of the Security Council, having been 'compiled in accordance with the Chatham House Rules under

---

and others still made their views known on Indonesian actions in Timor (see below Chapter 6, n 108 and 109); by 1999, in response to post-vote violence conducted or condoned by the Indonesian military, Geoffrey Robinson notes that in just a few days Kofi Annan received 'thousands of messages ... from all over the world ... that many people believe that the United Nations is abandoning the people of East Timor'—and 'some sixty thousand email messages [was] a volume so great that the United Nations Department of Public Information had to set up a separate server solely for messages relating to East Timor' (see Robinson, below Chapter 6, n 92, 194 n 40, and associated text).

107 Tzanakopoulos (2014), above Chapter 2, n 87, 423; José Alvarez has also noted the scarcity of Council meetings 'during the first four weeks of the 1991 air war over Iraq'—Alvarez, above Chapter 3, n 1, 14. In a different kind of emergency, as presented by the COVID-19 pandemic and the UN's location in New York (one of the epicentres of the pandemic), the Council might again be said to have retreated behind closed doors, even though the long term implications are not yet known (see above n 80).

108 The report does not list all attendees, but its wording implies attendance by the incoming E10 plus the majority of other Council members. Counting those commencing at least one E10 term since the workshop was inaugurated, plus those likely to have participated as outgoing E10 members in the inaugural session who have not served again since, indicates around 60 states would have had the opportunity to attend the workshop—and, from the tone of the reports, very likely took it.

the sole responsibility of the Permanent Mission of Finland'.[109] While the report is 'not intended to represent an agreed position of the participants or the organizers',[110] it does provide a synopsis of unattributed commentary and discussion at that year's event, in line with nominated topics.[111]

The series of reports thus together covers a significant slice of UN membership, and the reports are based on states' pertinent experience as constituent members of the Council, so views reported might at least be taken as an indicative poll of those who empower the Council via the *Charter*.

These reports are notable for at least two things—relative frankness of commentary elicited, and years of consistent comments on certain aspects of Council decision-making. They show priorities in agenda-setting are a constant issue, for example, as is time management in Council meetings. In terms of the quality of Council discourse, there is a continual thread in which Council work was seen as 'overly choreographed and ritualistic'.[112]

The reports also show non-trivial concerns about patchy information flows, lack of E10 engagement in drafting resolutions, and not nearly enough process transparency.[113] Changes have certainly occurred over more than 15 years since the workshop's inception, and are acknowledged by its members, but the

---

109 *Letter dated 19 February 2004 from the Permanent Representative of Finland to the United Nations addressed to the President of the Security Council* S/2004/135 (20 February 2004), 1.

110 Ibid, 2.

111 At least nine out of 15 relevant annual reports put the workshop report in 'Part III: Other matters considered by the Security Council': see *Report of the Security Council: 1 August 2003–31 July 2004* UN GAOR, 59th sess, Supp No 2, UN Doc A/59/2 (29 September 2004), 176; *Report of the Security Council: 1 August 2004–31 July 2005* UN GAOR, 60th sess, Supp No 2, UN Doc A/60/2 (2005), 182; *Report of the Security Council: 1 August 2005–31 July 2006* UN GAOR, 61st sess, Supp No 2, UN Doc A/61/2 (2006), 189; *Report of the Security Council: 1 August 2006–31 July 2007* UN GAOR, 62nd sess, Supp No 2, UN Doc A/62/2 (25 October 2007), 195; *Report of the Security Council: 1 August 2007–31 July 2008* UN GAOR, 63rd sess, Supp No 2, UN Doc A/63/2 (2008), 210; *Report of the Security Council: 1 August 2014–31 July 2015* UN GAOR, 70th sess, Supp No 2, UN Doc A/70/2 (20 October 2015), 188: *Report of the Security Council: 1 August 2015–31 December 2016* UN GAOR, 71st sess, Supp No 2, UN Doc A/71/2 (29 August 2017), 246; *Report of the Security Council for 2017* UN GAOR, 72nd sess, Supp No 2, UN Doc A/72/2 (2018), 197; *Report of the Security Council for 2018* UN GAOR, 73rd sess, Supp No 2, UN Doc A/73/2 (2019), 183.

112 *Letter dated 6 May 2013 from the Permanent Representative of Finland to the United Nations addressed to the President of the Security Council* S/2013/280 (9 May 2013), 22.

113 Such as in relation to obtaining chairs of the Council's committees operating as subsidiary bodies, where one 'newly elected member first heard about the results from a website and did not accept the assignments, and those committees did not meet for a year'—*Letter dated 26 May 2016 from the Permanent Representative of Finland to the United Nations addressed to the President of the Security Council* S/2016/ 506 (2 June 2016), 26.

Council's inability to change its processes featured in most reports (including addressing Council accountability in many of these).

Even allowing for eyes jaundiced by the prevailing geopolitical environment, this does not give a clean bill of health on Council agenda-setting, or for handling and concluding important matters with appropriate despatch and substantive results. One could take the Council's approach as more arcane than dysfunctional in its genuinely idiosyncratic circumstances, since the evidence for either status is not clear. But dissatisfaction on the part of constituent members of the Council certainly is not to be dismissed lightly—especially when considering what being accountable might bring to the prospects for enhancing Council productiveness.

On a wider front, evidencing that Council decisions matter by the results they achieve calls for dividing off what the Council should own and what might be left at the door of another—including that parties to a 'situation' (or a conflict or crisis or dispute) always retain ownership of their part in bringing it to an end. Even so, there is a paucity of examples showing Council action has resolved (or materially aided in resolving) the matter, or that could be said to show the Council was effective in attempting to avert or curtail the threat or use of force in international relations.

In fact, *Summary Statement* editions over approaching 75 years cover a plethora of armed conflicts not impacted upon by Council attention when they received it,[114] and these are a subset of those with trans-border effects where violence was, or is still, unabated after Council attention.[115]

An indication of results that matter might still be found if implementation of a Council decision achieved general participation by states. Measures associated with combatting terrorism might be a contemporary example, though little consolidated data is published (yet). More importantly, these calls are inherently qualified to the extent of opportunity arising for implementation: even if the call is made generally to states, opportunity may prove to be patchy or sporadic, so their implementation is not a reasonable indicator of support for that genre of Council decisions.

A better example is likely to be calls for troop contributions to peacekeeping missions. These are a routine feature of the entire post-Cold War period, so many now consider mounting such operations to be integral to the Council's

114 See, for example, Dunbabin, above Chapter 2, n 18; see also the discussion in Chapter 6.1 and 6.2 about the Council response in 1975–1976 to Indonesia's action in Timor.

115 See Vaughan Lowe, Adam Roberts, Jennifer Welsh and Dominik Zaum (eds) *The United Nations Security Council and War: The Evolution of Thought and Practice since 1945* (Oxford, 2008), Appendix 7.

functional capacity. There is no minimum qualifying contribution of troops and quite a variety of needs arise, so any state might participate by contributing individuals from its armed forces or police.[116] The first barrier to be hurdled is, however, persuading states to participate at all. No treaty status obligation to provide the UN with troops arises after the stillbirth of Article 43, and calls for peacekeeping troops are not said to be framed as an obligation under Article 25.[117] This means participation is voluntary at every turn: states decide on each element of every mandate, and this remains open to renegotiation whenever a mandate is renewed. Choosing to contribute troops thus serves as a not unreasonable proxy indicator for willingness by states to implement this genre of Council decisions—in the first instance, the fact of contributing troops is enough testimony for implementation.[118]

Significant expansion of peacekeeper numbers after the Cold War could, on first blush, suggest substantial and continued implementation of peacekeeping missions. That does not, however, show whether the increase was sufficient for the mandates at hand, nor signify the extent of difficulties in raising the quantum of troops needed. To detect the underpinning support for Council decisions, one might instead ask whether the 1990 pattern of contributions follows the increasing scale of operations: do contributors in earlier times continue to provide numbers of troops in keeping with the pace of growth in the scale of deployments?

Statistics on troop contributions are published by the UN on a reasonably consistent basis from 1990 onwards.[119] That data shows total troops fielded leapt from around 10,000 in 1990 to over 50,000 in 1992, then grew more steadily for some years before tripling again from December 2000 to December 2015. After 25 years the troops fielded thus stood an order of magnitude greater, being over 100,000 in December 2015, or about ten times the 1990 level (noting that since then the tide has turned to a degree, the total number receding to under 90,000). This means illustration of support for Council decisions on peacekeeping needs to allow for skewing from the significantly different scale

116 The embrace of police in peacekeeping has further opened up the opportunity for participation, including for those states with constitutional limitations on the nature of their permitted armed forces—such as Japan and Costa Rica.

117 The usual form of words captures the voluntary nature of participation—see for example SC Res 2149, UN SCOR, 7153rd mtg, UN Doc S/Res/2149 (10 April 2014), [20].

118 Which, for the purposes at hand, thus need not be connected to, for example, the specific situation being addressed by peacekeeping, or questions of Council productiveness more generally.

119 United Nations Peacekeeping *Troop and police contributors* <https://peacekeeping.un.org/en/troop-and-police-contributors>.

of total operations. On the other hand, contributors 'keeping pace' need not mean increasing by an entire order of magnitude by 2015, since UN membership was also growing and more states could get involved—plus, of course, there are also practical limitations on participation in the circumstances for each state.

As one approach to unpacking this, in 1947 the working assumption for implementation of Article 43 was that five states (the P5) would provide 'most' troops, say 75 per cent, the rest to come from a 'few' others.[120] Emulating the 1947 logic provides one way to show whether and how states' support for Council decisions would manifest in action to contribute troops, by looking at contributors amounting to 75 percent of the troops in the field. Based on numbers for December of each year, states' contributions were accumulated beginning from the largest, and adding others in descending order of quantum until cumulatively representing 75 per cent of the troops deployed.

This is illustrated in Figure 5, where names are weighted by the proportion of UN troops in the field in December of that year which were provided by that state.[121]

Figure 5 shows most states from 1990 very soon receded from view, so they were not close to keeping pace with the growth in troop contributions called for by the Council. It further illustrates turning points in the pattern of contributions, leaving no doubt that countries contributing the lion's share of troops changes significantly over time, even if contributors from earlier times continue to provide some troops.[122]

This says little, and quite possibly nothing at all, about causality in states' support for Council decisions on peacekeeping. What is, nonetheless, abundantly clear is that expansion in numbers of troops fielded is no cause for congratulations that the Council decisions are being implemented willingly and well.

Moreover, while 'mystery still surrounds the UN force generation process',[123] the record on filling this bill over the years is not encouraging. It has long been impolitic to openly admit defeat in raising sufficient troops, but official documents still furnish examples—such as when, in 2009, overtures by the Secretariat to '49 troop contributors and 12 potential troop contributors' still did not

---

120 See above Chapter 1, n 35.

121 The years selected were for the purposes of clear illustration—years omitted were consistent with the same trends.

122 However, see also below n 134, and associated text.

123 Marina Henke 'Great powers and UN force generation: a case study of UNAMID' (2016) 23(3) *International Peacekeeping* 468, 468.

FIGURE 5 States constituting 75 per cent of troops fielded
SOURCE: DERIVED FROM UN DATA[124]

---

124 United Nations Peacekeeping *Troop and police contributors* <https://peacekeeping.un.org/en/troop-and-police-contributors>

garner enough troops for the authorised level.[125] Now, talk of shortfalls is not at all novel,[126] 'capability gaps are an almost constant feature' of peacekeeping missions,[127] and a formal summit was convened in 2015 to address the issue.[128]

The long term implication is that the collection of states engaged has acquired a different character. Since 1990 this has moved away from established contributors, but, since around 2000, also away from developed countries more generally. Beyond just the sufficiency of numbers provided (noting the adequacy of the authorised quantum of troops remains a separate, and significant, question),[129] this raises several concerns—about states' willingness to implement generally, the fragmentation of contributions more specifically, and, in the end, making peacekeeping operations matter by meeting their mandate if resourcing remains stretched and difficult.

First, these results confirm what the Assembly has asserted—there is now a 'lack of participation by developed countries.'[130] Many do choose to contribute funds instead and, assuredly, funding is also essential. Funds mean little without enough arms and legs to animate a Council mandate, however. Moreover, there may be no legal obligation for states to implement such decisions in the way that Article 43 agreements presumably would have provided, but as Christine Gray asks:

---

125 *Letter dated 27 January 2009 from the Secretary-General to the President of the Security Council* S/2009/52 (27 January 2009), 1. He was responding to the increased deployment authorised for MONUC—see SC Res 1843, UN SCOR, 6018th mtg, UN Doc S/Res/1843 (20 November 2008).

126 For example: United Nations 'Overburdened, Underfunded, Overstretched Peacekeeping Operations Create 'Yawning Gap' between Expectations, Performance, Fourth Committee Told at Close of Debate' (General Assembly Meetings Coverage, GA/SPD/465, 27 October 2010).

127 Adam C Smith and Arthur Boutellis *Rethinking Force Generation: Filling the Capability Gaps in UN Peacekeeping* (Providing for Peacekeeping No. 2, International Peace Institute, May 2013), 1.

128 See for example—James Reinl 'UN nations pledge 40,000 peacekeepers' *Al Jazeera* (online) 29 September 2015 <https://www.aljazeera.com/news/2015/09/40000-peacekeepers-150929000643036.html>.

129 As one example of the difficult politics involved, and the pressure to paper over those difficulties that arise before even seeking contributions from states, when establishing the UN Assistance Mission in Rwanda (UNAMIR), the commander, General Dallaire 'had originally envisaged 8,000 peacekeepers, hoped for 5,000, but finally *agreed to request only 2,500* as *a feasible number that might be approved* [by the Security Council]': Howard Adelman and Astri Suhrke 'Rwanda' in David M Malone (ed) *The UN Security Council: From the Cold War to the 21st Century* (Lynne Rienner Publishers, London, 2004), 483, 491 (emphasis added).

130 United Nations 'Lack of Participation by Developed Countries in UN Peacekeeping Missions Raised in Fourth Committee' (General Assembly Press Release, GA/SPD/199, 8 November 2000).

> [How] far is it legitimate for developed states to pay their peacekeeping contributions, to provide commanders and perhaps logistical support and transport, but not to provide significant numbers of actual troops for UN operation?[131]

Second, contributions are very fragmented with most UN members providing only modest troop numbers, and each seeking its own version of the arrangements put forward under UN policy. For one notional mission involving five countries, this means the Council engages in five distinct relationships; 15 such missions involving five states each thus produces 75 situationally distinct relationships, even if there is some overlap between them. Contemporary peacekeeping involves added complexity: contributions to a specific mission may also involve multiple force elements from a single country—individual police, military experts, staff officers, formed units of police, formed units of armed forces personnel, and so on. Each force element potentially relates to its national government in a different way, due to its domestic legal and institutional arrangements, meaning that different command and control arrangements may apply in each case and create further variation in how forces operate when deployed on UN work.

To illustrate the current situation on that basis, as at December 2019 contributions of personnel for peacekeeping operations could be summarised as shown in Figure 6. The relevant operations are those which, by organisational arrangements from Secretary-General António Guterres, are promulgated as such and led by the UNs Department of Peace Operations (a subset of 'peace missions', which now also includes those led by the UNs Department of Political and Peacebuilding Affairs).[132] Taking this perspective better highlights the Council's situational relationships, which, in effect, go beyond what is indicated by the number of troop contributing countries per se. It is particularly worth noting that:

(a) the quantum of troops in the field in December 2019 is significantly less than December 2015–82,036 as compared to 107,088; *but*

(b) that still involves as good as the same number of countries—117 compared to 123.

---

131 Christine Gray 'Peacekeeping and enforcement action in Africa: the role of Europe and the obligations of multilateralism' (2005) 31(S1) *Review of International Studies* 207, 223.

132 United Nations *United Nations Peace Missions* <https://www.unmissions.org>. See also United Nations *United Nations Peace Missions—Where We Operate* <https://peacekeeping.un.org/en/where-we-operate>.

Mission	Total Personnel	Countries	Force Elements
MINURSO	202	35	38
MINUSCA	13,312	57	131
MINUSMA	13,695	59	144
MONUSCO	15,346	60	127
UNAMID	6,482	43	95
UNDOF	1,070	10	16
UNFICYP	861	26	36
UNIFIL	10,315	43	70
UNISFA	3,786	34	66
UNMIK	16	10	11
UNMISS	16,761	72	162
UNMOGIP	42	10	10
UNTSO	148	25	25
Combinations from 13 missions		484	931
Total for 13 missions	82,036	Uniformed personnel, including individuals and formed units from armed forces and police	
Originating from	117	Troop contributing countries	

FIGURE 6 Summary of troop contributions by country, December 2019
SOURCE: DERIVED FROM UN DATA[133]

Then, combinations of country and mission imply 484 potentially different links to the Council, and, beyond that, arrangements made may well be specific to each force element from a country—meaning those links may have been as high as 931 as at December 2019.

This confirms that the number of countries that the Council must address and interact with, to gather the authorised quantum of peacekeepers, has increased significantly since 1990, but also that this set of interactions has acquired a significantly more complex and time-consuming makeup as contributions have become rather more fragmented.

133 United Nations Peacekeeping *Troop and police contributors* <https://peacekeeping.un.org/en/troop-and-police-contributors>

Thus, while larger numbers of deployed forces might—superficially—speak to the Council engaging a diversity of countries, a more nuanced view concerns the seriousness of consequent workload and issues associated with having effective command and control arrangements. In fact, each such interaction carries workload almost regardless of the scale of troops contributed, Together, these realities are potential impediments to this central element of the Council's work being as productive as it might be—so it might well be said that the Council's approach is much more of a 'make work' rather than a 'get results' exercise.

In that light, Katharina Coleman's view that many small contributions arise without a question of capacity becomes more important in discussing Council productiveness. Describing these as a 'token' contribution, she observes that:

> [This is] a deliberately chosen and distinctive mode of participation [but this] distinctiveness is rarely recognized, because tokenism is widely and uncritically attributed to resource scarcity: states are simply assumed to make token contributions only because they cannot make more substantial ones. [However] the sheer number of token contributions militates against viewing tokenism as a residual category of troop contributions.[134]

Focus on growth in total numbers deployed, as an indication of healthy Council activity, thus appears misplaced. To begin with, it masks at least two distinct systemic issues:

(a) willing support, to implement Council mandates for peacekeeping, is lacking (to varying degrees) from a majority of states; and

(b) highly fragmented force generation is itself a potential drag anchor attached to Council effectiveness—from the much greater complexity of administrative effort required to deploy a mission, but also creating consequent opportunities for delay, error, omission, misconduct, and so on, in related operations.

Beyond that, making peacekeeping missions matter calls for them to meet their objectives (at least in general terms). Given the typically (and unsurprisingly)

---

134 Katharina P Coleman 'Token Troop Contributions to United Nations Peacekeeping Operations' in Alex J Bellamy and Paul D Williams *Providing Peacekeepers: The Politics, Challenges, and Future of United Nations Peacekeeping Contributions* (Oxford Scholarship Online, 2013), 47, 48. Of course, parsing or disaggregating a state's reasoning is not readily done—for example, see below Chapter 6, n 5.

fraught contexts in which peacekeeping takes place, and the undoubted role of those involved to settle their differences, this still looks to be very much an uphill battle.[135] Insufficient troops are a general malaise, but specific mandates are, not infrequently, roundly questioned.[136]

In the end, not all states can participate in peacekeeping operations, but many (perhaps most) of those that can, don't, or do so only on a token scale. So again, there is no clean bill of health here for the Council, which weighs in the balance against such decisions mattering as much as they ought to. No surprise then that a view from unnamed Council members was that 'the biggest challenge [in 2017] would be implementation',[137] and the record of Council work in 2017 suggests that this proved to be the case. Discussion so far indicates that this is not a new phenomenon for the Council, however, and this chapter further suggests this state of affairs is interlinked with strengthening needed in relation to Council capacity to set its agenda and make decisions in the first place. Thus, one might well ask would its decisions matter more if the Council accounted for its conduct, to elicit more, and more complete, implementation of its decisions by states? If so, what might the Council account for towards such ends?

5.4 What Matters in Being Accountable?

Discussion in this chapter so far shows that, as a socio-legal construct created to serve a purpose, the Council's effectiveness hinges on its capacity to identify and address what matters to its raison d'être by setting an appropriate agenda. From that capacity, its capability is metered in what it delivers, meaning that

135 As reflected in review of all operations up until 2012, chapter by chapter in Koops et al, above Chapter 3, n 59. One vexed issue is the use of force—for further background, see James Sloan 'The Evolution of the Use of Force in Peacekeeping' (2014) 37(5) *Journal of Strategic Studies* 674; Ian Johnstone 'When the Security Council is Divided: Imprecise Authorizations, Implied Mandates, and the "Unreasonable Veto" ' in Marc Weller (ed) *The Oxford Handbook of the Use of Force in International Law* (2015).

136 Again see mission critiques in the various chapters of Koops et al, above Chapter 3, n 59; see also, for example, Thierry Tardy 'A Critique of Robust Peacekeeping in Contemporary Peace Operations' (2011) 18(2) *International Peacekeeping* 152; Frédéric Mégret 'Between R2P and the ICC: "Robust Peacekeeping" and the Quest for Civilian Protection' (2015) 26(1) *Criminal Law Forum* 101; Peter Nadin, Patrick Cammaert and Vesselin Popovski 'Role and development of robust peacekeeping' (2014) 54(449) *Adelphi Series* 75.

137 See *Letter dated 30 May 2017 from the Permanent Representative of Finland to the United Nations addressed to the President of the Security Council* S/2017/468 (1 June 2017), 13.

setting an agenda and producing Council outputs are necessary, but not sufficient, conditions for productive results: implementation of Council decisions remains essential (and, I would suggest, ditto on Council recommendations). Beyond such implementation, what goes towards realising its Functions or contributing to UN Purposes is also a product of what may get in the way of that result—a wide range of legal, institutional, and practical, realities that are enmeshed in the operating context of the Council. These may deter, dilute, or detract from, action that should follow to achieve a salutary result from Council efforts.

Taken together, this points to what else may matter in the Council being accountable. A successful legal challenge to a Council decision really is not in prospect, for example, but practical limitations on what can be realised from Council efforts may arise even without a demonstrable institutional or legal impediment to heeding Council directions. States may be faced with the prospect of domestic political fallout over dubious legality, or a spectre of legal challenges about whether implementation would be rightful in their particular circumstances. In response, some may stint in complying with Council directions,[138] or, it must be said, others may use this as convenient, respectable clothes for their own (less salutary) political purposes—but these come to much the same thing in lack of implementation.

Moreover, a less-than-desirably productive Council, which does not explain or justify its agenda, outputs, and results, has an effect on attitudes to its authority and perceptions of its legitimacy—and, again, asserting a shortfall in Council legitimacy may be convenient cover for those with no real intention of meeting the obligations on states under the *Charter*.

As the long-running reform debate shows, no other actor is placed to impose solutions on it, so the Council not acting to remedy its situation is one aspect of how its legitimacy, and the role of accountability in bolstering that, interconnects with the good faith principle as an element of states' dealings in the international legal order. As Michel Virally has said:

> Nobody can ignore that good faith forms part of the foundation of the whole international legal structure without running the risk of reducing international law to a set of hollow legal formulas.[139]

138 Shown in the ongoing tale of counter-terrorism sanctions, as an extension of the discussion arising from Resolution 1267—see Chapter 6.2.2.

139 Michel Virally "Review Essay: Good Faith in Public International Law" (1983) 77 *American Journal of International Law* 130, 134.

In its peculiar politico-legal role, the Council relies fundamentally on such legal formulas for the capacity that it has to assert its will and expect its views to be respected. What accountability stands to add to that picture arises in significant part from better showing that the Council is doing what it can with the powers that it has, to see its Functions realised towards the UN's Purposes.

To such ends, Council habits might be adjusted to give better evidence that:

> [The] expressed will be consistent with the real will and, more generally, that the legal reality be consistent with what it seems to be (that is, consistent with the appearances created by the declarations or the behaviour of legal actors). Good faith excludes any separation between reality and appearances.[140]

One could certainly argue that in its corporate practice, evidencing a due rationale for Council decisions would show good faith towards establishing 'conditions under which justice and respect for the obligations arising from treaties and other sources of international law can be maintained'.[141] This means, inter alia, that whether or not it is bound by such treaties and other sources of international law, the better question for the Council to consider is what it may lose by contravening them, or even just being seen to be careless of their provisions. To engender compliance with its decisions, showing due care for such provisions would instead call for conduct standards against which the Council might explain its decisions and take stock of activities carried out in its name.

To better serve UN Purposes, conduct standards probably need not embrace the full flower of values associated with a 'thick' rule of law concept, but many would be wary that nothing meaningful, or perhaps nothing at all, would be added by bare procedural correctness from a 'thin', formalist approach.[142] This calls for cognisance of how the rule of law is conceptualised in international law. For example, Ian Hurd notes three ways:

> The first is anchored on the obligation of states to comply with their international legal obligations. The second draws on an analogy with the domestic rule of law. The third begins from the observation that states

140 Ibid, 131. A particular difficulty is, of course, the Council's well-known penchant for much-negotiated texts, including the embrace of 'constructive ambiguity' which does not prove to also be 'productive ambiguity'(see below Chapter 6, n 188 and 189, and associated text).

141 *Charter*, third preambular paragraph.

142 See above Chapter 2, n 82.

> invoke international law to explain and justify their policies—from this it expands into a model of law as integral to political legitimation.[143]

All may be relevant to the Council: the third adds to the power of the Council to pursue the first, mutually reinforcing the *Charter* design and the Council's Functions in that. These appear sufficient, even independent of the second, but the second remains a source of importable maxims of the kind that are relevant here.[144] For example, it may be uncontroversial to want transparency, or its close cousin, openness, as a feature of the Council's processes, because opacity and closed dealing obscure information which is crucial to accountability.[145] Nuancing is needed, though, as unlimited visibility readily amounts to all possible assistance short of actual help for accountability—just as the Council's annual report gives all possible documentation short of any explanation of Council decisions. An excess of formalist transparency will serve more to consume considerable resources—for a result that is well short of an actual critique, and likely to be just as ambiguous as the proceedings which are reported.

Requiring proportionate responses would also be unremarkable, consistent with proportionality as 'a general principle of law' and 'found in most legal systems', as Christopher Michaelsen observes.[146] The issue for a system of Council accountability is not so much to be able to see *one* determination as proportionate or otherwise: potentially it needs to be able to construe *any or all* of them in such a fashion, and do so promptly, consistently, and with due regard to its complex circumstances.

Of course, articulating a standard would start something that the Council needs to finish by changing its habits, and being seen to do so. This could possibly include:

- holding its members to standards in casting their votes—so working to restrain an excess of self-interest that may run counter to UN Purposes; or

143 Ian Hurd 'Three Models of the International Rule of Law' (2015) 23 *Eidos* 37, 37.

144 Where the extent to which 'rule of law' has a coherent meaning at the national level requires its specific political context—see, for example Simon Chesterman 'An International Rule of Law?' (2008) 56(2) *American Journal of Comparative Law* 331.

145 For a detailed analysis on one aspect of how this impacts on Council activities, see Kihara-Hunt, above Chapter 2, n 98.

146 Christopher Michaelsen 'Human Rights as Limits for the Security Council: A Matter of Substantive Law or Defining the Application of Proportionality?' (2014) 19(3) *Journal of Conflict & Security Law* 451, 465; see also Thomas M Franck 'On Proportionality of Countermeasures in International Law' (2008) 102(4) *American Journal of International Law* 715.

– framing its decisions so as to somewhat approximate a *ratio decidendi*—so as to provide something of a replicable, and thus assessable, basis for deciding, albeit without implying a precedent.

The same might also be said of the Council avoiding arbitrary decisions, at least as a contribution to 'conditions under which justice and respect for the obligations arising [from] international law can be maintained'.[147] That this is conduct desired or desirable from the Council, as one guardian of the international legal order, is an idea that ought not be contentious—including since, as Christine Chinkin and Hilary Charlesworth observe:

> If international law is understood as a method of controlling the use and abuse of power, it can provide protection against arbitrary determinations and unfettered discretion and therefore a basis for accountability.[148]

That much said, the nature of the UN's power architecture is fairly put as 'not government', and the Council is, in fact, idiosyncratic; the Council also has remarkable formal powers and potentially very significant power that flows from their exercise. Accordingly, the Council might start by heeding Martin Krygier, who sees the rule of law as 'opposed to arbitrariness in the exercise of *significant* power, whoever is doing the exercise', including 'oligarchs, Mafiosi, warlords, tribal elders, Al-Qaida, business executives or university administrators'.[149] Crucially, when judicial review of Council decisions remains unlikely, it is worth noting his view that:

> Arbitrariness is a specific and obnoxious vice when added to power ... There are many other vices which depend on the substance of the law, but arbitrary power is vicious enough even without them and moreover can be vicious even when the substance is fine.[150]

While not uncommon as a politico-legal adjective, the challenge is to interpret 'arbitrary' more specifically, so that it might serve as a standard for Council conduct. The International Court of Justice has made at least one decision

147 *Charter*, third preambular paragraph.

148 Christine Chinkin and Hilary Charlesworth 'Building Women into Peace: the international legal framework' (2006) 27(5) *Third World Quarterly* 937, 943.

149 Martin Krygier 'The Security Council and the rule of law: some conceptual reflections' in Jeremy Farrall and Hilary Charlesworth (eds) *Strengthening the Rule of Law through the Security Council* (Routledge, 2016), 24 (emphasis added).

150 Ibid, 20.

which deals with defining 'arbitrary'. In *Elettronica Sicula SpA* (*ELSI*),[151] a majority held that:

> Arbitrariness is not so much something opposed to a rule of law, as something opposed to the rule of law … It is a wilful disregard of due process of law, an act which shocks, or at least surprises, a sense of juridical propriety.[152]

It is not self-evident what might shock their honours from time to time, and only modest scholarly attention has since been given to that decision,[153] so it may be more pragmatic to ask the Court to advise further in the context of Council decision-making.

These are by no means the only characteristics that would be interesting in Council decisions: the point is more that principles, including legal principles, have a role to play in engendering the legitimacy that stands to aid Council productiveness, but the body of work from the Council continues to show a 'focus on crises [which] produces an impoverished set of substantive principles in international law', as Hilary Charlesworth puts it.[154] In that light, a dilemma in the Council's work mattering more is that it would be rather naïve to suggest that the Council can resolve the related gaps without authoritative assistance (even if it is not binding), but, equally, concluding that nothing more can be done to resolve them certainly would seem to be unduly cynical.

5.5 Mattering More

Ultimately, the whole world may be the worse for misuse, abuse, disrepair, or desuetude, of the Council's remarkable formal powers, and potentially very significant power that flows from them. Consistent with the aspirations ascribed to the UN, this should not be suffered to continue. One element, and perhaps a primary element, of curtailing that is a suitable account of Council

151 *Elettronica Sicula SpA* (*ELSI*) (United States of America v Italy) (Judgment) [1989] ICJ Rep 15.

152 Ibid, [128].

153 For example, Mann summarises that 'there had to be evidence to show that the act was unreasonable, capricious, incapable of rational foundation'—see F A Mann 'Foreign Investment in the International Court of Justice: The ELSI Case' (1992) 86(1) *American Journal of International Law* 92, 99.

154 Hilary Charlesworth 'International Law: A Discipline of Crisis' (2002) 65(3) *Modern Law Review* 377, 390.

doings. Discussion in this chapter first suggests suitability would be measured by how well the account identifies the extent to which the Council is doing what it was created to do, and making the impact on international peace and security that was intended when states collectively chose to create it under the *Charter*. From the desiderata of how the Council occupies its days (and, to be fair, many nights), these things warrant an explanation, but are hardly an exhaustive list.

Towards making that explanation, discussion in this chapter further suggests what is wanted is the orderly application of a neat fleet of conduct standards, constructed and deployed to explain or justify the Council's work. This is because accountability is not assisted by a gaggle of disjunctive assertions—affirmative or negative—often left bobbing in the Council's wake during politicised debates. Nor is a jumbled flotilla of qualities helpful, though each may be individually estimable and somehow necessary to Council work. Instead, to enhance legal and institutional accountability arrangements, so as to both better enable the Council's efforts and duly restrain the power that it embodies, that neat fleet needs to represent a collegial understanding of principles *agreed* as being valuable if applied proactively in the Council's work. Those principles at least need to be agreed by the Council's members as applying to its practice, if formal *Charter* reform continues to lack consensus among those states collectively empowering the Council.

Once adopted, such conduct standards would also likely need to be amended or adjusted, added to or subtracted from, over time and tide of geopolitics. There are thus two component parts needed in a response: first, an understanding of what to account for, and then second, a means of asserting that, which will—crucially in the Council's particular circumstances—accommodate the changing nature of both the UN and the world around it.

An overarching concern is that decisions, and the process of deciding, are both readily impoverished without due regard for rightful elements of the matter at hand, and equally may be impinged upon by undue individual self-interest exercised by states voting in Council decisions. Standards for what is rightful are needed, shaped by expectations of what the Council should answer for—at least to those empowering it, but more valuable for also answering concerns of others affected by activities, and inactivities, of the Council as a decision-making collective.

In that vein, the record of its practice suggests that the Council prefers to pronounce on the obligations of others rather than to settle the nature of its own: Council obligations, and those of its constituent members, are largely in abeyance even after approaching 75 years. Does this amount to the Council not providing itself with adequate and sufficient ways and means to meet its obligations, in part from reluctance to determine proactively how, and with what, to equip itself, and perhaps even why? If so, the Council lags further behind the mark noted by Clyde Eagleton.[155] Moreover, not only does it seem to disappoint expectations among those who empower it (if the reform debate is any guide) and leave wanting for help many of those it affects by its work (as many from Trieste to Timor would attest), but the Council faces gaps of its own making and others that it could close but hasn't (yet).

It is also a pragmatic reality that, in the absence of an agreed standard on implementation of Council decisions, and a prescribed means of asserting that, *being arbiter of what is rightful will fall to each actor doing the implementing.*

Since the non-permanent members of the Council emanate from the group of states collectively empowering it, the same group on whom implementation rests in largest part, the role of the E10 here is interesting. As with every Council decision now,[156] and distinct from whatever a P5 veto may render, the E10 has the weight of numbers to see a decision made (by lending their votes to support it) or not made (by voting against it, abstaining, or not participating in the voting).[157] In that light, should these 'representatives' then be taken to task for how they use (or do not use) their votes? Should they answer for their role in acquiescing to decisions,[158] including those which are then insufficiently implemented—such as approving peacekeeping mandates that are perilously flawed and/or not endorsed via implementation by the wider membership of the UN? Or should the E10 instead insist on improvements—for example, more enforceable conduct standards requiring all personnel on peacekeeping missions to uphold the good name of the UN in their standard of conduct, perhaps by withholding E10 assent to commence or continue the operation if conduct standards are not included and likely to be effective in the UN's operating circumstances?[159]

In wanting to assert the need for greater accountability in relation to Council work, such questions point to the fact that under the *Charter* as it stands, a key challenge is that no actor has a *right* to do so—and, as put by Simon Chesterman:

---

155 See above Chapter 2, n 95.

156 Indeed, for all since the increase in Council size to 15 members—see also Chapter 6.2.

157 To 'exercise the rarely seen but conceivable "veto" that the Council's non-permanent members wield' as Alvarez puts it (see Alvarez, above Chapter 2, n 70, 199), or the 'sixth veto', to use Colin Keating's phrase, being 'the collective no-vote of at least seven elected members'—see Keating, above Chapter 4, n 118, 145.

158 Through their 'concurrence or passivity' as Colin Keating puts it—ibid.

159 Or, equivalently, anywhere else the UN is 'represented' by those in a subsidiary organ.

> Accountability should not simply be a reaction to a scandal, however. To be effective it should normally exist as of right, which requires the creation of institutions, the elaboration of standards, and the potential for sanctions.[160]

Even before, or without, such a right being created by *Charter* reform, cause for hope is found in some wins by E10 members, originating in the relatively recent innovation of 'penholding'.[161] This is where a Council member takes the lead on drafting resolutions and steering the negotiating process to agree wording in 'consultations' of the Council. Some commentators note this role emerged primarily as a province of the P5, and a goodly measure of cynicism would certainly not be misplaced since there have been some side effects:

> Elected members were left out of the drafting process altogether and were brought into negotiations only at the very end—and were often discouraged from making meaningful amendments because they might disturb the wording agreed to among the P5 …[162]

A recent episode nonetheless provides a contrast: as violence in Syria continued to escalate in 2013, E10 members Australia and Luxembourg developed a proposal in relation to humanitarian access to assist hundreds of thousands of people displaced in Syria and/or unable to access necessities.

Though working in the rather long shadow of a probable veto, these states successfully crafted a presidential statement saying, in part:

> [The Council] condemns all cases of denial of humanitarian access, and recalls that arbitrarily depriving civilians of objects indispensable to their survival, including wilfully impeding relief supply and access, can constitute a violation of international humanitarian law.[163]

Commentators noted that achieving such access was 'one of the most contentious topics [over] several months' in the Council, but:

160 Chesterman, above Chapter 3, n 80, 43.

161 See Security Council Report *The Penholder System* (Research Report No. 3, Security Council Report, 21 December 2018); see also Security Council Report, above Chapter 1, n 76.

162 Ibid.

163 *Statement by the President of the Security Council* UN Doc S/PRST/2013/15 (2 October 2013), 2. For background, see above Chapter 2, n 20 to 23 inclusive, and associated text; see also, for example, *Letter dated 25 April 2013 from the Permanent Representative of Jordan to the United Nations addressed to the President of the Security Council* S/2013/247 (25 April 2013).

> [Many] Council members are also encouraged that two [elected] Council members drafted the text and led the process and that the text was not shepherded by [permanent members who] draft the majority of Council outcomes.[164]

As those in need in Syria spiralled into the millions, material lack of change prompted redoubled efforts in early 2014.[165] Jordan had joined the E10 and worked with Australia and Luxembourg as continuing Council members. Mutual efforts of these E10 members led to Resolution 2139, despite wariness from China, and reports that Russia 'described the draft as a "non-starter" [and argued it] would have no positive or practical impact'.[166]

Resolution 2139 broke ground by demanding 'rapid, safe and unhindered humanitarian access [across] conflict lines and across borders'.[167] Syria remained reluctant, however, and proposals for a political solution to the conflict were not even getting to the stage of a Council vote, so these E10 members collaborated again. As penholders on what had been dubbed the 'humanitarian track', they produced Resolution 2165, effectively requiring the same thing as Resolution 2139, but going even further to explicitly engage Syria's obligation to carry out Council decisions under Article 25 of the *Charter*.[168]

As penholders, they brokered this with the P5, and in negotiations involving the whole Council that revealed serious dissension: China and Russia were still 'firmly flagging their objection to a Chapter VII resolution challenging state sovereignty', though others were said to argue that 'they could not agree to [Russia's proposed wording] describing ceasefires that had been reached after two years of government bombardment and siege tactics to starve the area into submission as a positive example of engagement between [Syria's] government and opposition'.[169]

---

164 Security Council Report 'Syria: Addressing the Humanitarian Crisis' on *What's in Blue* (2 October 2013) <http://www.whatsinblue.org>.

165 Recalling that a presidential statement does not constitute a resolution of the Council, and so would be problematic to construe as a binding decision under Article 25.

166 Security Council Report 'Draft Humanitarian Resolution on Syria and Briefing by Humanitarian Chief' on *What's in Blue* (11 February 2014) <http://www.whatsinblue.org>.

167 SC Res 2139, UN SCOR, 7116th mtg, UN Doc S/RES/2139 (22 February 2014).

168 SC Res 2165, UN SCOR, 7216th mtg, UN Doc S/RES/2165 (14 July 2014), ultimate preambular paragraph and [2].

169 Security Council Report 'Syria: Monday Vote on Draft Resolution on Cross-Border and Cross-Line Humanitarian Access' on *What's in Blue* (13 July 2014) <http://www.whatsinblue.org>.

Events since show that a political solution remained a dim hope, and Syria saw a rising tide of increasingly desperate need that, due to extensive destruction of infrastructure, cannot abate until reconstruction is possible, and effected in the years to come. Though not the end of this story, or my attention to it, at least at that juncture the tempo of humanitarian aid deliveries was positively affected by these Council resolutions.[170]

Sitting within the *Charter* design, this example highlights where E10 members proved influential in Council business. It also suggests that there are other opportunities—that is, it illustrates just one of the malleable aspects of Council working methods that provide openings for concerted efforts of the E10 to make a difference.

On the basis that a measure of explaining and/or justifying Council outputs could aid in their implementation and go towards obtaining salutary outcomes, this also points to options for how to negotiate an understanding of what the Council might account for, along with a means of asserting that—while also accommodating the changing nature of both the UN and the world around it.

This is particularly important because accounting for one decision may identify (legal) flaws in it, but overall productiveness stands to be aided by systemic, rather than occasional, accountability. Moreover, the process used for negotiating and resolving relevant questions could usefully take carriage of systematically agreeing, and then addressing, standards and what change may then be called for.

This is explored further in the next chapter, to uncover how the Council could be made more accountable via opportunities arising under the *Charter* as it stands, towards seeing its results matter more through the impact that they have upon international peace and security.

170 This story is picked up again particularly in relation to Resolution 2249 (see below Chapter 6, n 188 and 189) and Resolution 2504 (see below Chapter 6, n 190 to 195). For the present element of the discussion, this assessment is based on my analysis of UN data on numbers of convoys, their frequency, and the general composition in numbers of trucks/vehicles from reports for the operative time period—as published by the UN Office for the Coordination of Humanitarian Affairs as pages of its web site. However, such gains were, sadly, rather over-shadowed by lack of progress on a political solution and the spiralling number of those in need, plus the burgeoning variety of their needs arising from, for example, the destruction of infrastructure as illustrated by Sheena McKenzie and Mark Oliver 'How seven years of war turned Syria's cities into "hell on Earth"' *CNN* (online) 15 March 2018 <https://edition.cnn.com/2018/03/15/middleeast/syria-then-now-satellite-intl/index.html>. See also World Bank 'The Visible Impacts of the Syrian War May Only be the Tip of the Iceberg' (Press release, 10 July 2017).

CHAPTER 6

How Could the Council Be Made More Accountable?

To serve the purposes for which accountability is warranted, more is needed than having a right to assert that an actor be held accountable, or calling on them to explain or justify some part or aspect of their conduct. The common pivot point of holding an actor accountable is the capacity to assess whether change in conduct is needed, and to prompt change when it is. This may occur in more orderly fashion when formal procedures are used to test legal accountability in a court of law, compared to when less formal methods are used to, for example, probe reputational accountability in some free-for-all affray in the court of public opinion.[1] The nub of it remains the same, however: to look at conduct of an actor and, if gaps are seen in them meeting duties or obligations, or functions or responsibilities, cause those to be addressed.

The rub is that Council accountability might be framed legally, but, as discussed in earlier chapters, legal accountability mechanisms of the usual kind do not capture the Council's work, even to the extent that the international legal order does so for other actors, or may yet do so for international organisations.[2] In any case, it is not clear that remedying flawed decisions would materially help, because Council productiveness arises not from a single output (among dozens and dozens of substantive decisions that it now takes, or does not take, each year) but from the overall impact of its work upon international peace and security.

Accordingly, novel options are called for, which might be devised by returning to a broad concept of legal accountability in the international arena. For example, Jutta Brunnée argues that this involves:

> [The] legal justification of an international actor's performance vis-à-vis others, the assessment or judgement of that performance against

1 As shown in the variety of examples discussed, for example, by Grant and Keohane—see above Chapter 2, n 61. That urging is usually, but need not necessarily be, aligned to the societal context in which accountability is framed—electoral consequences often arise for elected officials, but these need not be entirely divorced from public reputational consequences, for example.

2 See above Chapter 2, n 88 to 93 inclusive, and associated text.

 | DOI:10.1163/9789004444300_007

> international legal standards, and the possible imposition of consequences if the actor fails to live up to applicable legal standards.[3]

In reviewing Council conduct and its legal justification, to assess if change is needed to enhance productiveness, the means used will, perforce, need to navigate some distinguishing features of its legal and institutional arrangements. First, no pre-existing right to hold the Council accountable can be relied upon, so a mechanism would need to allow for mediating who has a right to be heard and then on what they should be heeded. Similarly, given the Council's peculiar role in the international legal order, intersecting with its obviously political character as an actor in international relations, what is adjudged to be relevant will likely also need to be mediated and moderated—not least to address competing directions on what it should do, or not do. Third, to have a material impact, by obtaining relevant change in Council conduct, the means used must have some capacity to impose consequences: these may themselves be novel in contrast to more usual legal consequences, since the Council is not subject to such things. If, for example, states might be cast as imposing 'consequences' when holding back their compliance with, or support for, Council decisions, somehow orchestrating that could be one option.[4] As discussed in Chapter 5, such consequences are by no means trivial (as seen in relation to, for example, the ongoing quest to raise troops for peacekeeping), but there are real difficulties in linking cause from Council decision(s) to effect in states' conduct. In understanding the 'cause', Council habits in documenting its decisions mean it is quite challenging to discern an unambiguous rationale from the surrounding verbiage, and, in terms of an 'effect', it is just as difficult to extract relevant elements from the decision calculus of individual states.[5]

---

3 Brunnée, above Chapter 2, n 53, 55. See also above Chapter 2, n 63 and associated text on 'consequences'.

4 Not dissimilarly, Antonios Tzanakopoulos has argued that disobedience to Council directions is a rightful response to wrongful sanctions—see above Chapter 2, n 85.

5 For example, rationales motivating a state to provide peacekeepers, and related inhibiting factors, are 'political, security, economic, institutional, and normative'—see Alex J Bellamy and Paul D Williams 'Explaining the National Politics of Peacekeeping Contributions' in Alex J Bellamy and Paul D Williams *Providing Peacekeepers: The Politics, Challenges, and Future of United Nations Peacekeeping Contributions* (Oxford Scholarship Online, 2013), 417, 436. See also above Chapter 5, n 134 and 135, and associated text. For the Council's part, one might look no further than Resolution 2249, which illustrates the ambiguity of both what the Council did, and why—see below n 188 and 189.

That much said, the core of that approach points to interpretive challenges likely to arise on a wide front. For example, organising principles are needed to facilitate some process of assessment, otherwise views from states, speaking as those empowering the Council, may never amount to more than a 'cacophony of unstructured participation ... frequently dominated by the groups that shout the loudest'.[6] Other actors would not necessarily do better when speaking about those affected, but such voices probably do now need to be heard even if not all need necessarily be heeded in the same way or to the same degree. On any of these points, principles and rules for deploying them would help to avoid a running contest which usurps substantive debate. Similarly, not every element of what the Council does, and how, necessarily calls for a detailed critique, but, for those that do, consistency or a constant standard is needed—lest each become mortgaged to unproductive debate over what is relevant.

In short, even if one limits 'relevant views' to those of UN members, more glue would be needed to bind their reactions into a systemic response towards holding the Council accountable. This means that the greater challenge is likely to be ensuring that reactions accepted as relevant actually cohere into a systematic critique which is itself productive. Otherwise, views expressed towards Council accountability become merely additional noise in the conversation on performance already swirling around the Council,[7] including in reform debate which has been, so far, largely unproductive.[8]

The means or mechanism to be used thus first needs to be appropriate to the audience claiming some right to be heard on Council accountability. Discussion herein so far suggests this begins with explaining its decisions to the states which collectively empower the Council. Put on the public record that would then be available to other interested actors, so parts of such explanation would be retailed via contemporary journalism and social media for, one hopes, a salutary impact on the wider circle of those whom the Council affects.

Second, the crux of the question on subject matter is that an account need not be exhaustive in order to be sufficient, and being suitably selective may be more effective if it actually impacts upon what matters most in Council conduct.

Within that spectrum of selectivity, how effective Council action proves to be, and gaps left by Council inaction, are interconnected to the promise of UN

6 Chesterman, above Chapter 3, n 80, 49.

7 See Chapter 2.2, but also the work and projects of scholars, publicists and advocates—see for example, Cassese, above Chapter 1, n 5 and Chesterman, above Chapter 1, n 82; see also above Chapter 4, n 117 and 118, and Chapter 5, n 96, and associated text.

8 See discussion in Chapter 2.2.

members embodied in Article 2(4). By that provision, states eschew the threat or use of force in international relations, which 'represents, beside the protection of human rights, the major achievement of the international legal order in the twentieth century [and] features as the cornerstone of that order and an undisputed core principle of the international community'.[9]

To show due fidelity to the *Charter*, it seems clear that the Council should, in particular, explain or justify its response to breaches or abrogations of that promise. Recalling that decisions voiced may carry baggage in decisions that are entailed, but unvoiced,[10] such a critique would advisedly need to include how the Council interpreted what appears to be threat or use of armed force to which it did not respond per se.[11]

Together this suggests that a means for Council accountability will need to progressively chart the waters of Council work. To my eye, the priority should be a critique to show how, and how well, Council action aligned to its signature Functions in the *Charter* design, its 'primary responsibility for the maintenance of international peace and security' under Article 24(1). However, that alone will not suffice for obtaining due Council effectiveness. This is because, like so much of the institutional and legal arrangements around the Council, what else matters is bound to evolve over time and be coloured by the interest-laden context of geopolitics.

Nonetheless, that would guide selection of subject matter, at least in the broad strokes, if the account rendered was a critique informative for amending

9 Simma et al, above Chapter 1, n 29, 233; however, cf Ian Hurd 'The permissive power of the ban on war' (2016) 2(1) *European Journal of International Security* 1.

10 See above Chapter 5, n 86, and following text.

11 By its decisions or determinations on: conditions existing that may threaten or breach the peace or constitute acts of aggression (Article 39); applying provisional measures, and accounting for states' failure to comply (Article 40); using non-forceful measures (Article 41); deploying forceful measures (Article 42); whether all UN members are to take relevant action, the mutuality of that action among states that take it, plus a response to consequential economic problems for states (Articles 48, 49 and 50 respectively); and the relevance of self-defence in response to any armed attack against a UN member (Article 51). On a much wider front, it is worth keeping in mind the struggles of the Council to reach an accommodation on wording—for example, on what would have been an almost entirely hortatory resolution in support of the Secretary-General's hard-to-fault initiative calling for a global ceasefire during the COVID-19 pandemic (which fell foul of the interests of individual members of the Council—see above Chapter 5, n 105—to the extent that an explanation would have been well placed in relation to the Council's conduct over the course of that year). See also discussion of Resolution 2504 in January 2020—below n 190 to 195.

its conduct.[12] Discussion so far suggests an accountability mechanism could do this—if it were capable of addressing what needs to be understood about Council conduct in order to render it more productive.

Case examples from earlier chapters suggest that answering a series of accountability questions could address such concerns, and that these questions would include the following:

(a) To account for the agenda as apportioning Council effort to its Functions under the *Charter*, what does the record show on disposal of matters addressed to it:
  (a)(i) What is the present status of those items on which the Council has accepted carriage?
  (a)(ii) What was the reasoning in relation to those on which it did not?
  (a)(iii) As well as those raised by others, are there matters on which the Council could aid its own purpose by its own initiative?

(b) To account for effort said to be spent in pursuit of *Charter* Purposes, what do choices made in deliberating show:
  (b)(i) Where published decisions or determinations were made, to what main or primary ends were they directed?
  (b)(ii) Where a published determination was not made on a matter that others have addressed to the Council, why not?

(c) To account for realising ends sought actively, what do choices made in calling for implementation show about asserting the Council's capacity to reach compelling conclusions, including legally compelling decisions:
  (c)(i) Was the conclusion put in an acknowledged form, and made properly according to *Charter* law?
  (c)(ii) Was it clear who the relevant actors were intended to be, with (reasonably) unambiguous directions to those actors?
  (c)(iii) Do results show that the relevant actors were duly persuaded towards implementation, including to meet their obligations created by the Council's decision, or, with such urging from the Council, to meet obligations already arising under the *Charter* or other international law?

12 Encyclopaedic documentation, such as the present annual report by the Council, may have valuable purposes, but recording such a plethora of facts without critique becomes part of a debate on Council outcomes, rather than an answer to explain or justify them.

Mediating and moderating dialogue on the Council's work thus calls for an approach that is able to probe what the Council has done or not done, through layers of decisions of which that is comprised, to get answers on which to base conclusions about what, if any, change may be needed.

As a preliminary illustration, the difference is shown by asking: what would these accountability questions reveal about, for example, Council attention to its signature Chapter VII responsibilities, or in responding to the threat or use of force in international relations even if not expressly connected to Chapter VII?

To first account for the overall state of its agenda, and thus priorities it assigns to what competes for its attention—questions (a) and (b)—does the Council satisfactorily dispose of matters on which it accepted carriage, and was its reasoning satisfactory in relation to those things on which it did not?

On Chapter VII, as a general assessment the available data suggests that 'things on which it did not' is the larger category. Over the first 50 years of the UN,[13] it is possible, for example, to list some 300 episodes of 'major' armed conflict, 'major' connoting at least hundreds of related fatalities.[14] Comparison to Council meeting records shows that most of these episodes did not feature, and so no reasoning is reported about why not. Some might debate the extent to which these episodes impacted upon international peace and security as now understood, turning attention to a narrower subset addressed by John Dunbabin—those situations specifically said to impact upon international peace and security. Similarly looking across the first 50 years, these number over 100 crises and armed conflicts,[15] but again, most did not feature on the Council's agenda. Council meeting records since his analysis continue to support Dunbabin's assessment that 'only a minority of post-1945 conflicts have generated serious UN intervention' via significant involvement of the Council,[16] suggesting there is some work to be done on the Council's agenda-setting.

That these decisions were not explained on the record by the Council may be less pressing if those situations were resolved otherwise, or if time showed that a threat to international peace and security did not eventuate,[17] although

13 Acknowledging the extended time horizons often found in matters of geopolitics, and so not expecting that such situations can be addressed or resolved quickly—as amply illustrated in Chapter 6.1 on Timor.

14 Monty G Marshall *Major Episodes of Political Violence: 1946–2016* (15 June 2017) Center for Systemic Peace <http://www.systemicpeace.org/warlist/warlist.htm>. This list is synthesised from many sources of relevant scholarship.

15 See above Chapter 5, n 114, noting that list is not intended to be exhaustive.

16 Dunbabin, above Chapter 2, n 18, 494. Dunbabin's analysis casts the net widely on 'non-involvement' to cover any situation in which the Council did not play a significant role.

17 Again, allowing for the time horizons that have attended many such complex matters.

on both points there are certainly arguments to the contrary. That said, in all of the circumstances and politics of international relations, perhaps the most pressing concern is that when the Council does choose to engage it should prove to be effective.

Perusing the *Summary Statement* again suggests that Council outcomes are otherwise: question (c) on implementation of Council decisions routinely does not arise simply because the Council has proven to be unable to assist. Viewed now as history rather than current affairs, some such cases relatable to Chapter VII might be seen as self-explanatory 'orphans' of Cold War divisions—where the major powers were not engaged directly but a result nonetheless eluded the Council. In 1961, for example, established Portuguese enclaves along the western coast of the Indian subcontinent were seized by India using armed force.[18] This appears to be well inside the scope of the Council's signature work, but the Council could not assist Portugal because it was divided over competing proposals.[19] One, rejecting Portugal's complaint and effectively endorsing the action by India,[20] garnered only four affirmative votes including that of the USSR. The other, deploring India's use of force and urging both to work out a solution in keeping with the *Charter*,[21] obtained the minimum necessary affirmative votes,[22] but was vetoed by the USSR. The matter went into limbo on the *Summary Statement* until Portugal abandoned the problem in 1975.[23]

A central difficulty in accepting the 'orphan' explanation remains pertinent in the post-Cold War era: if the use of force in international relations, prima facie contravening the central tenet of UN membership under Article 2(4), does not motivate and mobilise the Council in its signature role, sufficiently to conclude a productive decision, what will? Moreover, in many, possibly most, cases, parties involved do not have, will not accept, or, arguably, should not even consider, abandoning the problem.

In any case, it remains that implementation is essential for a productive result, but the *Summary Statement* shows no few cases where the Council

---

18 For a contemporaneous account and view of the Security Council response, see Quincy Wright 'The Goa Incident' (1962) 56(3) *American Journal of International Law* 617.

19 UN SCOR, 988th mtg, UN Doc S/PV.988 (18 December 1961), 26–27.

20 *Ceylon, Liberia and United Arab Republic: joint draft resolution* S/5032 (18 December 1961).

21 *France, Turkey, United Kingdom of Great Britain and Northern Ireland and United States of America: joint draft resolution* S/5033 (18 December 1961).

22 Then still seven.

23 The matter was de-listed on request from the Portuguese government in late 1974, after it committed to decolonisation as a result of the 'Carnation' revolution—see *Summary Statement* UN Doc S/11593 (7 January 1975), 1. See also below n 46 and n 48.

engaged and made an active decision, which was not then implemented, so the Council was unable to obtain a definitive conclusion to the matter.[24]

Accordingly, examples were sought to show how the Council might be made more accountable by learning from cases with little or no doubt about the need for Council involvement, but also with contrasting outputs, outcomes, and observable results, that flowed from them. Of course, no case answers all needs in understanding *what* the Council should do, or *how* it should do whatever it does. Even in responding to the use of armed force in international relations, which sits at the heart of the Council's Functions, each case has distinguishable features due to the nature of the situation, the parties involved, the exact actions that were said to be taken—or even just the historical era in which it arose, as an important impact upon the political possibilities for addressing the situation.

In that context, the priority was to illustrate the products possible from answering accountability questions as put above, especially question (c), to see what difference might be made to Council productiveness by explaining or justifying its decisions.

As already mentioned, many cases lack Council attention, or a decision when they were noticed, or Council engagement did not come to a conclusion or otherwise still appears to be pending decades afterwards. If a possible case example did not suffer from imponderables clouding the analysis (due to inconclusive deliberations or an open-ended case), it should also illustrate the nexus between what the Council might account for and to whom (going beyond UN member states to include links to civil society and 'those affected'), and thus possibilities for a future means or mechanism by which to obtain a measure of Council accountability.

For the purposes at hand, then, a case was sought where, firstly, the threat or use of force in international relations left little doubt the Council should be involved; secondly, active Council decisions were made and expected to be implemented; and thirdly, the episode was concluded definitively by the Council closing off its engagement in another active decision.

Chapter 6.1 thus looks at Timor.[25] There was little doubt about the need for a Council response in 1975, the Council did actually respond in a way requiring implementation action by others, and the case was subsequently closed by a specific decision of the Council in 2016. In the first instance, discussion centres on what may be gained by answering the accountability questions listed

24 For a recent viewpoint on this, see above Chapter 2, n 25. The continuing situation in Syria also speaks to this point (see above Chapter 2, n 20 and Chapter 5, n 163 to 170 and associated text, and below n 188 to 195, and associated text).

25 See below n 44 on the naming convention used in this case example.

above, but this proved to highlight impacts upon Council productiveness from compliance—where Council outputs, outcomes, and results, may be compromised by lack of implementation. This suggested an additional accountability question, so the next step is Chapter 6.2.1, which looks again at Timor in terms of *what may have been added* by the E10 members taking the opportunity to address the accountability questions—since the E10 sits at a nexus of what the Council might account for and to whom. That perspective showed contrasts with what might have been done, to suggest some opportunities foregone that could have been important in enhancing outputs, outcomes, and results, seen to arise from the Council's work on Timor. It is still possible to take this discussion further, because in other cases a contrast arises in fact—as shown in different, more recent examples of the E10's *actual contributions* as set out in Chapter 6.2.2 and 6.2.3. Without necessarily suggesting the E10 intended to explain or justify Council conduct, these examples afford observation about what comes of E10 members heeding voices with something to say about that—both the larger UN collective of states that empowers the Council, and the wider circle of others in civil society connected to those affected by the Council.

Taken as a whole, this chapter thus proceeds, in turn, to consider how accountability could be brought to bear on the Council, and so how it could be made more accountable, by:

(i) refining accountability questions as set out above, the better to explain or justify Council decisions and actions, if the means could be found to address them;

(ii) considering the E10 as a means to address those questions by attending more closely to the possible and actual contributions from E10 initiatives on Council agenda-setting and reaching conclusions, in particular based on their supposed standing as 'representatives' of the states collectively empowering the Council via the *Charter*; and

(iii) acknowledging that the E10 is assisted by heeding more than just states, and in particular those voices from civil society that are somehow raised on behalf of those whom the Council affects—shown in cases where they have been influential in obtaining productive results from the Council.

6.1 Case Example: Responding to the Use of Force

In 2012, the Council almost 'mistakenly renewed the [peacekeeping] mandate in Timor-Leste without first consulting the leaders of the country or the troop-contributing countries.'[26] It was not, in fact, renewed, and was, by a Council decision, subsequently removed from the *Summary Statement* in 2016 after receiving no further Council attention for three years.[27]

The Council thereby closed an episode begun in 1975 by Indonesia's use of armed force in Timor,[28] which engaged its international relations with Portugal as the 'administering Power' for Timor.[29] Council decisions in this case were recorded in 1975/1976, and then in 1999 (and onwards).

From some vantage points, 'Timor-Leste was widely seen as a UN success story',[30] but, considering the arc of UN involvement from 1975 to 1999, consequences that may find their way to the Council's door seem principally, and profoundly, negative. This is shown by the devastation of the population. Timor had just 610,000 people at the 1970 census.[31] Estimated deaths attributable to the invasion,[32] or the subsequent occupation,[33] range from 50,000 to the more likely figure of well over 200,000 people.[34] Timor's population has

26 *Letter dated 27 April 2015 from the Permanent Representative of Finland to the United Nations addressed to the President of the Security Council* S/2015/292 (27 April 2015), 18.

27 *Summary Statement* UN Doc S/2016/10 (4 January 2016), 4.

28 For an account from the Indonesian perspective, see Ali Alatas *The Pebble in the Shoe: The Diplomatic Struggle for East Timor* (Aksara Karunia, Jakarta, 2006).

29 In the UN's move to decolonisation, the Assembly noted Portugal as the 'administering Power' in the list of 'Non-Self-Governing Territories within the meaning of Chapter XI of the Charter': see *Transmission of information under Article 73e of the Charter* GA Res 1542 (XV), UN GAOR, 15th sess, 948th plen mtg, UN Doc A/Res/1542 (XV) (15 December 1960).

30 For example, Michael Leach and Damien Kingsbury 'Introduction: East Timorese Politics in Transition' in Michael Leach and Damien Kingsbury (eds) *The Politics of Timor-Leste: Democratic Consolidation after Intervention* (Southeast Asia Program Publications, Cornell University, 2013), 3; cf Simon Chesterman *You, the People: The United Nations, Transitional Administration, and State-Building* (Oxford, 2004), 183, where he notes a range of flaws in 'missed opportunities and wastage' in his discussion of the 'politics of humanitarian development and assistance'. See also the assessment that 'the UN's performance was mixed'—Ian Martin and Alexander Mayer-Rieckh 'The United Nations and East Timor: from self-determination to state-building' (2005) 12(1) *International Peacekeeping* 125, 140.

31 The last census before the Indonesian occupation: see *Report of the Special Committee on the Situation with Regard to the Implementation of the Declaration on the Granting of Independence to Colonial Counties and peoples* (*Volume* 2) A/10023/Rev.1/[Vol.II] (1977), 34.

32 As put contemporaneously by at least one Council member—China (see below n 128), and by scholars—see for example Keith D Suter 'The Conquest of East Timor' (1978) 232(1346) *Contemporary Review* 134.

33 See below n 68.

34 See below n 111, but the exact number of deaths remains unconfirmed. Early press reports put the number at 60,000—see 'Fighting on Timor said to kill 60,000' *The New York Times*, 15 February 1976, 11. For a comparison of various estimates in context of the pre-conflict population, see Ben Kiernan 'The Demography of Genocide in Southeast Asia: The Death Tolls in Cambodia, 1975–79, and East Timor, 1975–80' (2003) 35(4) *Critical Asian Studies*

since recovered to be circa 1.3 million, but lingering effects include sociocultural ramifications and persistent structural fragility—not least from having 60 per cent of the population aged under 25,[35] even as the country attempts to nurture a cohesive polity, create a stable economy, and develop its infrastructure towards security and prosperity.

Indonesia and Timor are both former European colonies,[36] and the legacy of the colonial era is a pivotal aspect of the case. Christine Chinkin demonstrates this clearly in her evocative précis of Timor's travails from 1975 to 1999, which she frames as a 'drama of decolonisation'.[37] For the present discussion, nothing in the UN's process of decolonisation absolves the Council from its Chapter VII responsibilities, and prior decisions by the Council,[38] and the Assembly,[39] were clearly to the contrary.[40] Accordingly, without diminishing the importance of decolonisation, and consistent with Chinkin's discussion in any case,[41] the focus here is specifically on understanding how productively the Council responded to Indonesia's use of force and devastation that followed.[42]

---

585. In terms of Indonesian records, Kiernan also points to reports of 'official' estimates by Indonesia as high as 120,000 just for the first several years, up until November 1979 (at 594). See also Post-CAVR Technical Secretariat *Conflict-Related Deaths in Timor-Leste 1974–1999: The Findings of the CAVR Report Chega!* (Post-CAVR Secretariat in Consultation with Benetec [sic], 2008); Benetech 'Silicon Valley Group Uses Technology To Help The Truth Commission Answer Disputed Questions About Massive Political Violence In Timor-Leste' (Press release, 9 February 2006); see also below n 42 and 111.

35 As at estimates in 2020, which is basically double the proportion seen in western countries—see Timor-Leste 'People and Society' in Central Intelligence Agency *The World Factbook* <https://www.cia.gov/library/publications/the-world-factbook/geos/tt.html>.

36 For an overview in context of Timor, see John G Taylor *Indonesia's Forgotten War: The Hidden History of East Timor* (Zed Books, London, 1991).

37 Christine Chinkin 'East Timor: A Failure of Decolonisation' (1999) 20 *Australian Year Book of International Law* 35, 35.

38 For example, regarding the situation in the Middle East, where the Council emphasised 'the inadmissibility of the acquisition of territory by war': SC Res 242, UN SCOR, 1382nd mtg, UN Doc S/Res/242 (22 November 1967).

39 For example, *Definition of aggression* GA Res 3314 (XXIX), UN GAOR, 29th sess, 2319th plen mtg, UN Doc A/Res/3314 (XXIX) (14 December 1974).

40 It is also worth noting that nothing since overturns the tenet that the 'prohibition on the acquisition of territory by threat or use of force [is] not subject to qualification'—see Thomas D Grant 'Annexation of Crimea' (2015) 109(1) *American Journal of International Law* 68, 77. He also notes 'use of force is not a basis for title [to territory]; it is not even a basis for a claim to title' (at 87).

41 See below n 113 and associated text.

42 The most comprehensive documentation of this case is Comissão de Acolhimento, Verdade e Reconciliação de Timor Leste (CAVR) *Chega! The final report of the Timor-Leste*

Timor and Indonesia are located in a region sprawling along the equator north and north west of Australia, long home to a melange of ethnicities, languages, cultures, and religions. Indonesia encompasses a significant portion of the region's landfall: one principal island is now shared with both Malaysia and Brunei, and another with Papua New Guinea. The large island known as Timor lies in the region's south-east corner, more proximate to northern Australia than to much of its archipelagic neighbourhood. Set by treaty, the border dividing that island dates to 1859. Unchanged after 1914, it separated territories then administered by the Netherlands and Portugal,[43] colonies known as Dutch Timor and Portuguese Timor respectively.[44]

Indonesia's emergence as a state predates concerted efforts of the UN towards decolonisation. A possession of the Netherlands for centuries, the colony was effectively abandoned by the Dutch on surrendering to the invading Japanese army in 1942. A unilateral push to declare independence followed the Japanese surrender in 1945. Not before a bloody contretemps,[45] the Dutch recognised Indonesia's independence in 1949, and UN membership followed in 1950.

For Timor, 'the attitude of Portugal towards self-determination was a negative one: until 1974, it denied [that right to] the peoples of its colonies'.[46]

Commission for Reception, Truth and Reconciliation (CAVR) (KPG in cooperation with STP-CAVR, 2013) ('*Chega!*'). On this point—Volume 1, Part 3: History of the Conflict, on 'Encirclement and annihilation': the final stages of Operation Seroja 1977–1979.

43 See United Nations Department of Political Affairs, Trusteeship and Decolonization 'Decolonization: Issue on East Timor' (Report, August 1976). For a brief synopsis, see Chinkin, above n 37, 37 n 6; see also 'Timeline of Political Developments in Timor-Leste' (2012) 4(1) *Asian Politics & Policy* 7.

44 For brevity, 'Timor' is used to denote the territory of the sovereign state and member of the UN, now Timor-Leste but formerly Portuguese Timor and later East Timor. The word is derived from Malay and Indonesian, 'timur' meaning east. In Portuguese, 'leste' also means east. 'Timor' herein signifies the former Portuguese territory, distinct from the former colony of Dutch Timor, later Indonesian Timor or West Timor.

45 Which featured heavily in the early deliberations of the Council—see, for example, selected meetings in the latter half of 1947 for voting on related proposals: UN SCOR, 171st mtg, UN Doc S/PV.171 (31 July 1947), 1616 (Australia) (reporting the outbreak of hostilities and placing the item on the agenda); UN SCOR, 173rd mtg, UN Doc S/PV.173 (1 August 1947); UN SCOR, 178th mtg, UN Doc S/PV.178 (7 August 1947); UN SCOR, 181st mtg, UN Doc S/PV.181 (12 August 1947); UN SCOR, 184th mtg, UN Doc S/PV.184 (14 August 1947); UN SCOR, 193rd mtg, UN Doc S/PV.193 (22 August 1947); UN SCOR, 194th mtg, UN Doc S/PV.194 (25 August 1947); UN SCOR, 195th mtg, UN Doc S/PV.195 (26 August 1947); UN SCOR, 207th mtg, UN Doc S/PV.207 (3 October 1947); UN SCOR, 217th mtg, UN Doc S/PV.217 (31 October 1947); UN SCOR, 219th mtg, UN Doc S/PV.219 (1 November 1947).

46 Miguel Galvão Teles and Paulo Canelas de Castro 'Portugal and the Right of Peoples to Self-Determination' (1996) 34(1) *Archiv des Völkerrechts* 2, 10.

Counter to the Assembly's headline resolution on decolonisation,[47] Portugal kept this stance until the Armed Forces Movement overthrew the government in 1974.[48] Portugal then turned to support decolonisation, albeit with little preparation for an orderly transfer of power.[49] Timorese politics crystallised as more parties were formed in 1974, and others became more visibly active: most notably conservative UDT, pro-Indonesia Apodeti,[50] and pro-independence Fretilin.

Towards independence, negotiations sponsored by Portugal were held in Macau in June 1975,[51] identifying 'a basis for a new constitution' and planning towards an election for October 1976, with independence to follow in October 1978.[52]

Fretilin boycotted some negotiations, holding out for a more accelerated timetable, but that process was then derailed anyhow: UDT seized key installations in August 1975, precipitating civil war. Fretilin 'won' the initial confrontation in a few weeks: fighting continued in September 1975, but by late that month Fretilin was said to control most of the colony.[53] Portugal called for international assistance;[54] the UN Secretary-General responded calling for a cease-fire and negotiations.[55]

---

47 From which other resolutions and actions followed as implementation: *Declaration on the granting of independence to colonial countries and peoples* GA Res 1514 (XV), UN GAOR, 15th sess, 947th plen mtg, UN Doc A/Res/1514 (XV) (14 December 1960).

48 Where colonial conflict in Portuguese colonies was central to initiating the Armed Forces Movement: see Suter, above n 32, 135; see also the *tour d'horizon* in C A R Hills 'Portugal and Her Empire: 1497–1997' (1997) 271(1578) *Contemporary Review* 10.

49 Chinkin, above n 37, 38.

50 Some relevant political parties are known by acronyms (eg. UDT), others by portmanteau terms generated from the Portuguese name of the party (eg. Fretilin and Apodeti). Authors variously treat portmanteau labels as acronyms to be capitalised, or as proper nouns with only an initial capital. For convenience, the latter approach is taken here.

51 Unless otherwise noted, dates are taken from 'Chronology, 1974–1976', in Department of Foreign Affairs and Trade *Documents on Australian Foreign Policy: Australia and the Indonesian Incorporation of Portuguese Timor 1974–1976* (Melbourne University Press, 2000), xviii.

52 Suter, above n 32, 135.

53 See United Nations Department of Political Affairs, Trusteeship and Decolonization, above n 43, 23; Paul D Elliott 'The East Timor Dispute' (1978) 27 *International and Comparative Law Quarterly* 238, 239. Writing in 1978, Elliott gave due regard to reports from the USA, UK, Australia and elsewhere from 1974 to 1977—see 238 n 3 therein.

54 For example, see *Letter dated 23 August 1975 from the representative of Portugal to the Secretary-General* UN Doc S/11813 (25 August 1975); *Letter dated 28 November 1975 from the Charge d'affaires a.i. of the Permanent Mission of Portugal to the United Nations addressed to the Secretary-General* UN Doc S/11887 (29 November 1975).

55 For a detailed account see *Chega!*, above n 42, Volume 1, Part 3 'History of the Conflict'.

To this juncture, Timor's struggles are, sadly, not especially novel as a quest for independence or the process seen if communities are seeking self-determination. Much is in common with the story of other colonies, and, as elsewhere, violence was sparked in sundry measures by internal divisions, rival factions, and competing claims to territory.[56] Timor may thus have continued down a fratricidal, internecine path, after Fretilin declared Timor independent on 28 November 1975, UDT and Apodeti signed a declaration for integration with Indonesia the next day, and Portugal rejected both initiatives on 30 November.

Timor did not, however: just a week later there came an unmistakable point of departure from internal wrangling, when Indonesia launched military action against Timor. Despite 'a strict news blackout', it soon became clear that, on 7 December 1975, 'naval bombardment of Dili was followed by the landing of seaborne Indonesian troops; simultaneously, paratroops from the elite Kostrad command dropped in and behind the city.'[57] That is, Indonesia's armed forces, not 'irregulars', 'militias', or 'volunteers', were quite visibly involved.[58] Portugal immediately broke off diplomatic relations with Indonesia, on 8 December advising the UN of Indonesia's actions. Particularly describing events in Dili, Portugal requested an urgent Council meeting.[59]

The Council was thus confronted by clear reports of armed military action by Indonesia that would, in many views, constitute an invasion of Portugal's (colonial) territory. Some might take this more expansively as an 'incursion'—action that was not necessarily a breach of the peace, for example. Be that as it may, there is little doubt that Indonesia's military was using armed force in Portugal's territory. Accordingly, Indonesia's actions place this squarely in the Council's Chapter VII bailiwick, where the Council is expected, even obligated, to deploy its *Charter* powers to regulate the threat or use of force in international relations.

On agenda-setting, accountability question (a) in the previous section concerns the Council's disposal of matters addressed to it, the status on the agenda

56 Such as by Senegal for what was then Portuguese Guinea, now Guinea-Bissau—on the former Portuguese colonies, see generally 'Portugal oversea [sic]: A struggling empire' (1962) 52(206) *The Round Table* 147; see also Hills, above n 48. Note that Indonesia was *not* such a claimant—see below n 64.

57 Adam Schwarz *A Nation in Waiting: Indonesia in the 1990s* (Allen & Unwin, Sydney, 1994), 204.

58 See below n 70 and 77.

59 *Letter Dated 7 December 1975 From the Permanent Representative of Portugal to the United Nations Addressed to the President of the Security Council* UN Doc S/11899 (8 December 1975).

of matters on which it accepts carriage, and why it does not accept carriage of others. In relation to these, the Council seems to have dragged its feet in even deciding whether to accept that this incident should be on its agenda. Informal 'consultations' may have gone on off the record, but no Council response eventuated if they did.

After debate on 12 December, an Assembly resolution showed that the collective membership of the UN was unsatisfied:

> *Deeply concerned* at the critical situation resulting from the military intervention of the armed forces of Indonesia in Portuguese Timor, [the Assembly, inter alia]
>
> 6. *Draws the attention* of the Security Council, in conformity with Article 11, paragraph 3, of the Charter, to the critical situation in the Territory of Portuguese Timor and recommends that it take urgent action to protect the territorial integrity of Portuguese Timor and the inalienable right of its people to self-determination ...[60]

The Council then met on 15 December 1975, deliberating in another four meetings over the following week.[61] Resolution 384 was adopted unanimously on 22 December,[62] one operative part calling on Indonesia 'to withdraw without delay all its forces from the Territory'.[63]

So once this situation was on the agenda, Council attention did reach a clear result. To answer accountability question (b) above, on the ends to which decisions or determinations are directed, this was aimed at ending the conflict. Equally, to meet question (c)(i), about deciding in line with *Charter* requirements, a Council resolution adopted unanimously at a formal Council meeting clearly meets the mark for being reached and recorded in a recognisable and accepted form.

Beyond that, however, problems become evident. Accountability question (c)(ii) asks both for addressees of the decision to be clear, and for the decision to give directions that were (at least reasonably) unambiguous. Resolution 384

---

60 *Question of Timor* GA Res 3485 (XXX), UN GAOR, 30th sess, 2439th plen mtg, UN Doc A/Res/3485 (XXX) (12 December 1975) (emphasis in original).

61 UN SCOR, 1864th mtg, UN Doc S/PV.1864 (15 December 1975); UN SCOR, 1865th mtg, UN Doc S/PV.1865 (16 December 1975); UN SCOR, 1867th mtg, UN Doc S/PV.1867 (18 December 1975); UN SCOR, 1868th mtg, UN Doc S/PV.1868 (18 December 1975); UN SCOR, 1869th mtg, UN Doc S/PV.1869 (22 December 1975).

62 UN SCOR, 1869th mtg, UN Doc S/PV.1869 (22 December 1975).

63 SC Res 384, UN SCOR, 1869th mtg, UN Doc S/Res/384 (22 December 1975).

does specifically address Indonesia and Portugal, but phrasing of it may well have muddied the message sent to the relevant actors.

In the first place, the Council did not characterise Indonesia's conduct in Chapter VII terms, or otherwise engage Chapter VII directly—or even indirectly by the effect of the wording of its decision. Formed units of Indonesian military were, however, unequivocally reported to be in Timor's main city of Dili. Indonesia was not a competing claimant to the territory of (Portuguese) Timor,[64] and made no case for purporting to act in self-defence under Article 51.

In response, while the Council 'deplor[ed] the intervention of the armed forces of Indonesia in East Timor', Indonesia escaped any stronger language addressing its use of armed force contrary to Article 2(4). Then, the Council called on Portugal to 'co-operate fully with the United Nations so as to enable the people of East Timor to exercise freely their right to self-determination.'[65] Rather than Portugal being a complainant rightfully seeking Council assistance in the face of armed force used by another, this seems to cast Portugal as something of a 'co-defendant' with Indonesia. Moreover, Indonesia's violent intrusion into Timor was a rather more remarkable impediment to its self-determination than Portugal's belated support for the decolonisation process—and not forgetting, of course, that Indonesia was, all the while, infringing on Portugal's territory and interfering in its domestic affairs.

These ambiguous directions mean the Council's decision has an effect that is rather awkward to explain. A harsher view is that the Council's power was somehow misused to shield Indonesia: the resolution's wording seems to smack of following *Charter* form, but winking to Indonesia on the substance.

Whichever may be closer to the truth, some such nuances are not unexpected in the geopolitical context, turning attention to what result the Council's decision proved able to elicit. That is, in relation to question (c)(iii) above, did

---

64 Claims of the Dutch and the Portuguese had long since been settled in the border treaty noted, and, as a former Dutch colony, Indonesia had no claim to be a 'successor' to the Portuguese. Moreover, at least until mid-1974, Indonesia had 'officially disavowed any interest in East Timor'—see Schwarz, above n 57, 201. See also *Chega!*, above n 42, 160[63] which confirms that 'before 1975, at no point did Indonesia claim that it had the right to incorporate the territory'. It is worth noting that the extent to which Indonesia was already interfering in Timor was at issue: for example, there were public assertions that Indonesia was planning an invasion or involved in fighting in Balibo, Timor—Frank Cranston 'Timor "builds arms" against invasion' *The Canberra Times* (Canberra), 24 June 1975, 1; Frank Cranston 'Action by Indonesia believed inevitable' *The Canberra Times* (Canberra), 12 September 1975, 7;' "Indonesian" Attack: Five Australians missing' *The Canberra Times* (Canberra) 18 October 1975, 5.

65 SC Res 384, UN SCOR, 1869th mtg, UN Doc S/Res/384 (22 December 1975) [3].

what happened next show actors were duly persuaded to meet their obligations from the Council's decision, or those that they had already (including under the *Charter*)?

In fact, the Council did not obtain any change at all in Indonesia's conduct, and Indonesia soon also transgressed the Council's legally-empowered decision.

Portugal formally reported that 'on 28 January 1976 cars and helicopters were unloaded in Betano, with eight Indonesian ships in proximity, and Indonesian land forces were present in the region between Same and Betano.'[66] Dili is on the northern facing coast of Timor, and both towns are on the far side of the island's mountainous interior: Betano is adjacent to the southern facing coast and Same is approximately 25 km inland from Betano; crucially, both are located well and truly east of the border with Indonesia's province of West Timor.[67]

Other than consolidating Indonesia's military occupation,[68] no purpose for this activity of the Indonesian armed forces presents itself.

Resolution 384 also required the Secretary-General to despatch a special representative for an 'on-the-spot assessment' and to ensure implementation of the resolution. His report was eventually made available to the Council in March 1976.[69] The report was long on already known context (five pages) and describing travel and activities (three pages), but short on analysis (perhaps half a page) or recommendations (one sentence). Most particularly, the special representative could not report Indonesia's compliance with the Council's resolution, only that Indonesia 'pointed out that the presence of the Indonesian volunteers in East Timor was upon the request of Apodeti, UDT [and others] to give whatever assistance was necessary to restore peace and order'.[70]

---

66 *Letter dated 30 January 1976 from From the Deputy Permanent Representative of Portugal to the United Nations Addressed to the Secretary-General* UN Doc S/11955 (31 January 1976), which also pointed out that these events had been 'amply recorded by the mass media and information services', and that Indonesia's actions had raised 'new problems' for work by the Secretary-General's special representative.

67 For a relevant map, see *Chega!*, above n 42, xix.

68 Though some may scruple to say it, in hindsight 'occupation' would be the appropriate term, and some scholars certainly said it at the time—for example, Thomas Franck did not delay in drawing a parallel between the use of force in the Western Sahara and 'the Indonesian occupation of East Timor, another place where historic, geographic, and ethnic claims were assessed out of the barrels of rifles.' See Thomas M Franck 'The Stealing of the Sahara' (1976) 70 *American Journal of International Law* 694, 695.

69 *Report by the Secretary-General in Pursuance of Security Council Resolution 384* (1975) UN Doc S/12011 (12 March 1976).

70 Ibid, 9 [39]. Leaving aside whether such parties had any right to request Indonesian assistance, which is really rather doubtful, Geoffrey Robinson notes while 'some of the

Thus far, it would be quite difficult to justify an assessment that Indonesia was persuaded to meet obligations placed on it by the Council's decision in Resolution 384, especially given that Portugal's report gave evidence directly to the contrary.[71]

Then, after seven more meetings over the course of ten days in April 1976,[72] a proposal, from Guyana and Tanzania,[73] was adopted by 12 votes to none.[74] Resolution 389 called on Indonesia 'to withdraw without further delay all its forces'.[75] An amendment, put up by Japan, attempted to change the reference to be 'all its *remaining* forces'.[76] This proposal was unsuccessful, but serves to underscore that Council members no doubt understood that Indonesia's military action continued, thereby contravening its fundamental *Charter* undertaking as well as Resolution 384.[77] Accordingly, the Council could not, to this stage, be counted as effective in reminding Indonesia of its obligations as a UN member in relation to Article 2(4), nor in compelling Indonesia to carry out the Council's directions, to show conformity with legal obligations to do so that it may have had under Article 25.

In Resolution 389, the Council also requested 'the Secretary-General to follow the implementation of the present resolution and submit a report to the

militias were in fact pro-integration Timorese … most were Indonesian soldiers dressed as Timorese, described as "volunteers", and carrying letters to that effect. The Timorese militia force was, in reality, nothing more than a deception.' See Geoffrey Robinson 'People's war: militias in East Timor and Indonesia' (2001) 9(3) *South East Asia Research* 271, 293.

71 In parallel, the question of Portugal's compliance could be mothballed as long as Indonesia occupied Timor. Compliance by the Secretary-General is also not irrelevant to accounting for Council decisions, and it should be noted that he had carried out the directions given. However, that is peripheral here anyway, as he was, in effect, an acting as agent of the Council, not a party to the crisis.

72 UN SCOR, 1908th mtg, UN Doc S/PV.1908 (12 April 1976) through to UN SCOR, 1914th mtg, UN Doc S/PV.1914 (22 April 1976).

73 *Guyana and the United Republic of Tanzania: draft resolution* UN Doc S/12056 (21 April 1976).

74 Japan and the USA abstaining; Benin did not participate in the voting.

75 SC Res 389, UN SCOR, 1914th mtg, UN Doc S/Res/389 (22 April 1976).

76 *Japan: amendment to draft resolution contained in document S/12056* UN Doc S/12057 (22 April 1976).

77 Geoffrey Robinson also documents that the reality of 'militias' being Indonesian military personnel was known to, for example, Australian authorities in 1975—see Robinson, above n 70, 293 n 73, and associated text. Other documents confirm that Indonesia's intentions were known to the USA and UK—see Brandon Mark 'Acknowledging Our International Criminals: Henry Kissinger and East Timor' (2003) 32(1) *Denver Journal of International Law & Policy* 1; William Burr and Michael L Evans (eds) *East Timor Revisited: Ford, Kissinger and the Indonesian Invasion, 1975–76* (National Security Archive Electronic Briefing Book No. 62, December 2001) <http://nsarchive.gwu.edu/NSAEBB/NSAEBB62/>.

Security Council as soon as possible'. A report was circulated to the Council on 22 June 1976,[78] which recorded, inter alia, that Indonesia 'declared that "Indonesian volunteers" were "in the process of leaving"' Timor and that this would soon be completed, but the special representative concluded 'it was not possible to assess accurately the prevailing situation in [Timor], particularly as regards implementation' of Council resolutions.

Unremarked by the Council, Indonesia in fact kept to its path: the very next month President Soeharto declared Timor a province of Indonesia.[79]

In summary, when faced with action contrary to the *Charter*, the Council made active decisions, but Indonesia simply did not comply—in fact, those decisions were publicly spurned by President Soeharto's declaration purporting to annex Timor. Whatever it discussed behind closed doors, the Council did not, however, reconvene on this matter. The Council retained this situation on its agenda but did not invest further in persuading or compelling Indonesia to meet its obligations to at least behave in accord with Article 2(4).[80] For example, in the annual report for 1976–1977,[81] related correspondence joined the list of matters brought to the attention of the Council but not discussed.[82]

The Assembly clearly wanted further Council attention to the matter, as shown in resolutions citing Article 11 of the *Charter*, in December 1976,[83] November 1977,[84] and December 1978.[85] The Council did not acknowledge this correspondence other than by listing them in the annual report. The Council is not obliged to agree with the Assembly's views, of course, but by its silence towards the Assembly, neither answering nor even declining to consider the

---

78 *Report by the Secretary-General in Pursuance of Security Council Resolution 389 (1976)* UN Doc S/12106 (22 June 1976), annexing the special representative's further report.

79 Which the General Assembly specifically rejected: see below n 83 and 84.

80 Were it to be argued, for example, that the Council did not make a decision clearly engaging Article 25.

81 *Report of the Security Council: 16 June 1976-15 June 1977* UN GAOR, 32nd sess, Supp No 2, UN Doc A/32/2 (29 November 1977), 49; similarly over the next two years—*Report of the Security Council: 16 June 1977-16 June 1978* UN GAOR, 33rd sess, Supp No 2, UN Doc A/33/2 (4 December 1978), 47; *Report of the Security Council: 16 June 1978-15 June 1979* UN GAOR, 34th sess, Supp No 2, UN Doc A/34/2 (7 December 1979), 58.

82 Principally, from the Secretary-General or the special representative, but also various notes from Benin and Mozambique on the one hand, and Indonesia on the other.

83 *Question of Timor* GA Res 31/53, UN GAOR, 31st sess, 85th plen mtg, UN Doc A/Res/31/53 (1 December 1976).

84 *Question of East Timor* GA Res 32/34, UN GAOR, 32nd sess, 83rd plen mtg, UN Doc A/Res/32/34 (28 November 1977).

85 *Question of East Timor* GA Res 33/39, UN GAOR, 33rd sess, 81st plen mtg, UN Doc A/Res/33/39 (13 December 1978).

question, in terms of accountability question (a) above the Council opened a gap in its own agenda-setting.

With the Council's stance set to silence and inaction, the Assembly dropped reiteration of this request from its next resolution on Timor, and turned to the Secretary-General for assistance.[86]

In 1982, this phase closed with an Assembly resolution on Timor. Indonesia's Foreign Minister, Ali Alatas, alone spoke to the proposal, in part saying:

> The unmistakable conclusion to be drawn from this year's vote ... is that the time has come to view East Timor on the basis of facts and of realism rather than of baseless accusations and wishful thinking. It is high time the Assembly dispensed with the sterile debate that has been going on for almost seven years on an issue that should never have been on its agenda in the first place.
>
> While expressing the hope that the General Assembly will next year be able to strike this so-called question of East Timor from its agenda once and for all, my delegation is again compelled to reiterate its rejection of the resolution just adopted.[87]

One could safely assume that in rejecting this Assembly resolution, Indonesia was also rejecting any obligation to comply with the Council's directions in Resolutions 384 and 389—or, indeed, to recognise its *Charter* obligations to eschew the threat or use of force in international relations.

No further Council response could be taken as the Council abdicating its role to make legally compelling decisions in this case, at least at this stage. This disengagement left the people of Timor legally cast adrift, much as the people of Trieste had been by an impasse in the Council three decades earlier. The circumstances of the Timorese people were, however, rather more dire than having clouds over the civil and political status of their community. On top of the death toll already noted,[88] under Indonesian administration the Timorese people suffered widespread rape and sexual slavery,[89] brutal repression,

---

86 *Question of East Timor* GA Res 34/40, UN GAOR, 34th sess, 75th plen mtg, UN Doc A/Res/34/40 (21 November 1979).

87 UN GAOR, 37th sess, 77th plen mtg, UN Doc A/37/PV.77 (23 November 1982), 1282 [158]-[159].

88 See above n 34 and associated text; see also Mark, above n 77.

89 *Chega!*, above n 42, Volume III Part 7.7 deals with the widespread and systematic rape, sexual slavery and sexual violence perpetrated by Indonesian forces. See also Susan Harris Rimmer 'Wearing his Jacket: A Feminist Analysis of the Serious Crimes Process in

looting, significant displacement of the population more than once, plus starvation and disease said to arise from Indonesian actions during what was eventually a quarter century of occupation.[90]

The Assembly continued its efforts, the 1982 resolution having also asked the Secretary-General 'to initiate consultations [to explore] avenues for achieving a comprehensive settlement of the problem'.[91] Years of effort were nugatory until an 'astonishing' policy shift by Indonesia's then-new President, B J Habibie, in early 1999.[92] This volte-face allowed the Secretary-General's efforts to culminate in agreements between the governments of Indonesia and Portugal, providing steps to a 'popular consultation [to] accept or reject' a status of special autonomy within Indonesia. Further legal steps would then be taken to either finalise Timor's incorporation into Indonesia, or to transfer authority to the UN for a transition to independence from Portugal.

The Council then re-engaged with Timor's situation. As tabled for a Council meeting on 7 May 1999, the Secretary-General's report foreshadowed the need for a related UN mission, and expressed concerns about the security situation.[93] In relation to the completed agreements, the Secretary-General noted that they stipulated:

> [A] secure environment devoid of violence or other forms of intimidation is a prerequisite for the holding of a free and fair popular consultation, [and] the appropriate Indonesian authorities have the responsibility to ensure such an environment as well as for the maintenance of law and order, [where] the United Nations will ascertain whether the necessary security exists for the peaceful implementation of the consultation process.[94]

Timor-Leste' (2009) 16(1) *Australian International Law Journal* 81; Michele Turner *Telling East Timor: Personal Testimonies 1942–1992* (New South Wales University Press, Sydney, 1992); Clinton Fernandes 'Accomplice to Mass Atrocities: The International Community and Indonesia's Invasion of East Timor' (2015) 3(4) *Politics and Governance* 1.

90 See generally *Chega!*, above n 42, Volume I Part 6—'The Profile of Human Rights Violations in Timor-Leste, 1974–1999'. For what was in evidence before that inquiry, see, for example, Amnesty International *East Timor: Amnesty International Statement to the United Nations Special Committee on Decolonization August 1991* (6 August 1991) Amnesty International (Document ASA 21/14/1991) <https://www.amnesty.org/en/documents/asa21/014/1991/en/>.

91 *Question of East Timor* GA Res 37/30, UN GAOR, 37th sess, 77th plen mtg, UN Doc A/Res/37/30 (23 November 1982).

92 Geoffrey Robinson *"If You Leave Us Here, We Will Die"* (Princeton, 2010), 94.

93 *Question of East Timor: Report by the Secretary-General* UN Doc S/1999/513 (5 May 1999).

94 Ibid, 2 [4], copies of the completed agreements being attached to his report.

In his further report of 22 May 1999,[95] the Secretary-General highlighted ongoing security concerns, including that 'credible reports continue to be received of political violence, including intimidation and killings, by armed militias against unarmed pro-independence civilians', and those militias were 'believed by many people to be operating with the acquiescence of elements of the [Indonesian] army ... Truckloads of pro-integration militia are able to roam about freely in the towns and to set up checkpoints [without] any intervention from the army or the police'.[96] He noted an essential condition for its success was that the UN mission monitoring the popular consultation needed the 'full cooperation of the Indonesian authorities'.[97]

In June 1999, the Council endorsed Ban Ki-moon's related proposals by Resolution 1246, in part stressing Indonesia's responsibility:

> [To] maintain peace and security in East Timor, in particular in the present security situation referred to in the report of the Secretary-General, in order to ensure that the popular consultation is carried out in a fair and peaceful way and in an atmosphere free of intimidation, violence or interference from any side and to ensure the safety and security of United Nations and other international staff and observers ...[98]

The Timorese people voted in favour of independence by a three quarters majority,[99] but what then actually transpired was that Indonesia oversaw a 'destructive rampage throughout East Timor',[100] by Indonesian forces and associated 'militias'.[101] Besides many more killings, forced evacuations and relocations, and widespread terror and violence that continued to tear down what little was left of Timor's social fabric,[102] its economic fabric was sundered when a significant majority of buildings were destroyed.[103]

---

95 *Question of East Timor: Report by the Secretary-General* UN Doc S/1999/595 (22 May 1999).

96 Ibid, 5 [23].

97 Ibid, 2 [5].

98 SC Res 1246, UN SCOR, 4013th mtg, UN Doc S/Res/1246 (11 June 1999) [9].

99 UN SCOR, 4041st mtg, UN Doc S/PV.4041 (3 September 1999), 2.

100 Martin and Mayer-Rieckh, above n 30, 131.

101 Simon Chesterman observes that this occurred 'under the direction of the Indonesian military, if not the government itself'—see Chesterman, above n 30, 62.

102 See *Chega!*, above n 42, Volume I, Part 3, 299 for the section on 'Indonesia departs: scorched earth'.

103 Estimates range around three quarters of, literally, all buildings in Timor—see for example, Samantha Power *Chasing the Flame: Sergio Vieira de Mello and the Fight to Save the World* (Penguin Books, London, 2008), 288; Robinson, below n 106, 87.

Putting aside the Council's earlier efforts, events in 1999 could be set as a fresh political phase in the case of Timor. From that viewpoint, an explanation of Council conduct in line with accountability questions (a) to (c) above could say that:

- the case returned to the Council's agenda promptly, at the first request from the Secretary-General;
- a clear decision was reached without undue delay;
- it was directed towards restoring international peace and security; and
- it was made in a way conforming to acknowledged *Charter* practice.

That the Council did not mention Chapter VII is not necessarily remarkable, especially if the use of armed force in international relations is glossed over; the wording also gives Indonesia unambiguous directions—so far, so good. However, the same problem arises from question (c)(iii), on obtaining due compliance with the Council's legally-enabled decision: Indonesia simply did not comply by fulfilling the new obligations placed on it by Resolution 1246. Moreover, for due fidelity to the *Charter*, Council decision-making in 1999 cannot reasonably be corralled away from its decisions in 1975, Resolutions 384 and 389 languishing unimplemented, and all the well known consequences that Indonesia's non-compliance had wrought.

It is worth recalling here that, whatever Indonesia might say, the world still regarded Timor as Portuguese (colonial) territory,[104] and this as an issue of international relations involving the use of armed force. So the Council decisions could be seen as rather less than faithful to the *Charter* for allowing Indonesia, the instigator in using armed force contrary to the *Charter*, to have responsibility for security. Nor does it seem nearly enough to say that there was no practical alternative, since many would hold that part of the Council's job is to equip itself as needed to meet its *Charter* Functions,[105] and, as Geoffrey Robinson notes, 'the violence had been widely predicted'.[106] In any case, Indonesia's violent record in Timor was already widely known around the world,[107] which rather suggests it was a highly ill-advised decision. By 1999, thanks to

104 Australia being one of the few to 'accept Indonesia's disputed claim over East Timor'—see Robinson, above n 92, 63 (including the related note); see also Thomas D Grant 'East Timor, the U.N. System, and Enforcing Non-Recognition in International Law' (2000) 33(2) *Vanderbilt Journal of Transnational Law* 273.

105 Including those sympathetic to an approach developed from the views of Clyde Eagleton—see above Chapter 2, n 95.

106 Geoffrey Robinson 'If You Leave Us, We Will Die' (2002) 49(1) *Dissent* 87, 87.

107 Causing some to criticise Council decision-making for not having learned its lesson from trusting the Serbs to guarantee the safety of Bosnians in Srebrenica—for example, see Power above n 103, 295.

contributions from civil society that record was public knowledge from, for example:

- credible reports, ongoing from the mid 1980s, of serious human rights violations on an egregious scale by Indonesia's military and/or militias associated with it;[108]
- eyewitness accounts of depredations by Indonesian forces published by Amnesty International, which had progressed to weekly updates by the time of the infamous 1991 'massacre' at Dili's Santa Cruz cemetery;[109]
- video footage of that particular event, shot by documentary cameraman Max Stahl, which was famously aired in Britain in January 1992;[110] and
- highly visible acknowledgement of such things, including in the 1996 Nobel Peace Prize being awarded jointly to Carlos Filipe Ximenes Belo and José Ramos-Horta—the press release saying, inter alia, 'Indonesia took control of East Timor and began systematically oppressing the people [and] it has been estimated that one-third of the population of East Timor lost their lives due to starvation, epidemics, war and terror'.[111]

Use of armed force by Indonesia, in its international relations with Portugal, was key to both phases of the case, and lack of implementation of Council decisions in the first phase might be taken as the cause of the second and the further depredations it involved. On the whole, then, when looked at in terms of the accountability questions put above, it is difficult to explain Council decisions or justify the Council's response as completed work in the earlier phase, but nigh on impossible to do so in the latter.

After the popular consultation vote, Timor duly spent a period under UN administration as had been agreed to by Portugal. Timor became a sovereign

---

108 Non-government organisations played a crucial role in highlighting the situation—see for example Amnesty International *East Timor: Violations of Human Rights—Extrajudicial Executions, 'Disappearances', Torture and Political Imprisonment* (1 January 1985) Amnesty International (Document ASA 21/016/1985) <https://www.amnesty.org/en/documents/asa21/016/1985/en/>. Photo essays were also widely available—for example, see Steve Cox and Peter Carey *Generations of Resistance: East Timor* (Cassell, London, 1995). The narrative from Oxford historian Peter Carey includes, for example, Indonesia's 'encirclement and annihilation' strategy and the 1991 'massacre' in Dili's Santa Cruz cemetery.

109 Amnesty International *East Timor: The Santa Cruz Massacre* (14 November 1991) Amnesty International (Document ASA 21/23/1991) <https://www.amnesty.org/en/documents/asa21/023/1991/en/>; Amnesty International *East Timor: After the Massacre* (21 November 1991) Amnesty International (Document ASA 21/24/1991) <https://www.amnesty.org/en/documents/asa21/024/1991/en/>. See also a synopsis of related developments in Robinson, above n 106, 82.

110 'Cold Blood: The Massacre of East Timor' *Yorkshire Television* (UK), 7 January 1992.

111 Norwegian Nobel Committee 'The Nobel Peace Prize 1996' (Press Release, 11 October 1996).

state and UN member in 2002, with successive Council mandated missions until 2012.[112] Its recovery has also relied on considerable assistance, some still ongoing, from civil society and governments around the world. As Christine Chinkin says:

> [W]e can speculate how much less would have been needed to establish an independent state [and] how many lives would have been saved if the members of the international community had insisted that Indonesia comply with its obligations under international law at a much earlier date and had not themselves been complicit in its violations.[113]

Answering accountability questions thus illustrates the importance of suitable agenda setting, proper process, and clear decisions. Crucially, they also show that implementation is paramount to Council effectiveness: conduct such as Indonesia's non-compliance, flaunted in purporting to annex Timor and flouted in rejecting Council resolutions, is a challenge to the Council's basic function as a decision-making body, and one it failed to answer.

With due regard to the *Charter* design and purposes, non-implementation of Council decisions then begs the question of why this was so—were its powers insufficient, for example, or found to be inaptly applied, or circumvented in some way? Did some other actor not keep faith with their part of the *Charter* bargain? Whatever the case might have been, what was done to prevent the *Charter* design (and perhaps international law more generally) from being usurped?

This case example thus shows the need to close the loop on whether implementation was obtained, and sufficient, including whether those instructed by a Council decision are duly persuaded to meet the obligations put on them, as per question (c)(iii).

This calls for further explanation which might be addressed by adding a question to the earlier list:

(d) To account for compliance with the *Charter* design, in its Purposes and specific provisions, as well as observing international law more generally (as applicable), what explanation is given for non-compliance, non-conformity, or otherwise less than complete implementation:

112 Those missions were vital, but only related to Chapter VII rather indirectly, so are not explored further here in terms of Council accountability issues.

113 Chinkin, above n 37, 54.

(d)(i) What was the reasoning for a UN member not meeting its obligations, when created by Article 25 of the *Charter*, or for non-implementation or non-conformity as may otherwise be applicable?

(d)(ii) Was the assistance of other actors—including the General Assembly, the International Court of Justice, or regional organisations—engaged under the *Charter*, and, if so, to what effect? If not, why not?

(d)(iii) Could other action, such as the Council making an explicit decision framed expressly in Article 25 terms, or using Chapter VII powers to specify other requirements, better engender adherence to the *Charter* generally or the Council's decision specifically? If so, was this action taken? If not, why not?

Further to those questions, unanswered interest from the Assembly underscores the importance of *questions being both asked and answered, which is the essential function of an accountability mechanism*. Of course, the Assembly has no supervisory role over the Council. However, it remains a relevant venue for states that collectively empower the Council, and it does have a *Charter* right to ask questions which strongly indicates that there is associated value to be had from the Council answering them.

This case also serves as a due reminder that, even if there is no identifiable obligation for the Council to answer such questions, it remains that for the Council to be powerful outside its walls, voting power must first be exercised by individual Council members within those walls. In the search for an accountability mechanism this turns attention back to the decision rights of its members in the conduct of the Council's business—which is, in effect, the underlying determinant of whether the Council can, or will, make any decision at all. The point here is not to pierce the institutional veil—perhaps to see if one or other Council member may bear some legal responsibility for what the Council has done. The aim is just to lift that veil to observe dynamics in Council power used (or not) towards its *Charter* Functions (or otherwise).

To look at what it may mean where implementation is lacking,[114] but left languishing for want of Council attention,[115] one question is *how* the Council's decision-making might be scrutinised—to see, for example, if it at least shows

114 Whether opposed openly in principled recalcitrance, or resisted in a stinting answer of subtle lip-service, in situations mooted by Antonios Tzanakopoulos, to justify disobeying the Council—above Chapter 2, n 85.

115 Where the importance of implementation and 'follow through' remains a very fresh issue—for example, see *Letter dated 14 February 2019 from the Permanent Representative*

fidelity to the *Charter* design and to UN Purposes, but, preferably, also shows due lawfulness—enough to propagate Council legitimacy towards fulfilling its Functions. Another question is *when* it may be advisable to scrutinise Council work—perhaps proactively,[116] or just more progressively,[117] than, for example, would be done in a periodic assessment or the occasional legal initiative.[118] Some may argue that accountability comes only after the fact,[119] and in other places a proactive approach is more usually put under the heading of having 'checks and balances'.[120] However one may choose to describe it, for discussion about the Council the important point is *providing and using opportunities to adjust its course of action* (or inaction), to ensure better effect, and so a more productive Council.

As discussed in the next section, in the Council's circumstances, and given the nature of its work, potential consequences of Council work show the advisability of being accountable after the fact. However, they also strongly suggest that it would be an improvement to duly 'explain or justify' its actions and inactions in the course of decision-making processes—a measure of *prevention that is needed simply because cure is so unlikely*.[121]

6.2 Case Examples: Lifting the Veil on the Council

In terms of decision rights of Council members, the *Charter* design of the Council is to have:

(i) five permanent members, by their right of being member states named in Article 23(1);[122] and

of Finland to the United Nations addressed to the President of the Security Council S/2019/144 (15 February 2019), 18, in which a member of the Council (a participant at the annual workshop for newly elected members) said that there is 'a pressing need ... to devote more attention to implementing the Council's decisions [which is] a prerequisite to boosing the Council's legitimacy'. See also above Chapter 3, n 118.

116 See, for example, Selznick, above Chapter 2, n 86.

117 If, for example, the Council's annual report were to be taken and developed this way.

118 Whatever might come of that—for example, see above Chapter 2, n 97.

119 Which is certainly usual in conventional legal accountability, and, for example, seen in the description in Grant and Keohane, above Chapter 2, n 61.

120 See, for example, Klabbers, above Chapter 1, n 52.

121 Noting rectification or remediation are difficult to pursue and probably even more so for an omission than a wrongful act—see generally Ian Brownlie *The Rule of Law in International Affairs* (Martinus Nijhoff, 1998), Chapter IX. On Council-related peculiarities of reparation, see also Tzanakopoulos, above Chapter 2, n 85, 144.

122 Leaving aside the wrangles over China's representation—see above Chapter 4, n 66, and Chapter 5, n 69 and associated text, and questions over 'succession' to the USSR by Russia—see above Chapter 1, n 96 and associated text.

(ii) ten non-permanent members, by virtue of them being member states elected in keeping with the Assembly's right under Article 23(1), and the Assembly's relevant procedures.

These are features of *Charter* law that, in practical effect, contribute to two main tenets of the conventional wisdom on Council accountability, namely that:

(a) P5 members are said to control the Council by dint of their veto power under Article 27(3), bolstered by their right to membership that nothing can overturn short of *Charter* reform, or their expulsion from the UN; and

(b) the Council is said to escape legal accountability, shielded by UN immunities and not subject to judicial or constitutional review, a view bolstered by lack of provisions for removing Council members (again, short of *Charter* reform or expelling the state from the UN)—the P5 ever, or the E10 before the expiration of their term.

While the veto power and UN immunities are facts, they obscure the truth that there is more to Council decisions than the wishes of the P5, and more to its accountability than a day in court might achieve. In particular, nine affirmative votes are always necessary for Council decisions, meaning, inter alia, powerful actors must have cooperation from the less powerful for any decision to be made.

Looked at in terms of decision rights, for ten Council members their rights are contingent on their status—being elected by the UN membership and conventionally seen to 'represent' them. They have no right ever to become a member of the Council, but if they are elected, their term will expire and their record stands for all to see should they ever seek re-election. Taken together, this suggests that those who do the electing should express their expectations and that those elected should be responsive, perhaps especially if they harbour aspirations to a future term.[123]

Put another way, one does not need to be a hardened cynic to see that the Assembly's suasion over the P5 will probably remain quite limited, but, on the other hand, neither is it unduly naïve to suggest that the right to elect the E10 provides, to the collective of states in the Assembly, an opportunity to exert considerably more suasion over states aspiring to that office. This lever might well be applied during the election process, but also through their term of office.

---

123 As sovereign nations, of course one might reasonably assume such responsiveness will be circumscribed by also responding to their national community on geopolitical activities, in line with whatever legal responsibility the regime has to respond on domestic matters, but the point stands.

Crucially, the E10 as a group has the weight of numbers for a Council decision before a negative P5 vote morphs into a veto. That is, E10 members have the power to be powerful via their votes, not individually so much as collectively: even if all the P5 agree to a proposal, their wish is not a decision without some of the E10 to make up the nine affirmative votes needed to adopt a Council resolution.

This answers both *how* some means of Council accountability might arise—through use of E10 voting power, and also *when*—whenever they can arrange concerted voting action. The E10 thus could become a distinctive influence engaged to answer questions from the Assembly.[124]

Even with the veto unreformed, two main avenues appear to be available for such initiatives: these are a decision of the Council and/or a decision of the Assembly.

In the Council, concerted action by the E10 could, for one example, take the initiative to adopt a Council resolution to add explanations to its decisions or in its reporting. On practice to date, this procedural matter would not be subject to the veto, and could be done by adding to the Council's *Provisional Rules of Procedure* (or to its working methods). Adoption of amended *Provisional Rules of Procedure* has, so far, been treated as a procedural question,[125] but it is conceivable that the 'preliminary question', on whether it is a procedural question, might come in to play.[126] If it did, some of the P5 might be willing to spend political capital on a 'double veto'—to cast the question as substantive and then veto the change. Such incidents have largely been confined to the early years of the UN,[127] but if one or more P5 members did go this route, it remains open to the E10 to nonetheless informally govern their practice to that effect. If E10 members did, this might be more impactful if assisted by the Assembly.

In line with the legal basis for electing them, the Assembly thus might—additionally or alternatively—formally call on E10 members to explain or justify what is done in the Council, where voting by the E10 somehow occurs to voice the interests of a wider membership that they are taken to 'represent'. Again, the Assembly cannot expect to change the conduct of the P5 in this, but could very well assert suasion over how the E10 members act while in office.

124 As a relevant forum in which those states empowering the Council convene on related matters, and quite distinct from questions that are, in the usual course of events, put by one member of the Assembly—and which should be taken as no different from any other way that such a state would raise a question with the Council.

125 See Simma et al, above Chapter 1, n 29, 1031 [MN 10 and 11].

126 See Sievers and Daws, above Chapter 5, n 78, 318.

127 See Simma et al, above Chapter 1, n 29, 904.

This may come to the fore more if such states again seek election in the future, but it remains open for the Assembly to take action as the principal actor with the opportunity to formalise expectations in this regard.

Either way, E10 accountability would then turn on what the Assembly wants from them, which may be further illustrated by gaps seen in the Council's response on Timor, and thus the contrast created if the E10 had been able to obtain a measure of accountability when it was seen to be needed.

6.2.1 *Could the E10 Have Helped Timor Sooner?*

As discussed in Chapter 6.1, the Assembly repeatedly called for more action on Timor in a series of Article 11 requests to the Council. The benefit of an E10 obligation to explain Council decisions to the Assembly, as a venue for states which collectively empower the Council, may thus be found in what greater part the E10 could have played in obtaining a response with the speed and on the scale that the Assembly adjudged as appropriate in the circumstances—or at least some explanation of the hold up.

Firstly, the Assembly clearly did want more and faster action by the Council, and further formal meetings on the matter after April 1976. UN member states may collectively have accepted that, even having support from China,[128] *Realpolitik* meant the E10 could not overcome the combined lack of interest in more Council action from the USA and the UK, as major sellers of arms and military material to Indonesia.[129] At least a majority would, nevertheless, quite possibly have wanted E10 members to show energy and initiative in mooting this on the record to account for the Council's approach.

Next, long before 1999 the UN membership may well have wished the E10 to tax the USA on interfering with the Council's legitimate business. That it had done so was no secret as early as 1979, from memoirs published by Daniel Moynihan, who was the USA Ambassador to the UN in 1975/1976. Specifically in relation to, inter alia, Timor, he (in)famously said that:

> [The] United States wished things to turn out as they did ... The Department of State desired that the United Nations prove utterly ineffective ...

128 China (by then the People's Republic of China) led the call for stronger Council action, making censorious comment on Indonesia, whose 'dispatch of troops for armed invasion of East Timor has laid bare Indonesia's attempt to annex East Timor, which constitutes a direct violation of the Charter'—see UN SCOR, 1869th mtg, UN Doc S/PV.1869 (22 December 1975), 2 [14].

129 For example, see Robinson, above n 92, 59—saying USA arms sales 'quintupled from 1974 to 1975, and that roughly 90 percent of the military equipment used in the invasion was supplied by the United States'.

> This task was given to me, and I carried it forward with no inconsiderable success.[130]

Again, as part of specifically obliging the E10 as their 'representatives' in Council doings, a majority of states quite possibly would have wanted the E10 to take issue on this, and to press harder for the resolutions to be implemented—or provide an explanation for why not and thus at least bring the situation further into the light of day.

Thirdly, Indonesia purported to annex Timor as Indonesian territory, a position that the Assembly expressly rejected. The Council's inaction worked in opposition to the Assembly's view, in effect buttressing Indonesia's position as time marched on from 1976 to 1999. E10 members explaining why the Council did no more, in particular to counter Indonesia's claim of sovereignty over Timor, would have gone at least some way to respecting the position supported by a significant number of UN members (as formally shown in an Assembly resolution).

As a last example here, in 1999 Indonesia asserted that an international force in Timor would require its permission, for which Simon Chesterman notes there appeared to be no legal basis.[131] Geoffrey Robinson summarises the situation thus:

> [Indonesia's] military remained adamantly opposed [to this as] an unacceptable violation of Indonesian sovereignty [so despite] the dubious legal basis for Indonesia's claim to sovereignty in East Timor, most major powers ... made it clear they would not move ahead without Indonesian approval.[132]

Many, if not most, UN member states may have accepted it was not, by that late stage, possible to overturn Indonesia's position—due in large part, perhaps almost entirely, to the effect of Council inaction. If so, the option left would be to adopt Resolution 1246 despite Indonesia's record in Timor. The post-vote violence thus may not have been avoidable if the E10 had not already been successful in influencing the Council as a whole to make other decisions. Rather than promoting alternative outcomes, such possibilities go more to highlight the importance of accountability being a process woven into Council decision-making. This is vital to obtaining the benefits of prevention in relation to misuse, abuse, disrepair, or

130 Daniel Patrick Moynihan *A Dangerous Place* (Secker & Warburg, London, 1979), 247.

131 See Chesterman, above n 30, 62.

132 Robinson, above n 92, 191.

desuetude, of Council power—whichever way one might choose to characterise the consequences of its decisions being unimplemented in 1975–1976, and prolonged Council silence and inaction in the face of, for example, Indonesia purporting to annex Timor and publicly rejecting the UN's position entirely.[133]

If the larger geopolitical environment of those days may not have allowed any better results than those speculated upon here, what actually followed is far more encouraging in terms of the influence that the E10 can assert by owning its Council role (distinct from what such states may say in their own right during Assembly sessions).

After the initial post-vote violence in 1999, Russia, China, and the USA, all remained resistant to intervention by an international force,[134] even as a Council mission was travelling in Indonesia and Timor. Led by E10 member Namibia,[135] the Council mission was in country as the post-vote violence continued despite Indonesia declaring martial law in Timor. In among responses from other organisations, and diplomatic initiatives by individual countries, that mission is credited with 'forceful diplomacy' and a 'stinging report' that 'unquestionably influenced opinion within the Security Council and the United Nations more generally'.[136] The Namibian representative, for example, is purported to have challenged Indonesia's General Wiranto, who claimed martial law was 'choking off the turmoil', by replying 'We don't believe you. You are not convincing us.'[137]

In fact, the E10 might reasonably be given significant credit for the next Council decision, because:

> The field mission, and in particular the delegation's willingness to challenge the Indonesian military's narrative of events on East Timor, was an integral part of a broad international effort to address the crisis. [The] visiting mission cabled back their analysis before the Security Council met

133 See above n 79 and 87, and associated text. Of course, Indonesia is not alone in having taken such a tack, but the fact is that this conduct has not subsided into history (as it might have if Bizerta was the only example—see above Chapter 3, n 132) but remains relevant in recent times (see Grant, above n 40).

134 Robinson, above n 92, 192.

135 With representatives of the E10 Malaysia, Netherlands and Slovenia, plus representatives of the UK and the Secretary-General.

136 Robinson, above n 92, 196. See also his synopsis of diplomatic efforts (ibid, at 192), and, for example, the contemporaneous reportage by Mydans, below n 137.

137 Seth Mydans 'Cry From Besieged City: Don't Forget East Timor' *The New York Times* (online) 12 September 1999 <http://www.nytimes.com/1999/09/12/world/cry-from-besieged-city-don-t-forget-east-timor.html>.

> in open session. Member states then lined up to condemn Indonesia for failing to keep the peace and called on Jakarta to accept an international mission.[138]

Official records show that in two sessions of the Council's 4043rd meeting,[139] even while China and Russia continued to say Indonesia would have to approve international intervention, some 40 nations spoke their piece, mostly to reinforce the view from E10 members: that, inter alia, the post-vote violence offended the UN itself. Faced with such diplomatic pressure,[140] President Habibie shifted stance to agree that an international force in Timor could proceed under the Council's imprimatur. Authorised by unanimous adoption of Resolution 1264,[141] INTERFET was led by Australia and saw over 20 other countries involved.[142]

Returning to the accountability questions set out earlier, question (d) concerns compliance, as may be applicable, with the *Charter*, Council directions, and international law more generally. This brief application of that question suggests that if such influence from the E10 is possible in one situation, to see a modicum of implementation in answer to question (c), it may be indicative of a broader possibility that the E10 can be influential in Council decision-making—perhaps especially if inspired by the UN membership wanting them to be, and holding them accountable as their 'representatives' in the Council.

That this could be so, because the E10 has capacity to be more influential than may be supposed from focus on the veto as power,[143] is illustrated by

---

138 Jim Della-Giacoma 'U.N. Security Council Should Make Better Use of "Road-Trip" Diplomacy' on *Global Peace Operations Review* (21 March 2016) <http://peaceoperationsreview.org/commentary/u-n-security-council-should-make-better-use-of-road-trip-diplomacy/>. See also Robinson, above n 92, 197.

139 See UN SCOR, 4043rd mtg, UN Doc S/PV.4043 (11 September 1999); UN SCOR, 4043rd mtg, UN Doc S/PV.4043 (Resumption) (11 September 1999).

140 In his discussion of the meaning of consent in relation to peacekeeping operations, Ian Johnstone fairly includes Timor as one of three examples where 'the consent granted was hardly an act of volition and indeed verged on duress'—see Ian Johnstone *The Power of Deliberation: International Law, Politics and Organizations* (Oxford, 2011), 140. On the other hand, it might be argued that the world had not accepted Indonesia's annexation of Timor, so Indonesia's consent was not strictly necessary and sundry UN members were rightly, if belatedly due to Council disengagement, taking the opportunity to assert suasion in keeping with the Assembly's rejection of that annexation (see above n 79).

141 See UN SCOR, 4045th mtg, UN Doc S/PV.4045 (15 September 1999), 2.

142 SC Res 1264, UN SCOR, 4045th mtg, UN Doc S/Res/1264 (15 September 1999).

143 Though without at all doubting that, one way and another, the veto is a significant factor in Council decisions, so focus at other times is certainly warranted.

discussing accountability question (b) about Council choices in deliberating on questions arising about the effectiveness of Resolution 1267.

6.2.2 *E10 Initiative on the 1267 Ombudsperson*

Resolution 1267 was adopted unanimously in October 1999,[144] the Council acting under Chapter VII in an attempt to more effectively assert sanctions over the Taliban (including to facilitate apprehension of Osama bin Laden). In particular, this established the *1267 Committee*,[145] to be comprised of all Council members, and to, inter alia, consider implementation of the resolution and states' compliance.[146]

After several years of practice on imposing such sanctions, the 2005 World Summit was attended by a significant majority of UN members.[147] Informed by Kofi Annan's report *In Larger Freedom*,[148] it culminated in the World Summit Outcome document, which was then adopted by the Assembly.[149] Reflecting concerns with practices as they had developed, this called, inter alia, for the Council 'to ensure that *fair and clear* procedures exist for placing individuals and entities on sanctions lists and for removing them'.[150]

There was no formal Council response—for example, a direct initiative to add this to its agenda. When briefed on the *1267 Committee* report in October 2005,[151] E10 member Brazil instead got the ball rolling by opining that the 'mechanisms for listing and delisting leave significant room for improvement in transparency, effectiveness and fairness'.[152] Then and at the next briefing,[153] other Assembly members intervened,[154] to underscore the World Summit

---

144 SC Res 1267, UN SCOR, 4051st mtg, UN Doc S/Res/1267 (15 October 1999); UN SCOR, 4051st mtg, UN Doc S/PV.4051 (15 October 1999).

145 As it was then, the 'Security Council Committee established pursuant to resolution 1267 (1999) concerning Al-Qaida and the Taliban associated individuals and entities' ('*1267 Committee*').

146 Noting that, as with other such subsidiary bodies of the Council, committee meetings are not recorded as official meetings of the Council despite having the same membership, so their discussions are accessible only via the reports made available for Council deliberations on the record.

147 For further information, see above Chapter 3, n 47.

148 Ibid.

149 Ibid.

150 Ibid, *2005 World Summit Outcome*, 26 [109] (emphasis added).

151 UN SCOR, 5293rd mtg, UN Doc S/PV.5293 (26 October 2005).

152 Ibid, 10.

153 UN SCOR, 5375th mtg, UN Doc S/PV.5375 (21 February 2006).

154 As in the usual course of Council practice, under Rule 37 of the *Provisional Rules of Procedure*.

Outcome points, and in May 2006,[155] E10 members Greece,[156] Qatar,[157] and Japan,[158] all pressed for more response on procedural fairness and/or 'fair and clear procedures'.

Against that backdrop, while President of the Security Council for June 2006 Denmark scheduled a thematic debate on 'Strengthening international law: rule of law and the maintenance of international peace and security'. In a 'non-paper' circulated to 'help guide the discussion',[159] Denmark put forward three issues meriting special attention—one being enhancement of efficiency and credibility of sanctions regimes.

This may have prompted informal engagement with correspondence from 19 May 2006,[160] sent by Germany, Sweden, and Switzerland (none of these states then being in the E10). This furnished a report commissioned 'to analyse current sanctions committee practices and recommend proposals to strengthen [UN] targeted sanctions regimes'.[161] To 'address shortcomings' of sanctions committee procedures, in part this compared a range of options for a review mechanism,[162] where an ombudsman was one of those recommended for consideration.[163]

Added weight to the occasion of the debate was given by Denmark's Minister for Foreign Affairs, Per Stig Møeller, taking the chair, and Judge Rosalyn Higgins, President of the International Court of Justice, attending to intervene in accordance with Rule 39 of the *Provisional Rules of Procedure*.

In session, each of the E10 mentioned the need for better procedural fairness, and/or 'fair and clear procedures', in sanctions regimes. In particular, Japan gave the majority of its comments to this point, Ghana drew a direct connection to the World Summit Outcome, Slovakia said that the 'transparency

155 UN SCOR, 5446th mtg, UN Doc S/PV.5446 (30 May 2006).

156 Ibid, 10.

157 Ibid, 14.

158 Ibid, 16.

159 *Letter dated 7 June 2006 from the Permanent Representative of Denmark to the United Nations addressed to the Secretary-General* S/2006/367 (7 June 2006).

160 It was not formally discussed and so joined the annual report list of correspondence received but not discussed at meetings of the Council: see *Report of the Security Council: 1 August 2005–31 July 2006* UN GAOR, 61st sess, Supp No 2, UN Doc A/61/2 (2006), 203.

161 *Identical letters dated 19 May 2006 from the Permanent Representatives of German, Sweden and Switzerland to the United Nations addressed to the President of the General Assembly and the President of the Security Council* A/60/887-S/2006/331 (14 June 2006). It was prepared by the Watson Institute Targeted Sanctions Project at Brown University (Rhode Island, USA), and included legal analysis by Larissa van den Herik and Nico Schrijver.

162 Ibid, 51.

163 Ibid, 62.

and effectiveness of listing and delisting procedures are becoming a yardstick for the work of numerous sanctions committees',[164] and Greece went so far as to say:

> The sanctions committees should amend their guidelines to bring them in line with procedural fairness and effective remedy requirements. In that respect, we would like to emphasize the important contributions of Council members France and Denmark [noting that the recent report] sponsored by the Governments of Switzerland, Germany and Sweden, provides many useful options to that effect, and we urge the sanctions committees to take those options into consideration.[165]

When the Council was briefed in September 2006 by the *1267 Committee*, Greece again spoke to such concerns remaining unaddressed:

> We urge the [1267] Committee to embark upon consideration of these issues at the earliest opportunity, also taking into account the proposals submitted to the Committee by Denmark and France, as well as the various options offered by recent academic discussions on this issue. As we have stated on many occasions, ensuring fair and clear procedures will ultimately strengthen the effectiveness of targeted sanctions.[166]

Late in 2006, France's proposal for a sanctions 'focal point' was adopted unanimously.[167] In a meeting lasting only 15 minutes, Greece nonetheless again took the opportunity to reinforce the need for further steps:

> We believe, however, that the sanctions committees should continue to improve their delisting procedures, particularly in the direction of establishing a review mechanism along the lines of the useful suggestions made recently by member States such as Denmark ...[168]

Its term of office on the Council expired at the end of 2006, but Denmark still remained visible in initiatives for improving sanctions regimes. In 2007,

164 UN SCOR, 5474th mtg, UN Doc S/PV.5474 (22 June 2006), 12.
165 Ibid, 24.
166 UN SCOR, 5538th mtg, UN Doc S/PV.5538 (28 September 2006), 25.
167 SC Res 1730, UN SCOR, 5599th mtg, UN Doc S/Res/1730 (19 December 2006).
168 UN SCOR, 5599th mtg, UN Doc S/PV.5599 (19 December 2006), 3.

in the context of briefings by the Council's subsidiary bodies on sanctions, Liechtenstein (intervening) noted that:

> Many Member States still have concerns regarding the requirement of "fair and clear procedures" [in] the Council's use of targeted sanctions. [To] facilitate a constructive discussion on that issue, we organized a round table on de-listing on 8 November 2007 [sponsored] by the missions of Denmark, Sweden and Switzerland ...[169]

In 2008, Denmark, Germany, Liechtenstein, the Netherlands, Sweden, and Switzerland, again urged attention to delisting procedures—including via another paper, elements of which Denmark, Liechtenstein, Sweden, and Switzerland, had discussed with the *1267 Committee*.[170]

On 30 June, when the Council adopted Resolution 1822 to further promote the 'focal point',[171] E10 member Costa Rica made the only substantive comment, the representative concluding that:

> ... although the establishment of a focal point [was] an important achievement, it is also necessary to establish a review mechanism. We believe that the States members of the Security Council should seriously consider the proposal made by Denmark, Germany, Liechtenstein, the Netherlands, Sweden and Switzerland aimed at agreeing mechanisms to fully protect the basic rights of listed individuals.[172]

During the Presidency of Belgium in August 2008, discussion on working methods was guided back to the issue of transparency by the related note from the representative of Belgium.[173] Intervening, also on behalf of Denmark, Finland, Norway and Sweden, here it was Iceland urging further work:

> ... moves towards truly fair and clear procedures should include the introduction of an independent advisory input to the work of the Security

169 UN SCOR, 5779th mtg, UN Doc S/PV.5779 (14 November 2007), 28.

170 *Identical letters dated 23 June 2008 from the Permanent Representative of Switzerland to the United Nations addressed to the President of the General Assembly and the President of the Security Council* A/62/891-S/2008/428 (2 July 2008).

171 SC Res 1822, UN SCOR, 5928th mtg, UN Doc S/Res/1822 (30 June 2008).

172 UN SCOR, 5928th mtg, UN Doc S/PV.5928 (30 June 2008), 3.

173 *Letter dated 4 August 2008 from the Permanent Representative of Belgium to the United Nations addressed to the Secretary-General* S/2008/528 (6 August 2008).

> Council Committee established pursuant to resolution 1267 (1999), especially with respect to requests for de-listing.[174]

Liechtenstein (also intervening) added to the transparency theme, saying:

> ... access by non-members to the sanctions committees remains a crucial topic [but] practice leaves room for improvement. Earlier this year, we asked to meet with the 1267 Committee, as part of a group of States, to discuss relevant matters. However, the request was only taken up after extensive consultations within the Council. ... We believe that improved access to the sanctions committees would benefit the Council and the implementation of sanctions.[175]

Later that year, Switzerland intervened to press the point in sanctions committee briefings:

> Unfortunately, we must voice our disappointment that no progress has been made on what we consider to be a serious shortcoming of the current system, namely, the lack of an independent review mechanism concerning delisting decisions.[176]

There were similar mentions in subsequent briefings by the chair of the *1267 Committee*, and in the 2008 report on implementation of Resolution 1822, but also in a thematic discussion under the Presidency of Croatia, addressing 'Threats to international peace and security caused by terrorist acts'.[177] Switzerland (again intervening) returned to the point in May 2009, during briefings from Council sanctions committees, saying:

> Critics see the continuing lack of fair and clear procedures within the current sanctions regime as undermining the effective implementation of targeted sanctions [and] Member States find themselves in a dilemma when national or regional courts question the legality of domestic measures to implement sanctions.[178]

---

174 UN SCOR, 5968th mtg, UN Doc S/PV.5968 (27 August 2008), 29.

175 UN SCOR, 5968th mtg (Resumption 1), UN Doc S/PV.5968 (Resumption 1) (27 August 2008), 14.

176 UN SCOR, 6015th mtg, UN Doc S/PV.6015 (12 November 2008), 25.

177 See, for example, UN SCOR, 6034th mtg, UN Doc S/PV.6034 (9 December 2008), 11.

178 UN SCOR, 6128th mtg, UN Doc S/PV.6128 (26 May 2009), 27.

Liechtenstein (also again intervening) took a similar line, to remind Council members of what they had done as UN member states, and the 'long-overdue target we set ourselves in the Summit Outcome Document of 2005'.[179] At the next briefing, E10 member Costa Rica stepped up to say:

> The increasing number of trials around the world seems to confirm the need to provide the regime with an independent apolitical review mechanism that would come from within this Council, not from judicial, regional or international bodies outside it. With that in mind, Costa Rica has worked with Germany, Denmark, Liechtenstein, the Netherlands, Sweden, Switzerland, Belgium, Finland and Norway to produce a working document with a number of options to improve the due process within the sanctions regime.[180]

At the same meeting, the Netherlands representative (intervening) gave a synopsis of the efforts of the group of like-minded states noted by Costa Rica, saying, inter alia, that:

- those states mentioned by Costa Rica suggested still more was needed to meet 'the requirements of impartiality, independence and the ability to provide an effective remedy';
- open and inclusive dialogue was essential for improvements to enhance the prospects for implementation, 'thereby securing the effectiveness of a sanctions regime that may otherwise be at risk'; and
- national developments pointed to inadequate human rights protections in the Resolution 1267 arrangements, noting 'this question is a challenge to the efficiency, legitimacy and credibility of the entire United Nations sanctions regime'.[181]

The Netherlands representative wrapped up by saying:

> We firmly believe that the required improvements to procedures can be achieved without in any way compromising the authority of the Council. The new draft resolution on sanctions ... will constitute an important step to that end.[182]

179 UN SCOR, 6128th mtg (Resumption 1), UN Doc S/PV.6128 (Resumption 1) (26 May 2009), 16.

180 UN SCOR, 6217th mtg, UN Doc S/PV.6217 (13 November 2009), 15.

181 UN SCOR, 6217th mtg (Resumption 1), UN Doc S/PV.6217 (Resumption 1) (13 November 2009), 7–8.

182 Ibid, 8.

Resolution 1904 was adopted unanimously on 17 December 2009, establishing the role of an Ombudsperson for the *1267 Committee* (as part of updating its procedures).[183]

Taken in isolation, the transcript of that very brief meeting might suggest that Council impetus for this step came from Council members drafting the proposal. However, Costa Rica again mentioned cooperative work by like minded states (noted previously),[184] and the representative of Austria acknowledged the USA as the 'main sponsor of the resolution', but went on to particularly mark this as being the culmination of collective effort, saying that:

> ... special thanks are due to many other United Nations Member States that have actively supported this process over many years, in particular the group of like-minded States and the friends of the rule of law.[185]

Overall, from an accountability point of view there is much to laud in this episode, including:

- concerted efforts by states that were aimed at making Resolution 1267 productive—even as E10 members came and went over the operative years;
- E10 members duly 'representing' those that empower the Council, the UN's membership—including by spearheading efforts needed to make initiatives in international peace and security *effective via proper implementation by states*; and
- perseverance in pursuing an objective agreed by the Assembly as its collective will (from the 2005 Summit, endorsed in an Assembly resolution), against the lack of interest of individually more powerful actors—which could be taken as evidence that there really is more to Council decisions than the wishes of the P5.

This shows that although one E10 member may not be powerful, and two years is but a moment in Council business, the E10 does have power collectively, especially when asserted via coherent, principled action that supervenes their terms of office.

As an illustration of responding in terms of question (b), which calls for explaining the Council efforts in deliberating, this also shows interconnection to other accountability questions. For question (c)(iii), on the pivotal need to persuade actors to meet their obligations, it highlights the necessity that the

183 SC Res 1904, UN SCOR, 6247th mtg, UN Doc S/Res/1904 (17 December 2009), [20].

184 UN SCOR, 6247th mtg, UN Doc S/PV.6247 (17 December 2009), 3.

185 Ibid, 2.

Council answer questions and resolve issues so UN members will, or possibly can, duly implement its decisions. It is particularly noteworthy that answering questions was essential to accommodate legitimate concerns over Resolution 1267 and the lawfulness of the measures—which was expressed (repeatedly) well ahead of legal cases on relevant points. On accounting for compliance in line with (additional) accountability question (d) above, this case example also shows the benefit from proactive assessments made by E10 members that Resolution 1267 was at risk of being unproductive: in line with (d)(i), they formed a view that Resolution 1267 may not deliver the results wanted while states felt hampered by features of the listing and delisting processes, making the resolution possibly inappropriate for states to implement in due cognisance of their obligations on human rights or their own constitutional strictures. In line with (d)(ii), the response engaged the wider Assembly audience, to achieve action consistent with implementation in line with (d)(iii). Simple persistence to obtain this is also worth noting.

The example of the 1267 Ombudsperson illustrates what may be obtained by concerted E10 action, when states are duly moved to protect their citizens or others in their care. Returning to the main example of Timor shows what the elected members can do to give voice to those who are 'affected' by Council decisions, but who are less than perfectly served by the state of which they are (putatively) a part. Despite the efforts of Portugal, and support from the E10 in 1975, the people of Timor suffered mightily under the Indonesian regime, and could not be said to have been well-served by that state while Timor was purported to be a province of Indonesia. Urged on by civil society actors, however, in the end the E10 were instrumental in relieving the situation of the Timorese people in keeping with the Purposes of the UN. That example is, however, hardly without parallel then or since.

Indeed, more recent times bring this point into stark relief as the suffering of the Syrian people at the hands of their own government has continued for years despite the frequent attention given to the situation by the Council. As noted earlier, the Council's interest arises from the (potential) impacts upon international peace and security,[186] not least from such a colossal scale of refugee exodus to surrounding states, and the extent of the humanitarian crisis attending this situation which has continued to spiral as the Council has struggled to make any headway on a political solution.[187]

186 See above Chapter 5, n 163 to 170, for background, including the request from Jordan to consider this as a matter of international peace and security—this the Council has done under the broad agenda item 'the situation in the Middle East'.

187 See also above Chapter 2, n 23 and above Chapter 5, n 170, and associated text.

Resolution 2249 (2015) provides an example of how the competing interests of P5 members can tend to confound productive outcomes. This resolution addressed Islamic State in Syria and Iraq, as 'a global and unprecedented threat to international peace and security', and the resolution called upon states 'to take all necessary measures ... to redouble and coordinate their efforts to prevent and suppress terrorist acts committed specifically by ISIL'. It did not, however, go so far as to lend Council authority to any particular action nor did it specify a legal basis for states' use of force in response.[188] Moreover, the operative paragraph is such a long and circumlocutory sentence that it is arguable whether a clearly shared understanding of it is even possible—certainly, it would not meet the mark that I suggest in accountability question (c).

Labelled as 'constructive ambiguity' by Dapo Akande and Marko Milanovic,[189] the resolution seems to have been worded with the intention of providing political support for countries to take military action, without providing an endorsement for any given logic to underpin that. The larger problem confounding the situation, however, is that four out the five P5 members have been actively involved in the situation in Syria, at best putting them at cross-purposes and potentially courting outright conflict—from where I sit, the effect is that, rather than clarifying and directing some compromise, the resolution served more to let each continue to go their own way with just a (wafer) thin veneer of political cover which has produced precious little improvement to the situation on the ground. Thus Akande and Milanovic may have been on the mark to call this 'constructive ambiguity', but whether it was also 'productive ambiguity' is rather more of an open question as things have turned out—I would suggest not, particularly for the people of Syria whose situation remains perilous, and so I would further suggest the overall impact upon international peace and security is more that the Council abdicated its role in this episode, and should be required to explain or justify why it did so.

In fact, this is the more so because as recently as January 2020 efforts to continue humanitarian assistance provoked acrimony among the members of the Council, including those four P5 members that have been so heavily involved in Syria's situation.

The matter had been much debated in December 2019,[190] and the transcript of the Council's 8700th meeting in January 2020, when the resolution was

188 SC Res 2249, UN SCOR, 7565th mtg, UN Doc S/Res/2249 (20 November 2015).

189 Dapo Akande and Marko Milanovic 'The Constructive Ambiguity of the Security Council's ISIS Resolution' on *EJIL:Talk!* 21 November 2015 <https://www.ejiltalk.org/the-constructive-ambiguity-of-the-security-councils-isis-resolution/>.

190 Security Council Report 'Syria Briefing and Competing Humanitarian Draft Resolutions' on *What's in Blue* (19 December 2019) <http://www.whatsinblue.org>; Security Council

finally adopted, is replete with recriminations. E10 members, led by Belgium and Germany who were the penholders architecting the (eventually successful) draft proposal,[191] had to contend with a competing proposal from Russia.[192] By 11 votes to none, with abstentions by China, Russia, the UK, and the USA,[193] they were nonetheless able to extract from the situation at least some succour for a portion of the beleaguered people of Syria: Resolution 2504 continues the efforts earlier addressed by Resolutions 2139 and 2165, even though via much more limited means.[194] This mandate was, eventually, renewed for one year in July 2020, in the face of ongoing contention over humanitarian assistance and (unproductive) divergence on the situation of Syria more generally.[195]

Interestingly, the 'penholders' were acknowledged as playing an important part in that they came in for some serious ill-feeling expressed by Syria, showing (via the various mentions I have made) how this role has solidified and come to the fore over the course of the situation in Syria since 2011.

In contemporaneous contrast, an attempt to show solidarity with the Secretary-General's call for a global ceasefire in the face of the COVID-19 pandemic also fell foul of P5 interests that overtook the collective interest towards advancing international peace and security through such a ceasefire. For what would very likely have been little more than an hortatory gesture, six weeks of backroom back and forth—over the divergent views of P5 members on the culpability of actors for the pandemic—in the end came to nothing as no wording could be agreed that would not be vetoed by one of the P5.[196] Perhaps needless to add is that in accounting for Council conduct, Resolution 2249, and initial failure to support the call for a global ceasefire followed by months of delay in agreeing a form on words

Report 'Vote on Competing Humanitarian Draft Resolutions' on *What's in Blue* (10 January 2020) <http://www.whatsinblue.org>.

191 *Belgium and Germany: draft resolution* UN Doc S/2020/24 (10 January 2020).

192 *Russian Federation: draft resolution* UN Doc S/2019/962 (20 December 2019). The proposal from Russia was said to be almost unchanged when on the table for the 8700th meeting (see above n 190), noted in the transcript as UN Doc S/2020/25, but that draft has since been removed from the offical documents system and the number re-assigned to other correspondence, so the later draft is no longer accessible.

193 SC 2504, UN SCOR, 8700th mtg, UN Docs S/Res/2504 (10 January 2020), 3.

194 SC Res 2249, UN SCOR, 7565th mtg, UN Doc S/Res/2249 (20 November 2015). See also above Chapter 5, n 163 to 170.

195 Such contention is less visible in the public record due to special arrangements for COVID-19, but has not gone unremarked—see, for example, *Middle East: Syria* (29 May 2020) Security Council Report < https://www.securitycouncilreport.org/monthly-forecast/2020-06/syria-20.php>. For more on the renewal of the mandate, including the multiple failed proposals, see UN News 'Security Council extends for one year, lifesaving cross-border aid to Syria' (11 July 2020) <https://news.un.org/en/story/2020/07/1068181>.

196 See above Chapter 5, n 105, and associated text.

on this, are the types of results that would certainly warrant further explanation or justification—as is intended to be delivered by answers to the accountability questions that I proffer. As mentioned as the outset of this book, the point is to look at the Council's conduct, even where that is driven by the interests of an individual Council member, because the Council exists as a distinct entity not reducible merely to its component states. Towards the Council improving its own effectiveness, or productiveness, it should own the outcomes that it causes—the outcomes that it renders should be explainable via answers to the question I pose, and justifiable on their own merits (rather than in terms of actions by one Council member or another), including those results that emanate from what is, in effect, acquiescence arising from a failure to act by the Council.

Returning to accountability question (a), to account for apportioning Council effort to its purposes under the *Charter*, discussion of Resolution 1267 highlights E10 influence in setting the Council's agenda and thus all that might flow from it. Over years, various E10 members managed to re-insert 'fair and clear' procedures under quite a variety of agenda items, responding to question (a) by faithfully pursuing the Assembly's request from the World Summit to answer states' questions, and, in effect, also answering questions (c)(iii) and (d) towards obtaining productive results.

The importance of question (a) is underscored by a final case example, on selecting a new UN Secretary-General in 2016. This gives further indications of the influence of the E10 over Council accountability and what may come of asserting it proactively along the way in Council decision-making—as a voice for states empowering it, but, in this situation, also engaging with voices said to speak for 'those affected' by the Council.

6.2.3 *E10 Influence and Civil Society*

Similarly to Article 4 on accepting new members of the UN, Article 97 of the *Charter* provides that the Assembly appoints the Secretary-General 'upon the recommendation of the Security Council'. In 1946, the Assembly suggested it would be 'desirable for the Security Council to proffer one candidate only for the consideration of the General Assembly, and for debate on the nomination in the General Assembly to be avoided'.[197] The Council obliged and formed a habit of finding a candidate behind closed doors.[198]

---

197 *Terms of Appointment of the Secretary-General* GA Res 11 (1), UN GAOR, 1st sess, 17th plen mtg, UN Doc A/Res/11 (1) (24 January 1946) [4(d)].

198 In a veto-driven deadlock in the Council in 1950, the Assembly did take the initiative to extend Trygve Lie's term—he had resigned before the end of his term and he was the subject of Soviet vetoes leading up to the Assembly's initiative.

Five decades on, the Assembly attempted to re-assert its role in the broader reform groundswell of the mid-1990s—for example, saying that the process should be made more transparent and that:

> Without prejudice to the prerogatives of the Security Council, the President of the General Assembly may consult with Member States to identify potential candidates endorsed by a Member State and, upon informing all Member States of the results, may forward those results to the Security Council.[199]

But the Council's doors seemed rusted shut then and later when Canada attempted to promote such concerns in 2006.[200] Heading towards the next appointment, Canada's initiative did not appear to gain momentum and the 'President of the General Assembly seemed reluctant to add this issue to the already difficult set of reform problems confronting the United Nations in 2006'.[201]

The Assembly noted the need for the process to be 'inclusive of all Member States and made more transparent',[202] but it is moot whether the Council took heed. Whatever the true range of candidates then in the running, however much 'consultation' occurred along the way, the record shows just one formal meeting on the matter, in which the resolution to recommend a sole candidate was adopted 'by acclamation'.[203] Thus, if Ban Ki-moon was chosen from a wider field of candidates considered by the Council, that conclusion was nonetheless reached very largely off the record in informal sessions, including by use of the equally informal 'straw poll' procedure said to date to 1981.[204]

In the same vein, more recent commentary on the process for selecting the Secretary-General noted 'criticism by civil society that [it] lacks transparency

199 *Strengthening of the United Nations System* GA Res 51/241, UN GAOR, 51st sess, Agenda Item 48, 105th plen mtg, UN Doc A/Res/51/241 (22 August 1997), [60].

200 In an informal paper circulated by the Canadian delegation—that paper is not available as an official UN document. See Security Council Report *Second Report on the Appointment of the UN Secretary-General* (Special Research Report No. 2/2006, Security Council Report, 21 June 2006), 1.

201 Ibid, 4.

202 *Revitalization of the General Assembly* A/Res/60/286, UN GAOR, 60th sess, Agenda Item 116, 99th plen mtg, UN Doc A/Res/60/286 (9 October 2006, re-issued), 4.

203 *Official communiqué of the 5547th (closed) meeting of the Security Council* UN SCOR, 5547th mtg, UN Doc S/PV.5547 (9 October 2006).

204 Security Council Report *Appointing the UN Secretary-General* (Research Report No. 2/2015, Security Council Report, 16 October 2015), 3. By way of comparison in the same environment: under Article 4(1) of the *Statute of the International Court of Justice*, judges of

and needs updating as it is out of touch with best practices in high-level public sector appointments in most countries and other international organisations'.[205] Beginning in late 2014, civil society actors,[206] cooperating via the '1 For 7 Billion' campaign,[207] thus sought an 'open and inclusive selection process, with genuine involvement by all UN Member States'. As well as inertia from long-standing practice, this initiative faced a distinct lack of enthusiasm from the P5,[208] and a real distaste for the pace of events from Russia.[209] In September 2015, however, the Assembly took up the running by adopting a resolution that it, inter alia:

> *Requests* the Presidents of the General Assembly and the Security Council to start the process of soliciting candidates ... through a joint letter addressed to all Member States, containing a description of the entire process and inviting candidates to be presented in a timely manner ...[210]

Even catalysed by activism in civil society and then given some voice in the Assembly,[211] not much more may have eventuated without the E10 fostering the impetus for change—beginning with Spain, as President of the Security Council for October 2015, going ahead with a meeting that set the necessary wheels in motion. A draft was later circulated to Council members.[212]

---

the International Court of Justice are elected by parallel action in the Council and the Assembly. An excess of candidates is not unusual and competitive election of judges has long demonstrated just how much can be achieved without undue indignity for the candidates (arising in, for example, an open debate on their relative merits).

205 Ibid, 9.

206 Perhaps an exemplar of the potential role for the legitimating influence of civil society—see Scholte (2007) and Scholte (2016), above Chapter 4, n 119.

207 See 1 for 7 Billion, above Chapter 4, n 119 and 120.

208 China, Russia and the US favouring the status quo, France making no comment—see Security Council Report 'Informal Discussion on Selection and Appointment of the Next Secretary-General' on *What's in Blue* (20 July 2015) <http://www.whatsinblue.org>.

209 Ibid; see also Security Council Report 'Consultations on a draft joint letter for the appointment of the Secretary-General' on *What's in Blue* (18 November 2015) <http://www.whatsinblue.org>.

210 *Revitalisation of the work of the General Assembly* A/Res/69/321, UN GAOR, 69th sess, Agenda item 118, 103rd plen mtg, UN Doc A/Res/69/321 (22 September 2015), [35] (emphasis in original).

211 For example, see the 1 for 7 Billion alliance of non-government organisations campaign to 'find the best UN leader'—see 1 for 7 Billion *Who We are* <http://www.1for7billion.org/who-we-are/>; see also the various suggestions and inputs from the Accountability, Coherence and Transparency Group of states in the UN and The Elders global leaders group, now archived to <http://www.1for7billion.org/resources/>.

212 Security Council Report, above n 200.

At around the same time, E10 members Angola, Chile, Jordan, Malaysia, New Zealand, and Spain, urged greater accountability and transparency, via a joint statement in the annual open debate on Council working methods.[213] Delivered by the representative of Angola, this cast the net widely on change needed by all members of the Council and called for greater cooperation with other UN bodies. The statement concluded with specific reference to the process for selecting the Secretary-General, saying it 'is not acceptable that the Council has been slow to take up the necessary engagement between the Presidents ... especially relevant given the unequivocal call' from the Assembly.[214]

By then, civil society activism had already achieved something by lobbing the issue up well ahead of when it might have otherwise become visible on the Council's agenda. Given that the Assembly formally took a view, the E10 no doubt helped to give this much greater voice, including by duly 'representing' the collective wishes of the UN membership in the Council's machinations.

Noting resolve on the part of the individual ambassadors seems to have made a difference, the E10 as a group thus were pivotal in advancing towards something much more than what had been done before. In particular, they pushed ahead to set an approach agreed between the Presidents of the two UN chambers, with a clear message in terms of accountability questions (c)(i) and (ii) on implementation. The letter to all UN member state delegations gave specific commitments, such as:

> [We] invite Member States presenting candidates to do so in a letter to the President of the General Assembly and the President of the Security Council. [They] will jointly circulate to all Member States, on an ongoing basis, the names of individuals that have been submitted for consideration. [They] will offer candidates opportunities for informal dialogues or meetings with the members of their respective bodies, while noting that any such interaction will be without prejudice to those who do not participate.[215]

---

213 Although Angola was in only its second term on the Council, it is worth noting that the other five are not newcomers to Council work, having served between six and ten years each.

214 UN SCOR, 7539th mtg, UN Doc S/PV.7539 (20 October 2015), 8.

215 United Nations General Assembly *Procedure of Selecting and Appointing the next UN Secretary-General* (President of the 70th Session, undated), which linked to: <http://www.un.org/pga/70/wp-content/uploads/sites/10/2015/08/15-Dec-2015_Appointment-of-Secretary-General-15-December-2015.pdf>.

Thus, for accountability question (a), on agenda setting, this shows E10 members advanced the cause in the Council's formal proceedings, which proved crucial to having these steps included in the overall 'consultative process'.[216] This unfolded through 2016, and the results, seen in candidates and fresh information, left none involved the poorer for learning something germane—including by seeing candidates rehearse the role of Secretary-General in a number of open sessions hosted by the Assembly,[217] and by civil society organisations.[218] In terms of explaining how the Council's time is apportioned to its allotted tasks, accountability question (b) above, these events suggest that the Council both decided, and showed that it did so clearly, on a matter of great importance to the UN and for fidelity to the *Charter*. It also acted collegially and so without this taking up much more time in its own activities than it would have needed anyhow. Perhaps most importantly, in terms of accountability questions (c) and (d) above, and being able to address those proactively and progressively as needed, the Council here made promptly, *and saw implemented*, multiple decisions on how to proceed, and in the final result, the ends sought were realised.[219]

Connecting what the Council should account for to those to whom it might advisedly explain its conduct, this action accorded with the wishes of those empowering the Council by the *Charter*, (which was expressed via the Assembly),[220] in coherence with 'civil society' views put forward for 'those affected' (in effect, the entire world). Interestingly, the E10 might also be seen here to have delivered on their 'representative' role since, in keeping with the Assembly's 1946 request, the Council still made a single recommendation. This was, pivotally, balanced by being reached in a vastly more open process, explained and visible, so as to meet contemporary requests of the Assembly as

216 United Nations News Centre 'Selecting a new UN Secretary-General: a job interview in front of the whole world' (8 April 2016) <https:// news.un.org/en/story/2016/04/526302-selecting-new-un-secretary-general-job-interview-front-whole-world>.

217 United Nations News Centre 'United Nations begins informal briefings to select next Secretary-General' (12 April 2016) <https://news.un.org/en/story/2016/04/526502-united-nations-begins-informal-briefings-select-next-secretary-general>.

218 Such as a public debate which was co-hosted by The Guardian newspaper—see Julian Borger 'UN to hold secretary general job hustings for first time ever' *The Guardian* (online) 30 March 2016 <http://www.theguardian.com/world/2016/mar/30/un-general-secretary-candidates-compete-public-first-time>.

219 Thereby obviating the need to further consider question (d) above in this case.

220 United Nations News Centre 'The next UN Secretary-General: Assembly President says 'new standard of transparency' established' (15 April 2016) <https://news.un.org/en/story/2016/04/526832-next-un-secretary-general-assembly-president-says-new-standard-transparency>.

well—noting also that these results did not occur at the behest of P5 members, and were against the preference of some, such as Russia.[221]

The process still involved a notable lack of transparency in some parts of the Council's work, such as signalling decisions along the way that used the 'straw polls' approach.[222] Nonetheless, these developments can be taken as evidence of:

(a) the need for, and value of, concerted efforts and persistence in seeking more accountable processes—along the way, not just after the fact;
(b) the influence of the E10 in that pursuit, not least from the efforts of more than one E10 representative during their Presidency; and
(c) the helpful contribution from the resolve of individuals in key posts, not least individual ambassadors of E10 countries, and the President of the General Assembly for its 70th session, Denmark's Mogens Lykketoft.

Taken overall, for this cause to succeed E10 members had to aid it by rediscovering the value in process transparency, diversity of options, and informed choice, over that of mere unanimity.[223] The record shows that they did; moreover, that such influences should not be sold short as feasible means of achieving change—even in the UN.

6.3 Answering Accountability Questions

In this chapter, the accountability questions proffered are one approach to what the Council should account for. Discussion about answering them illustrates learning by critiquing Council decisions vis-à-vis *Charter* law, which opens the door to improving the legal and institutional arrangements around the Council. This was seen particularly in the aftermath of *not* making a due, and duly prompt, response to threat or use of force in international relations. Explaining Timor's plight in that way showed real and material gaps in making decisions that matter to Council effectiveness on a core *Charter* obligation, while deleterious outgrowths of Council decisions that were not

221 See above n 200.

222 Where some would say the Council 'should be ashamed by the lack of transparency'—see *Letter dated 30 May 2017 from the Permanent Representative of Finland to the United Nations addressed to the President of the Security Council* S/2017/468 (1 June 2017), 11.

223 See above Chapter 5, n 91 and associated text.

duly implemented served to underscore the manifold necessity that they should be.[224]

Harking back to the myriad matters finding their way into the Council's in-tray, as discussed in earlier chapters, additional examples show how a wider cross section of Council work is impacted upon in similar ways. Using these Council episodes to model answers to a structured series of accountability questions indicates that the Council could very well have greater capacity to be productive towards its *Charter* Functions—that is, more than might be supposed from its annual reports, the state of the permanent agenda seen in the *Summary Statement*, and the indeterminate status of many issues promoted for Council attention and/or somehow dealt with over the years.

As framed by these questions, the point of accountability is to engage that capacity of the Council in order to enhance productive capability which is brought to bear across the ambit of Council Functions. Discussion in this chapter further suggests this is better done by an ongoing process for being accountable, to progressively and proactively address the desiderata of international peace and security over time.[225]

This looks to be considerably more fertile ground than pursuing only conventional forms of legal accountability after the fact of an occasional scandal, outrage, or other spectacular failure of governance or practice.[226]

Additional case examples on Resolution 1267 and appointing a Secretary-General also show that the E10 has more capacity to be influential than may be supposed from focus on the veto as power.[227] They illustrated that, particularly when acting in concert, the E10 stands to contribute to agenda-setting and to Council outputs (decisions, determinations, recommendations, and so on), but also to be impactful is seeing those outputs brought to fruition in the outcomes that are realised over the course of time.

---

224 Whether or not Article 25 was specifically engaged. Of course, a lapse becomes a yawning gap when the Council cannot formulate action in response - on, for example, Russia's effective annexation of Crimea (see below Chapter 7, n 13).

225 One could reasonably expect that this would also then serve well when those matters arise in future, no matter the impetus for that, or how unexpectedly some such impetus emerges—as amply demonstrated by the COVID-19 pandemic presenting opportunities for procedural responses (see above Chapter 5, n 80) or attention to substantive matters, even if only as an hortatory gesture (see above Chapter 5, n 105).

226 Although doing that, even without avenues for judicial review, can still contribute to the overall picture of Council accountability, but simply will not capture some of the more obvious failures of decision-making, such as in response to Russia's action in Crimea - see below Chapter 7, n13.

227 Though of course that remains pivotal to Council decision-making capacity.

Connected to answering accountability questions, this could be seen as integral to prosecuting the largely unstipulated role of E10 members as 'representatives' of the collective of states that empowers the Council to exist. In illustrating this contribution to those necessary, but insufficient, conditions for the Council being productive—agenda-setting, reaching conclusions, and realising outcomes—the case examples further showed that E10 states have potential to play an important role in mediating and moderating legal, institutional, and practical, questions arising along the way in the Council's work, thereby removing that which may otherwise get in the way of obtaining productive results.

The E10 is placed to do this not only because these states are drawn from the collective empowering the Council via the *Charter*. Civil society actors of various stripes might provide an additional or alternative conduit to those whom the Council affects, in important part by prioritising what states may not. However, such actors cannot usually point to an established authority to speak on behalf of others (such as states are presumed to have for their citizens), or at least make a fair claim in that direction. This suggests a role for the E10 as a possible means to mediate and moderate when relevant matters are on foot—for example, to answer when, how, and how much, to engage with input from civil society in line with expectations that might be expressed by the collective of states that elects them.

In short, discussion in this chapter does not suggest that the Council is accountable to the E10 in some fashion, nor to the Assembly per se: rather, the idea is that the E10 may be the basis for a means or mechanism for making the Council more accountable in the usual course of its work. This is taken forward in the next chapter, in seeking a scheme for Council accountability that may help to break the Council habit of 'too many meetings without outcomes and too many outcomes without results'.[228]

228 *Letter dated 26 May 2016 from the Permanent Representative of Finland to the United Nations addressed to the President of the Security Council* S/2016/506 (2 June 2016), 31.

CHAPTER 7

The Council's Call: Hercules or Sisyphus?

The UN Security Council has an unparalleled place in the world, but not, so far, a compelling answer to what that is—at least, not one sufficient to instil confidence that it is doing what it is there to do under the *Charter*, if the ongoing reform debate is any sort of a guide. There is a central consideration to keep in mind, however: towards doing whatever it is there to do, the Council's power from its *Charter* powers materialises only if states implement the Council's wishes, seen when they comply with its decisions, conform to its recommendations, or otherwise carry out its directions. Discussion of case examples has highlighted a range of difficulties arising when states' support is not forthcoming enough, meaning that the Council then is not, and cannot be, effective in realising its Functions under the *Charter*—however that might be interpreted from time to time.

The importance of a normative belief that Council authority should be respected, and its directions heeded,[1] points to a leading reason for why one would want a greater measure of accountability from the Council. Sound implementation does not negate the Council's Herculean task—formidable, intractable, it is certainly not for the politically faint-hearted, but does bring prospects of a boon for all the world when international peace and security is maintained or restored. On the other hand, when opposed by principled recalcitrance, or resisted in stinting, lip-service responses, the Council's work turns Sisyphean—interminable, nugatory, a shield for international peace and security that is made flimsy as it is so much perforated by a lack of implementation or compliance.

Perceptions of the Council's legitimacy are crucial to tipping the scales from one to the other, which will very largely be the Council's call since the Council's own conduct is probably the single largest part of what weighs in the balance.

Accountability for conduct is an active ingredient in the alchemy of Council legitimacy, but assessing Council conduct is hampered by evolving institutional circumstances and the ever-shifting sands of the geopolitical landscape—a commensurately complex undertaking that will be complicated further simply by the breadth and depth of Council work. Together this means that the

1 See above (Chapter 3, n 129) and associated text.

 | DOI:10.1163/9789004444300_008

issue is not so much to assess Council conduct in a single incident, decision, or episode, as it is to have the facility to construe any or all of its work in some fashion to inform possible needs for change in aid of its productiveness.[2] In short, accountability questions raised need answers but, in the end, dialogue on accountability does not help unless conduct actually changes (if that is said to be needed).

Accordingly, this concluding chapter portrays a scheme, or model, to account for Council conduct, with an eye to the consequences from the Council's work that live long and scatter widely. It brings together questions about who the Council should heed and on what, to progressively negotiate what the Council is there to do, gauge how the Council is doing, engender action needed by answering the questions raised along the way, and then periodically take stock of what else might be warranted in the interests of Council productiveness.

This illustrates but one way of doing so, intended as confirmation of possibilities rather than some sort of prescription—but also to show that these possibilities can be found by reasonable navigation between outright naïveté on the one hand, and unduly world-weary cynicism on the other.

7.1 A Scheme for Security Council Accountability

Working through four corners of concerns on why, to whom, and for what, the Council should be accountable, and how accountability might be brought to bear on it, I have shown that obtaining a more accountable Council calls for some means or mechanism to negotiate, mediate, and moderate, the many and various views offered about what the Council does or should do, and how, including who should be heard on that and what conduct standards may be relevant.

Further, to my eye the need is to respond to the turn of geopolitical time and tide, so any such mechanism itself needs capacity to revise or adjust, add to or subtract from, such arrangements.

Models of accountability emanate from relationships between actors and pivot on the nature of those relationships. We have seen that scholars distinguish, for example, between delegation that creates a trust relationship, where accountability may serve to earn and re-earn that trust, and/or being affected

2 See, for example, above Chapter 5, n 146 and associated text.

by another actor, which may bring desire and/or capacity to participate in what that actor does, so as to have a say in how one may be affected.[3]

Though not placed in the *Charter* design so as to be supervised, per se, the Council was bestowed powers specifically, for purposes of maintaining or restoring international peace and security, and conditionally, those purposes to be pursued in keeping with principles in the *Charter*. States acting collectively to empower the Council via the *Charter* provide it with powers assertable directly over UN member states, and, less directly, power that may affect the entire world. Together this suggests, firstly, that UN member states are owed some explanation or justification for how the Council uses the powers that, collectively, they have given it, *simply because of that gift being given*; secondly, it is not irrelevant that interests of those affected by the Council may or may not coincide with those of states (or that are susceptible to being expressed by states), but that few ready means exist for reasonable participation in Council processes by those affected.[4]

The idea that the Council might usefully account for its conduct to states collectively empowering it then speaks to the reality of its productiveness: this is fundamentally a function of whether, and to what extent, states will comply with Council decisions, conform to its recommendations, or otherwise respect its legally-enabled authority by implementing its directions.

The less compliance must be coerced, the more it signals that a Council decision can be read as being perceived to be sufficiently legitimate and lawful,[5] and, I suggest, the ends sought and the means to be used are both relevant considerations. On the other hand, in the complex alchemy of legitimacy noncompliance is both an expression of a shortfall now, and a deleterious impact on future legitimacy—although the objective extent of either is unknown, and, I would suggest, unknowable.

To the latter point, one incident of noncompliance suggests an item of feedback on how a state may prefer to animate, ameliorate, or vitiate, an aspect of their *Charter* compact, and tolerating that may not be unreasonable so as

3 See, for example, above Chapter 2, n 64.

4 Whether—at all, such as was the case with the people of Trieste (see above Chapter 2, n 107 and 111, and associated text); or via the pleadings of non-government organisations, such as was significantly the case for the people of Timor (see above Chapter 4, n 10, Chapter 5, n 106), and Chapter 6, n 90 and 109, and associated text); or both, such as on Palestine where states and non-government organisations, and many others (not least the General Assembly) have been involved in articulating the case and the impact upon various actors (see above Chapter 4, n 72 to 78 inclusive, and Chapter 4, n 95, and associated text).

5 Perhaps especially where compliance or conformity is entirely voluntary, such as in contributing troops and funds for peacekeeping—see above Chapter 5, n 134 and associated text.

to accommodate immediate politics in differing opinions among sovereign states. If that is repeated, however, a pattern of noncompliant conduct emerges, further propagated if such non-compliance is emulated by others. No matter the desire behind it or reasoning for it, such a pattern stands to undermine the legal and institutional fabric of what states seek to create via the *Charter*, and may, in effect, hollow out important legal formulas—not least those by which the *Charter* design was intended to regulate the use of force in international relations, thus corroding the capacity of the *Charter* to compel a standard for states' conduct.

For the collective interests of maintaining or restoring international peace and security, the Council appears obliged to avoid such corrosion or, better still, to protect the *Charter* from it. The Council is, after all, the intended instrument for ensuring that states adhere to conduct standards under the *Charter*, for example, and feasible projects show that it can do so—to be obtained, not least, by ensuring compliance with Article 2(4), via which states eschew the threat or use of force in international relations.

On the whole, accounting for its conduct to UN member states looks to be an impactful starting point in aiding the Council's future productiveness. If that affords a measure of consideration for the views of those affected by the Council as well, so much the better.

Turning to what the Council should account for, a key consideration is how much accountability is enough: rather than exhaustively explaining or justifying each and every Council decision or action (or inaction), I have set out a modest series of accountability questions to identify and probe Council conduct,[6] in order to habituate, hone, and polish, that conduct over time and experience.

In each phase of its work,[7] the point is to establish what the Council is achieving,[8] and then relate this to how its productiveness may be addressed through being accountable.

Firstly, agenda-setting: creating an agenda aggregates procedural decisions, but it is not merely, or entirely, procedural and a function of what a decision-maker is legally-enabled to do. There is more at stake that many would see as worthwhile the Council explaining, especially with its inextricably politico-legal nature. Such choices may have substantive impacts upon myriad actors, including what arises from matters that are ignored, omitted, or delayed.[9]

6 See above Chapter 6, n 12 and 113, and associated text.

7 See discussion in the introductory section of Chapter 5.

8 Which is itself a rather complex question—see discussion in Chapter 3.2.

9 See, for example, discussion on membership applications in Chapter 4.1.

Fundamental decision-making capability of the Council thus is seen in how it selects matters to which it will attend, and then how it chooses to dispose of both matters addressed to it and those where Council attention was its own initiative. On the whole, the question is whether the Council is dealing well and promptly with managing the sphere of influence created by the ambit of its powers under the *Charter*.

Secondly, deciding: the Council has powers as an entity, something more than the sum of its parts and not only because of those parts (being the states that constitute the Council from time to time). From that the Council's functional capacity is embodied in how, and to what ends, it differentiates between what it decides and what it does not, which may arise from active or passive decisions.[10] In both procedural and substantive matters, the core is assessing how, and to where, the Council can or should lead those who are supposed to heed its directions—whether those are expressed or styled as a decision, determination, recommendation, or otherwise. This is itself the product of the efforts of and votes by all Council members—but still ascribable to the Council collectively, rather than to those members severally.[11]

Thirdly, results: the extent of its effectiveness is shown in whether those the Council would instruct will actually heed its directions when the Council gives them. The Council can be instrumental in its own productiveness by expressing directions so as to be readily and rightfully apprehended, but also in learning by experience should its directions prove to be less so.[12] This is indicated by what more the Council does to redress instances of less-than-complete implementation,[13] or to enjoin other assistance to such ends.

---

10 See, for example, above Chapter 4, n 96, Chapter 5, n 43, and Chapter 5, n 83 to 88 inclusive, and associated text.

11 See discussion in Chapter 5.2.

12 See Chapter 6.1 and 6.2.

13 Such as where these arise due to the legitimate concerns of states—see discussion of implementation of Resolution 1267 in Chapter 6.2.2, but also in the geopolitics of the day—see Chapter 6.1, for example. Of course, outright defiance is another matter entirely, as seen on Timor, where Indonesia simply did not heed the Council's directions. Much more recently, and in relation to a P5 member, the same might be said of the action by Russia on Crimea—for the initial question see *Letter dated 28 February 2014 from the Permanent Representative of Ukraine to the United Nations addressed to the President of the Security Council* S/2014/136 (28 February 2014); for background see Security Council Report 'Chronology of Events: Ukraine' Security Council Report (1 June 2020) < https://www.securitycouncilreport.org/chronology/ukraine.php>; for analysis see Thomas D Grant 'Annexation of Crimea' (2015) 109(1) *American Journal of International Law* 68; for a recent viewpoint, see Steven Pifer 'Crimea: Six years after illegal annexation' Brookings (17 March 2020) < https://www.brookings.edu/blog/order-from-chaos/2020/03/17/crimea-six-years-after-illegal-annexation/>.

Lastly, outcomes: the Council's systemic capability to do what it is there to do shows in the product of its agenda-setting and decisions, but such results may matter more or less to its Functions and the UN's Purposes depending on the eventual outcomes realised from them. Thus, capacity of the Council, to see outcomes realised that contribute to its raison d'être, hinges on who is supposed to do the implementing plus whether and how they will. In context of treaty-based international organisation, this then circles back to the question of legitimacy and authority to compel states to take meaningful action.

To such ends, an accountability framework needs a means for moderating and mediating the process, actors, and information, that it engages, centring on an actor as arbiter of what is rightful in the circumstances: by their response, they make the call on what is relevant to consider, who may consider it, and standards for that consideration.

In the absence of accountability arrangements, being arbiter of what is rightful falls to each of those who do the implementing of the Council's wishes—or not. Rather than hazard this to chance, given the myriad actors involved in seeing Council wishes come to fruition, my observations suggest that it is better to be deliberate in identifying an actor(s) likely to be an aid to, rather than a drag on, what the Council is attempting to do.[14]

The point of making such arrangements is to garner a fair reading of the situation from a suitably broad audience, but also to make being accountable a process that is conclusive and finite each time around. That is, negotiating these things is necessary, but it remains a means to other ends, so the process should not be unduly prolonged or resource-intensive relative to its results.[15]

If the form and quantum of explanations are apt, a selective approach to Council accountability thus may serve well enough if focussed on defining characteristics showing authentic outcomes and satisfactory dealings. Lawfulness is one such characteristic, at least to the extent of the *Charter* as treaty law, where even before being tested, assertions of unlawful conduct or consequences might reasonably prompt reactions that detract from Council effectiveness. The case on Resolution 1267, and slow progress in the face of states' well-founded concerns, suggests a larger question about the need to resolve such issues rather more proactively, as they arise.

Against that backdrop, development of rules is a particular clash of the naïve versus the cynical—between thinking that rules solve everything, or seeing that all the ways to avoid rules mean they solve nothing.

---

14 See above Chapter 5, n 155 and associated text.

15 As one might suggest the reform process has become—see Chapter 2.2.

From the vantage point of where related research has taken me, the inherently dialogic workings of an accountability mechanism seem set to assist by its role in navigating towards rules that order interaction and temper experience, to herald purposes being realised. In particular, rules for the interaction of actors serve to formulate an expression of expectations, by establishing parameters for the relationship against which eventualities might be tested. In short, if rules capture lessons learned from experience, they save the tears of relearning them—tears with which the *Summary Statement* might well be saturated. This is an eventuality that the Council would do well if it could avoid in the future, and which would stand to aid effectiveness accordingly.

When power is distributed unevenly, accountability is also all the more valuable for embracing the procedural in balance with the substantive: in a venue such as the Council, procedural rules carry more than their weight if they aid in diffusing and defusing power imbalances. Put in the hands of the less powerful, they are tools for obtaining an agreed standard of conduct from all comers, without needing to re-win that right at each turn.

An accountability system thus needs to collate suitably selected feedback and related explanation, and do so systematically in a systemic context so as to inform a larger discussion: whether the parties, their relationship, and its objectives, are in a satisfactory state, and how that continues with time and tide of the operating circumstances.

Then, actual accountability still needs a catalysing ingredient: the will of the actors, for some to call in the account and others to pay it. An account may spell endorsement or opprobrium, but this remains unknown until the account is rendered—albeit not entirely unknowable if the will can first be found to call the account in.

In that overall light, the *Charter* already provides at least two places with capacity to function as venues for better understanding elements of Council productiveness. These are the General Assembly and the International Court of Justice:

(a) Having plenary scope, topics for the Assembly encompass all those addressed in the Council and more, but it was not placed in the *Charter* design so as to supervise the Council. Nonetheless, it is not irrelevant that collective views from the UN membership, as gauged by decisions or actions of the Assembly, may be the closest thing obtainable to a voice for states empowering the Council and no new arrangements need be made to hear that.

(b) The International Court of Justice does not have direct capacity for the judicial review of Council decisions, or to initiate a formal interaction with it on matters of substance, but the Court can make

> authoritative comment on legal issues that attend Council work. If requested—by the Assembly, if the Council will not—such commentary could, for example, inform views on concerns about legality or lawfulness of the ends sought, or the means to be used in seeking those ends.[16]

Beyond the organisational awkwardness of this legacy of how and when the *Charter* was devised, accountability best flows with activity: even with a supervisory relationship to the Council, the opportunities for these chambers to assert it would need to be more frequent than suggested by their current workings. Put another way: if it is not based on an established and enforceable right, a system of accountability operates better as a regular and routine habit, followed with very few exceptions. The instrument by which to advance a scheme for improving Council accountability thus calls for a more continuous and accessible presence in Council processes than either chamber could provide without re-writing the *Charter*.

Accordingly, both the voice of, and the will for, Council accountability would usefully be drawn from those states who empower the Council under the *Charter*, but, in the interests of enhancing its effectiveness, this needs to be virtually omnipresent in Council activities—which suggests to me that it be found among constituent members of the Council.

Pivotally, if P5 members may have purposes other than serving the *Charter* as an expression of the collective view of the UN's membership,[17] E10 members should not.[18] The *manner* of electing the E10 means they are already conventionally seen as being elected to 'represent' the membership of the UN; the *process* of their election is an opening to further define that role to include engaging on Council accountability.

---

16 Of course, the Council itself is another such venue, if the process could somehow be dialogic (see above Chapter 2, n 59 and Chapter 3, n 106, and associated text), but such an approach seems likely to be stymied by a P5 veto, given, for example, P5 resistance to finalising the *Provisional Rules of Procedure* (see above Chapter 4, n 113 and 118, and associated text). And, as noted at the annual workshop for newly elected Council members: 'One monologue followed by another did not equal a dialogue'—see *Letter dated 14 February 2019 from the Permanent Representative of Finland to the United Nations addressed to the President of the Security Council* S/2019/144 (15 February 2019), 12. That comment was made about how the Council conducts its formal meetings, but, in my view, has clear applicability to the much larger body of practice in how the Council does it work more generally.

17 Not least, for example, Russia—see above n 13, or various P5 members—see above Chapter 6, n 190 to 195, and associated text.

18 Though each still needs to reconcile its own national interests with fulfilling its role as a Council member.

Such a process ought not, of course, seek to compel states to eschew entirely the pursuit of their national interests, but equally, they are not compelled to seek election in the first place and it is for each state to reconcile for itself any conflict or competition on this point.

The short step to the E10 becoming custodians of Council accountability thus could start from an Assembly commitment to characterising the E10's role to that effect, in an Assembly decision to set out relevant dimensions of their tasks.

Ideally, this would itself be done in a way susceptible to being accounted for in the E10 election process, and accompanied by rules for the specifics of how the E10 are to comport themselves in representing the UN collective of states in the conduct of Council business—not, I would suggest, as a monolith, but by continuing to embrace the diversity which is self-evident in that collective. Notwithstanding complexities from the ebb and flow of E10 membership, and their role being thinly characterised in or beyond the words of the *Charter*, their joint will to play this part is bolstered to the extent that the process of electing the E10 might pay heed to this point of them being on the Council.

Under Article 23(1), in the election of non-permanent members 'due regard [is to be] specially paid, in the first instance to the contribution [to] the maintenance of international peace and security and to the other purposes of the Organization, and also to equitable geographical distribution.' The E10 might thus be charged to have regard to certain aspects of Council activities, and the members electing them could then make their choice accordingly. That is, having regard *also*, rather than primarily, to geography, by making accountability a theme prevailing over successive E10 elections.

With such ends in mind, I note again that by their colloquy past E10 members have shown non-trivial capability as influential confederates, a capability which might also be bent to identifying and then answering the desiderata of conduct that should be explained or justified in the Council's work. Since such an answer is almost certainly a work in progress that would need to proceed over years, the means of answering needs its own means of functioning within the Council's work practice. Accordingly, the E10 may aid its own cause by continuing to reinvigorate rules for the conduct of Council business, all the better to broker agreement on substantive qualities desired in Council dealings and outcomes.

Capturing those politico-legal characteristics in rules, such as the Council's *Provisional Rules of Procedure* might provide, signals intent to be accountable. Such intent provides glue necessary to bind together an accountability system so that it may bear its own weight, seen in value added to the purposes at hand being in surplus over the effort that is required to be accountable. Of course, that intent must also come to fruition in due course, but documentation that merely retells, tabulates, or summarises, does not evidence such an intent. Hence, however much effort might be invested in it, documentation that lacks a principles-based critique mostly serves other purposes.

In good faith for realising *Charter* Purposes and Principles, such rules might begin with stipulating expectations for transparency and openness in Council dealings, endorse proportionate responses as a due ingredient of lawfulness, and expect clearly stated rationales which are sufficient to counter arbitrariness (or the appearance of it). These are by no means the only characteristics that would be interesting in this context—the point is that some be agreed and E10 members need to own the initiative on asserting them.

In the larger scheme of things, and the place of accountability in that scheme, the question for the E10 thus is not whether a P5 member could usurp a Council decision by veto, or speak on its own behalf on matters before the Council. Instead, the question for the E10 is what they will say and do when speaking and acting as representatives for states that collectively empower the Council via the *Charter*.

On the whole, this discussion suggests a system of Council accountability is within reach, though untold enterprise would be needed to navigate questions arising along the way and see it through to fruition. To design such a system may be unprecedented, but the approach further discussed in the following section is possible without formal *Charter* amendment—and it is hardly the only such formulation. This is so because the nub of change needed is to *identify duties and obligations of the Council's elected members*. That applies, for example, whatever their number may be, and whether or not the veto power is ever changed. Being accountable to enhance the Council's potential productiveness may, of course, still be aided further by changes to the construction of the Council under the *Charter*, and I also touch on that idea a little more in the next section.

Reform debates suggests strongly that none of this would be easily negotiated, so the best aid to facilitate and give coherence to such development is objectives for which that enterprise might aim—outcomes that would, in due course, signal to the world that accountability is alive and well and living in the Council chamber.

To illustrate further, some of those objectives are shown in the samples that I provide in the next section—set out as a 'future-scape', which is my speculation on how the UN's future might look if the will to seek it could be found. This speculation has not changed much from the original version in my doctoral thesis, finalised well prior to the COVID-19 pandemic. Accordingly I note also with great interest that, when the Council was pressed to cope with being at a pandemic epicentre in New York City,[19] the changes to work practice adopted incorporate various features which demonstrate, I would suggest, that my speculation is not so fanciful after all.

7.2 Modelling Accountability in a 'Future-scape'

Information about what an actor has done is a fundamental ingredient for understanding conduct. For a public actor, no simple answer says how much will be enough, so an accountability mechanism should also serve to help negotiate that—as illustrated in this first element of the 'future-scape'.

> *Early in 2026, the General Assembly's 80th session has on the agenda the 2025 annual report from the Security Council. A slim volume of rather less than 100 pages, it covers evaluation of both still-active matters and those concluded during the year, a synopsis of implementation of Council decisions, and a forward look at where a Council response to strategic circumstances and developing issues of international peace and security may be required.*

In its only E10 term to date (2001–2002), Singapore's advocacy for reform of the Council's annual report showcased positive leadership by an E10 member, and embodied the idea that critique and analysis of information—not mere documentation, however comprehensive that may be—remains fundamental to accountability.[20] Re-engaging with this initiative, and taking it further in a different approach to the report, would be a clear step towards being accountable.[21]

> *The focus throughout the annual report for 2025 is on explaining the priorities that the Council has pursued towards realising the purpose and principles of the Charter. Areas are identified in which UN member states could assist more, such as where further implementation of Council decisions could better support the outcomes sought.*

---

19 See above Chapter 5, n 80.

20 See UN SCOR, 4616th mtg, UN Doc S/PV.4616 (26 September 2002), for the culmination of that process.

21 Of course, that might also be achieved by instituting an additional reporting mechanism, but that quite likely would result in substantial duplication of effort if it is just another report.

In flagging steps by the Council towards being accountable, as an aid to the outcomes it can deliver, the dialogic nature of accountability means Council expectations of others are also relevant—and, I would suggest, more powerful for being set out in context of what the Council is planning to do. Analysis of the Council's activities which is fairly said to 'account' for the Council's decisions would incorporate into that dialogue concomitant responses needed from others (especially if they are somehow lacking up to that point).[22]

> *The annual report reflects emerging opportunities to contribute to international peace and security, such as those highlighted collegially by the Economic and Social Council from its interaction with non-government organisations. To be better informed about the views of states that collectively empower it, the Council invites the Assembly to express a consensus opinion on priorities for such matters, in comparison to the priorities currently being pursued by the Council.*

The Council's Herculean task is pursued with finite resources, so what is done occurs at the expense of what then cannot be done, but not just in terms of obvious issues of limited funding: time and effort dealing with conflict and post-conflict situations may be at the expense of conflict prevention; attending to a wide array of matters may come at the expense of those in its sole province; attention spread thinly over more issues is at the expense of deeper consideration on a smaller selection.[23] Undoubtedly, such calls are the Council's to make, but, equally, to achieve much at all means they are made daily, weekly, monthly, in the doing of the Council's work. As the reform debate highlights, inter alia, concern for the effectiveness of Council endeavours is unabated, and being accountable while making such calls would provide opportunity to have its choices nuanced by a perspective from those who collectively empower the Council. That cannot wait for an annual, retrospective stock-take of Council action, nor is that the best or the only means available. Of course, what the Council then does with such a perspective is, again, its call to make.

Taking another approach may also provide an opportunity for the Council to press its claims on those obliged to support it, and along the way negotiate due reminders that the Council and its subsidiary organs (including peacekeeping operations) do not have infinite capacity. As the reform debate

22 For example, see Schedler, above Chapter 2, n 59.

23 As expressed in a variety of relevant concerns from Council members—see above Chapter 5, n 111.

running over so many years demonstrates,[24] benefits from such dialogue need to be gathered formally, in a structured fashion, to actually help by appropriately informing the Council. Such debate needs a mechanism by which to be mediated and moderated, finitely and conclusively, so as to bear fruit for those concerned.[25]

> *Contributions to Council outcomes are noted in the annual report, including from troop contributing countries that are resourcing peace mission mandates, and from regional organisations performing their role under Chapter VIII of the Charter. Analysis by the Military Staff Committee critiques any gaps from a collective security perspective, and their likely impact—particularly in personnel and materiel fielded for missions.*

Taking effective action while being reliant on others for resourcing means the Council will always need to cut its cloth cleverly, but that is quite different to being forced to make clothes from nothing but scraps,[26] when the authorised level of resources could not be gleaned, promptly or at all, from UN member states.[27] Accounting for Council decisions includes acknowledging the impost of implementing them, in contrast to the downside of action which is delayed or denied—or action taken, but remaining demoralisingly ineffective.

> *Council members are now enjoined, by Assembly initiative and the Council's Rules of Procedure, to receive questions in their representative capacity, and bring them forward into formal Council meetings. To further propagate this practice, the report gives illustrative case examples from the past year. Answering questions in session is prioritised in accordance with the relative number of UN members sponsoring the question. The Council is considering a proposal for a regular 'question time', where speakers will be prioritised according to the number of UN members on whose behalf they speak.*

---

24 See Müller, above Chapter 2, n 29.

25 The prolonged activities of relevant Assembly initiatives showing how inconclusive (and, it must be said, rather less than fully productive) such a process can be otherwise—see above Chapter 2, n 30 and 32, and associated text, and above Chapter 2, n 44 and associated text.

26 As it not infrequently seems pressed to do in peacekeeping—for a specific example, see above Chapter 5, n 128.

27 On the general malaise over numbers of troops, see above Chapter 5, n 127, 128, 130, and 134, and associated text.

For the Council, being accountable turns on acknowledging that states have a right to their questions, and that, to aid its own cause, the Council should duly answer.[28] This is a means to the ends of Council productiveness, meaning that the essential accountability process of asking and answering questions still must be reasonably bounded by the contribution it makes to the purposes at hand. Article 11(3) of the *Charter* achieves this selectively on 'situations which are likely to endanger international peace and security'. Contemporary geo-politics suggests more is needed, but resources devoted to the process should always be moderated by the collective purpose it would serve. Such a facility should be no more of a podium for self-interested polemics, or for partisan filibusters, than a Council seat should be.

> *The Council's conduct standards for itself are now set out in the Council's Rules of Procedure, revised and finalised to embrace habits already shown as mutually accepted by being generally followed in practice. Taking due cognisance of concerns over evidencing proportionality and avoiding arbitrariness, these rules include a structure of considerations, agreed by the Assembly, for E10 members to use when setting out their reasons for voting in the Council. The Assembly earlier advised of what its Sixth Committee (Legal) saw as case study samples of proportionate responses potentially suitable to emulate. The Assembly's consensus view on sufficient transparency of activities, in the Council and its subsidiary organs, is being reviewed by the Military Staff Committee in terms of accommodating occasional restrictions for dealing with particularly sensitive material. The International Court of Justice gave an advisory opinion on questions raised by the Council about a fresh approach to setting out a rationale for its decisions. The advice was based on case examples chosen by the Council to illustrate concerns suggested by member states on possible impediments to implementation—such as by Council decisions appearing unlawful, or by being seen to be ambiguous or arbitrary to the extent of frustrating legal construction for effective implementation.*

Selective standards, applied in the course of conducting Council business, would aid in balancing the impetus for Council action with the reality that implementation rests on feasibility, which itself is interconnected to the lawfulness of both means used and and ends sought. Openness and transparency, proportionality and (avoiding) arbitrariness are by no means the only

28 As shown, for example, in relation to Resolution 1267—see Chapter 6.2.2.

interesting topics for standards and rules that would benefit the Council,[29] but they provide a meaningful starting point. Beyond being commonly in evidence in many and various state systems, their value is seen in what they might contribute to the Council's productiveness—by enhancing the likelihood that decisions exhibit due fidelity to the *Charter*, and to the UN's Purposes, as well as broadly in legitimating Council determinations by showing their appropriately lawful character.

By adopting conduct standards, and being seen to do so, the Council may well make more feasible any project it may have for asserting conduct standards over others. Not least, reinforcing its own legitimacy is a necessary part of asserting standards effectively over its own subsidiary organs, and, in turn, will be impacted upon by whether those standards are effective—all of which combine in the alchemy of legitimacy surrounding the Council and its work. As guardians of Council accountability, the E10 would be better equipped with a formal expression of conduct standards: putting rules in one place, publicly and unequivocally, would improve on what have been piecemeal directions to the Council's constituent members found in a miscellany of Council documents.[30] By no means least, this lowers barriers to effective participation by E10 members, giving a greater opportunity to 'hit the ground running'.[31]

> *After extended advocacy by Denmark, engaging with a broad cross-section of states involved in peacekeeping or concerned about its effectiveness, conduct standards have also now been set by the Council for all peacekeeping missions. These standards centre on concepts of 'conduct bringing disrepute on the United Nations' and 'conduct unbecoming of representing the United Nations'.*

The incidence of misconduct in peacekeeping (by uniformed personnel or civilians) may be presumed to be very low, but setting and enforcing conduct standards pays due heed to the ubiquitous *possibility* of misconduct incidents, and deleterious impacts of actual incidents on the UN's standing in the world

---

29 See discussion in Chapter 5.4. See also discussion of Resolution 2249—above Chapter 6, n 188 and 189, and associated text.

30 Though noting recent efforts of some states on this—see above Chapter 4, n 117 and 118, and associated text—but also noting again the changes (however temporary they might be) that have be made in the face of COVID-19 (see above Chapter 5, n 80).

31 See above Chapter 5, n 26 and 27, and associated text.

community.[32] The question for the UN is to what extent Member States are prepared to carry the cost to its reputation from misconduct or crime by persons associated with UN missions; the question for the Council is to what extent its effectiveness is undermined by the wider question being insufficiently answered. In relation to peacekeeping, it seems that more is needed because misconduct continues, and so far the Council does *not* appear to have done what it can, used the powers that it has, deployed tools within its grasp, and fully explored other options to obtain the results needed—namely, an appropriate standard of conduct, maintained across all missions in the Council flagship activity of peacekeeping.

> *Based on Denmark's proposal, the Assembly has specifically requested that the E10 ensure every peacekeeping mandate engages these standards, or that they not approve the mandate.*

If the Council will not reach determinations on this, perhaps the Assembly should feel obliged to do so. A formally expressed Assembly opinion might then be asserted on a more continuous basis by the concerted efforts of the E10.

> *It is a condition of a state's participation that both alleged misconduct by any persons (troops, police or civilians), and the command chain or employer response to that, is subject to a determination by the UN conduct tribunal. That determination addresses, on a balance of probabilities, whether the conduct occurred, and, if so, whether the misconduct, and/or the response made, constitutes 'conduct bringing disrepute on the United Nations' or 'conduct unbecoming of representing the United Nations'. If so, the individuals involved become persona non grata for future missions—both the individuals involved in the conduct objected to, and those making an inadequate or inappropriate response on behalf of the relevant institution. In keeping with an advisory opinion from the International Court of Justice, such exclusion is characterised as limiting a state's future discretion in choosing its personnel: it is thus an action impacting upon the state in its dealings with the UN, or a choice that the UN is entitled to make in contracting with other employers, rather than*

32 This was acknowledged in earlier reports (see particularly above Chapter 3, n 77) and is implicit in the approach more recently fostered by UN Secretary-General António Guterres—see, for example, *Special measures for protection from sexual exploitation and sexual abuse: Report of the Secretary-General* UN GAOR, 73rd sess, Agenda Item 132 and 150, UN Doc A/73/744 (14 February 2019).

an action against the individuals concerned. While asserting the right of the UN to protect its good name, and to combat impunity for acts done behind the aegis of its immunities, this approach thereby respects state sovereignty and avoids intruding on the state's rights and capacity for proceeding against individuals in keeping with the particular misconduct said to be involved.

Faced with the reality of misconduct in fact, as now regularly reported by the Secretary-General, willingness to hold the line on accountability helps,[33] especially by recognising the role of leaders in the military and bureaucratic structures under which peacekeeping proceeds. This underscores the importance of institutional or organisational failure to respond effectively to misconduct, as an issue separate to addressing the misconduct itself.

Rather than the Council, here it is the Secretary-General who has himself become Sisyphus in the full panoply of what peacekeeping now entails, at once attempting to fill the bill of troop numbers for the Council while also properly and effectively asserting conduct standards—across missions, the proliferation of states involved, and the admixture of force elements deployed (not to mention civilians and contractors).[34] The best prospects for re-rendering the Secretary-General's task to be merely Herculean may well come from the Council somehow matching its legally-enabled capacity, to mount such missions, with a corresponding mandate for conduct, to set standards and prescribe a mechanism for enforcing them. For example:

Always including one judge from a P5 state and two from E10 states to reflect the makeup of the Council, tribunal panels for uniformed personnel are completed by a judge from the state providing the person against whom misconduct is alleged, plus one from the state in which the alleged misconduct is said to have taken place.

---

33 Such as would be consistent with the more recent policy approach—see, for example, *Special measures for protection from sexual exploitation and sexual abuse: a new approach—Report of the Secretary-General* UN GAOR, 71st sess, Agenda Items 134, 139 and 149, UN Doc A/71/818 (28 February 2017), 16. See also progress, and many ongoing practical challenges, reported in *Special measures for protection from sexual exploitation and sexual abuse: Report of the Secretary-General* UN GAOR, 73rd sess, Agenda Item 132 and 150, UN Doc A/73/744 (14 February 2019); *Special measures for protection from sexual exploitation and sexual abuse: Report of the Secretary-General* UN GAOR, 74th sess, Agenda Item 129 and 148, UN Doc A/74/705 (17 February 2020).

34 Ibid, Annex v. See also Bowett, above Chapter 3, n 73, and associated text.

This is an interesting juncture at which the reality of the legal and political facets of Council work resurface, in light of whether and how international organisations engage with international law.[35] The UN undoubtedly has capacity to assert its requirements in the international legal order, but there is a long way to go before this will be of equal standing with that of states who desire to maintain the extent of their own sovereign discretion. So this becomes a case example where the Council getting a productive result for the UN may need to embrace national interests and politics to an extent, but I suggest this can be done in a measured way—allowing it to both preserve the benefits of an informed, collective critique, while also defraying unhelpful, unproductive, or ill-informed, feedback from individual states.

Some may be a little uncomfortable with allowing for national interests in this way, as indeed I am, but the point is that it might—not unreasonably—be done in the foreseeable future by setting out the UN's idiosyncratic approach to such things, in a way that is more likely to be enforceable. The point is to afford, by formally and openly stipulating it, a reasonable but balanced presence for states in matters of international cooperation because it affects their citizen (by a person possibly becoming *persona non grata* in UN circles). I suggest, in effect, that this can be obtained by emulating the approach to appointing judges ad hoc to the International Court of Justice.

> *Conduct tribunals are convened promptly by taking three judges from the primary pool—made up of one appointed by each Council member for a five year term. The others are taken from the additional pool, for which up to three judges from a 'provider' state are nominated on standby whenever it fields personnel in a peacekeeping mission, as are up to three from a 'host' state when it agrees to having a Council mandated peacekeeping mission, or peacekeeping mission support activity, conducted in its territory. States have discretion to nominate a mix of civilian and military judges according to their national approach to maintaining order in, and control over, their armed forces and police. In cases to date, some 'host' states have chosen to nominate a judge from the primary Council pool when circumstances prevented their national judges from being available to join the additional pool. Anticipating future challenges, on the Council's request the International Court of Justice has also advised on a proposed process for making a neutral appointment if the territory in question were not to be under the effective control of any state.*

35 See above Chapter 1, n 20, 21, and 22, and associated text.

This sketch of one institutional approach to answering misconduct is admittedly speculative, but still shows that forming the intent to overcome impunity, and do so quite directly, stands to be a powerful catalyst. Regardless of the detailed design of, or arrangements for, such a mechanism (and the extent to which one would choose to accommodate politics and national interests in that), the idea is to carry forward what is begun by obliging E10 members to agree mandates for peacekeeping only if they are satisfied that conduct issues are being suitably addressed as an unproductive, counter-productive, or otherwise deleterious, element of the Council's outcomes.

In short, if the states empowering the Council via the *Charter* are unsatisfied with its progress on resolving this issue, then perhaps the onus reverts to them—in particular, to elect 'representatives' based on specific expectations expressed to show that they should address it otherwise.

Past Council initiatives show that there is ample scope for establishing new mechanisms, limited less by the *Charter* per se and more by the policy-making will of the Council. A little creativity in how to frame a response from the Council would thus open a door to countering deleterious impacts on perceptions of the Council's productiveness, which would then behove the Assembly to inspire the E10 to walk through it.

> *If proven against a uniformed peacekeeper, misconduct is also assessed by the tribunal against the threshold level established by the Council for 'systemic' misconduct, in contrast to 'occasional' or 'recurring' misconduct that is associated with a state. This incorporates review of other cases associated with that state for the previous five years, along with the response in each case. If that threshold is breached, the assessment is reviewed by the Military Staff Committee. If confirmed as 'systemic', that state is suspended from all participation in fielding uniformed personnel for Council mandated missions, until the Council accepts advice from the Secretary-General that appropriate remedial steps are in effect. The Secretary-General is considering a parallel mechanism for civilian personnel.*

There is no doubt that bad apples sooner or later turn up in every conduct barrel in the world. The first step to an effective institutional response is genuinely acknowledging that this is so, and not over-reacting to an isolated incident; the next is not under-reacting to situations in which there are systemic or structural impedimenta in evidence—such as organisational responses that dissuade reporting, or that could be perceived as ignoring or condoning such conduct.[36] Importantly, what is done at the Council's behest is relevant to perceptions of its productiveness, so if it cannot intervene directly to overcome impunity which detracts from that productiveness, then perhaps it should find a way to do so indirectly. Various solutions might achieve this with uniformity and robustness across missions, and also without humiliating those very many peacekeepers whose conduct is untarnished. What is certain, however, is that more is needed than a Council resolution that is largely unenforceable, approving missions that cause serious harm to people they are intended to help, or allowing an inadequate response to itself further sully the name of the UN.[37]

In the end, the Council cannot expect to obviate all misconduct, but it can deploy the powers that it has to ensure that more effective steps are taken to deter conduct that works against the Council being as productive as it might otherwise be.

> *In 2025, much of the documentary compendium of yesteryear's annual report has been overtaken by complementary procedures, which both facilitate, and report on, prompt conclusion of Council business. Administrative matters, for example, are finalised out of Council session by 'circulating resolutions', which are then validated for the record at an open Council meeting regularly reserved for that purpose. That session covers feedback on effectiveness and efficiency of administrative processes, decisions in matters on which the Council has previously mandated a process—such as on nominations for the 'Captain Mbaye Diagne Medal for Exceptional Courage'—and*

36 See above Chapter 3, n 78; see also above Chapter 3, n 76—noting, again, initiatives of Secretary-General António Guterres go in this direction (see above n 33). Of course, beyond much-trammelled territory in addressing the general problem of sexual misconduct in armed forces, the passage of time and experiences of the wider community in many countries now means that there are significant fresh opportunities to learn—from the travails of other institutions that, for example, have failed to respond adequately to the abuse of children, where that failure is itself sometimes characterised as a further 'institutional abuse' of children. In addition to the many public reports on such matters, see, for example, Johanna Sköld 'Historical Abuse—A Contemporary Issue: Compiling Inquiries into Abuse and Neglect of Children in Out-of-Home Care Worldwide' (2013) 14(1) *Journal of Scandinavian Studies in Criminology and Crime Prevention* 5; Kathleen Daly 'Conceptualising Responses to Institutional Abuse' (2014) 26(1) *Current Issues in Criminal Justice* 5; Jodi Death 'Bad Apples, Bad Barrel: Exploring Institutional Responses to Child Sexual Abuse by Catholic Clergy in Australia' (2015) 4(2) *International Journal for Crime, Justice and Social Democracy* 94; Penny Crofts 'Criminalising Institutional Failures to Prevent, Identify or React to Child Sexual Abuse' (2017) 6(3) *International Journal for Crime, Justice and Social Democracy* 104.

37 See above Chapter 2, n 84, 97, and 98, Chapter 3, n 75 to 78 inclusive, and above n 32 and 33, and associated text.

follow up on the disposition of complaints about conduct on peacekeeping missions.

Handling volumes of correspondence and non-strategic decisions, and doing so in a timely fashion without undue impost on juggling the agenda, is an essential capability for any decision-maker.[38] As for other decision-making bodies, openness in this by the Council has its own accountability role in enfranchising those represented—not least because by being openly accountable for prosaic matters, a decision-making body may more generally build confidence in its work.[39]

In composing the Council's agenda, position papers from, and perspectives expressed by, a group of at least 25 states, not counting members of the Council, are given priority as correspondence with the Council. Feedback on that approach was taken in the first routine administration meeting of the Council in 2026, informing some further fine-tuning to unfold in the year ahead. Readily accessible ongoing updates confirm the status of items submitted to the Council as 'placed on the agenda', 'awaiting consideration', 're-directed' (*such as to another UN agency or an external organisation*)*, or 'answered'* (*such as when the Council declines to accept carriage of the matter, and advises the correspondent to that effect*).

Beyond organising its agenda to create opportunities for the Council to be effective,[40] a first step in eliciting their cooperation is engaging in dialogue with interested parties—a basic signal of the regard accorded to others by the Council. Openness about where it is placed in its deliberations is a courtesy allowing others to organise and plan their own part, so that action may be prompt and effective once the Council decides a way forward. Another such signal is being transparent about definite answers to questions raised in correspondence. This is a useful part of explaining the Council's approach to its

---

38 See, for example, see above Chapter 5, n 46 and 80, and associated text, as well as above n 19 in relation to the COVID-19 pandemic.

39 For example, see comments on lack of visibility in the UN force generation process—above Chapter 5, n 124 and 127—which suggest that closed dealing in not necessarily or entirely helpful in the difficult process of obtaining enough voluntary contributions of peacekeeping troops.

40 See discussion in Chapter 5.1.

work in a systematic fashion, and flagging this openly could provide salutary feedback for many parts of its organisational ecosystem.[41]

> *Correspondence asserting an emergency situation and the need for urgent Council attention is circulated immediately to Council members, for a decision on its priority at the next meeting as an item under 'any other business'. If none is scheduled within 24 hours, an additional meeting is convened in that period to decide its priority.*

With the best will in the world, emergencies still arise unexpectedly, as contemplated by the world view embodied in the *Charter*—and as seen often in more than 70 years of geopolitical machinations since it was drafted. Well-rehearsed procedure should mean the first step, of assessing the asserted emergency, is taken without delay—but, crucially, also without exception.

Perhaps the freshly-active Military Staff Committee is beginning to go in this direction,[42] but questions for the Council—and, I suggest, the E10 at the Assembly's behest—are around the cost of responding. Not the material cost, but the geopolitical damage from a litany of too little, too late in, for example, unsuccessful or highly compromised missions.

> *The Summary Statement is now organised by these priorities, where 'awaiting consideration' means that initial or further consideration is expected within six to twelve weeks. That part of the Summary Statement list is known as the 'long agenda', while the 'short agenda' embodies the immediate work programme, confirming those items 'placed on the agenda' for active consideration at a meeting scheduled within two to six weeks. New matters usually go on the long agenda as 'awaiting consideration', unless the President considers they will be disposed of as 'answered' or 're-directed'. Monthly, a summary of the latter items is circulated to Council members, to ensure they have no objection to the answer or redirection. If five constituent members of Council object, the matter is discussed at an administrative meeting and a formal vote taken, either promoting it onto the 'awaiting consideration' list or confirming it may be closed by an administrative response.*

In essence, this sketch of just one possible approach embodies the will to make, and be seen to make, procedural decisions in an accountable way.[43] More than

---

41 As suggested by discussion in Chapter 5.2 and 5.3

42 See above Chapter 3, n 49 and associated text.

43 See Chapter 5.1.

recommending a specific approach, this formulation of agenda management is intended to indicate that, as part of the dialogic process of accountability, an overt system is not impossible to devise nor necessarily a significant impost on those who will use it.

> *The Security Council's annual report now includes particular note of matters on the long agenda to which the Council does not attend within a year. The Assembly is invited to comment on the priority of these matters, relative to others on the long agenda, and to collectively recommend alternative action or adjusted priorities. The Assembly has made a variety of recommendations since this step was instituted—some that no further action was necessary; others that the actors involved should seek assistance from another organ of the UN or from a regional organisation with relevant capacity; and a few where there was an opportunity for a specialist agency, including selected non-government organisations, to gather information to better contextualise the options for proceeding.*

It remains that the Assembly has a vital role to play in the overall scheme of maintaining or restoring international peace and security—not as a chamber placed to supervise the Council, but as a relevant venue in which the temperature of the UN's membership can reasonably be taken, to flag the view of those collectively empowering the Council.

For their mutual part in its accountability, states may aid the Council by casting a wider net on inputs to its deliberative process,[44] but also using such inputs judiciously to explain their preferences for Council action or activities (by their shared judgement on relative priorities of matters competing for Council attention, for example).[45]

The active ingredient in this accountability dialogue comes from combining a concerted approach and a collective opinion: little will be added by debate that, for example, is all heat and no light and cannot be brought to a fruitful conclusion,[46] or degenerates into no more than an unvarnished pursuit

---

44 For example, by: seeking advice on issues of wider concern—see Chesterman, above Chapter 1, n 82, or above Chapter 6, n 161 (the report mentioned); or proactively pursuing themes of practical concern—see generally discussion of Resolution 1267 in Chapter 6.2.2.

45 As shown in relation to seeking a replacement for Ban Ki-moon—see above Chapter 6, n 207 and associated text.

46 See generally Chapter 2.2. See also discussion of Resolution 2249, for example—above Chapter 6, n 188 and 189, and associated text, or the Council's failure to support the Secretary-General's call for a global ceasefire amid the COVID-19 pandemic—see above

of base political advantage,[47] or provides an opening for individual states to take up Council time and effort against the express wishes of the broader UN membership.[48]

> *On general matters put before the Council, a publishing cycle for agenda papers makes available a synopsis on each substantive matter receiving active consideration by the Council. This includes peacekeeping mission options and estimates of associated troop contributions from the Military Staff Committee. UN members have a standing invitation to respond, to peruse position papers from other states' delegations, and to make contributions and submissions from their own perspective.*

The bulk of Council business proceeds in a (relatively) mundane fashion, and likely would be better served if more of its arrangements were designed with that in mind. Even for UN peacekeeping, it is disingenuous to continue arguing that feasibility is improved by keeping planning entirely secret. Unless one would suggest Article 43 might rise from the grave (and I, for one, am not so brave), most operations simply cannot proceed without involvement from multiple states. In fact, this is most often dozens and dozens of states—but force generation can (and, many would suggest, should) be approached separately from force deployment. Short term mandates, and a constant program of renewals, may be intended to signal missions are finite and temporary. The fact of routine renewals over years, and not infrequently decades, militates against the effectiveness of this as a political signal or as an organisational discipline. If force generation for peacekeeping is instead an open and strategically oriented process, states will have the opportunity to stand ready with troops and thereby assist the likelihood of timely deployments.

Of course, more peacekeepers may be readied than turn out to be needed (as may also have been the case in force generation under Article 43 agreements, which was designed to occur in advance of a need). That would, however, more likely be a cause for celebration than complaint.[49]

Chapter 5, n 105, or its ineffectiveness on a material matter of international law—Russia's annexation of Crimea—see above n 13.

47 Such as suggested by less optimistic assessments of the reform process—for example, see above Chapter 2, n 40.

48 Which would be unfortunately consistent with, on a wider front, the implications of those items that are so very long lived on the *Summary Statement* (albeit, perhaps, in hibernation)—see above Chapter 5, n 36 to 42 inclusive, and associated text.

49 See above Chapter 5, n 126, and Chapter 3, n 62 to 71 inclusive, and associated text.

> *Following debate on the 2025 report, the Assembly is expected to give priority attention to two significant developments affecting E10 elections. The first arises from formal advice to the Assembly that a new grouping of states wishes to break away from long-standing geographical groupings. This is set to have a profound impact on numbers in, and seats allocated to, geographical groupings.*

This example is, firstly, a reminder that although the wheels of the UN grind at a glacial pace, and seem to go inexorably in an established direction, seismic shifts are still never out of contention—even in relation to the Security Council.

> *Approaching 40 states, each with a population of no more than circa one million, the group has mutually acknowledged that their capacity for E10 membership is often subject to some steep resource barriers—in being elected and, more so, in holding office. Their compact is to not seek election in their individual right for the next ten years; instead they plan to contribute to international peace and security by supporting only those E10 candidates that will consult formally with them—regularly, as a group—and seed their views into Council decision-making. While the Assembly as a whole determines how to accommodate this new grouping, the states involved are considering their approach to choosing a representative—a like-state, meaning they will back one of their own number, or a like-minded state, meaning they will back a larger state perceived to be committed to relevant ideas. Current indications very strongly favour the latter approach, with Switzerland and other members of the Accountability, Coherence and Transparency Group mooted as possibilities.*

Secondly, the idea of departing from current Assembly practice is intended to re-engage with the *Charter* view that gives weight, over geography, to 'the contribution of Members of the United Nations to the maintenance of international peace and security' and other organisational purposes. In future, the question will be whether geography really has a contemporary role to play, if it even had a genuine benefit to begin with, beyond mere convenience.

There is also more to this than smaller states being ardent defenders of international law and the global order that it promises, although that is of abiding importance.[50] Even as UN members urge the P5 to re-think their approach to

50 See, for example, discussion in Adam Lupel and Lauri Mälksoo *A Necessary Voice: Small States, International Law and the UN Security Council* (International Peace Institute, April

the use of the veto, or to address other realities of their privileged position on the Council, it behoves them to also lead the way by addressing the effectiveness of the Assembly's contribution to the fabric of maintaining international peace and security. The way in which the Assembly is constructed leaves open the opportunity for even small states, by weight of numbers in the Assembly, to be quite influential in this—I suggest this will be all the greater if they share an objective to aspire to and to thus guide diplomacy conducted with relatively scare resources (in comparison to the P5, for example, or richer and more populous members of the E10).

The second development arises from the Working Group and intergovernmental negotiations under the Assembly's Decision 62/557 in September 2008. With some of the P5 still set against changing the veto power, and nothing achieved on voluntary renunciation of it, the breakthrough proposal was that five new-style elected seats be added to the Council. One is to be filled each year for a term of five years, with the possibility of being immediately re-elected. To make the transition over the first cycle of five years, as each seat is added to the Council one vote will be added to the majority required for a Council decision—going to 10 votes out of 16 initially, progressively up to 14 votes out of 20 when fully implemented. This proposal succeeded in large part by addressing the political imperative to avoid new seats becoming captive to named states, given how changing geopolitical fortunes play out over time and in an evolving organisational ecosystem. It also addressed a pragmatic need for greater continuity and preservation of a body of expertise among non-permanent members when faced with the ever more complex work of the Council. Both are duly balanced against the desire to ensure such representatives justify the trust placed in them when acting on behalf of other states, and that such a powerful position be re-earned regularly, with credentials to such ends being re-validated in that process. These considerations are now the core of an election process focussing on performance of duties and obligations identified for the role of all elected members, regardless of the length of their term. Several states are expected to make a strong case for taking one of the new seats based on Article 23(1)—evidencing their contribution to international peace and security by, amongst other things, their voting record in previous terms of office, troop contributions unmarred by patterns of misconduct, achievements in

2019). The authors provide illustrative examples of successful small state-led initiatives achieving material outcomes in the Council.

representing concerns of states not on the Council, and success in advocacy to ensure that the Council observes the spirit as well as the letter of its own conduct standards.

To answer the epithet of 'unrepresentative' there are few alternatives to expanding the Council, which would necessitate amending the *Charter*. But that is not the end of that story.

Unless the conduct of Council members is better regulated, enlarging the Council amounts to doing more of the same anyway, and so would be unlikely to deliver a more effective Council.[51] Indeed, a larger Council may well work to the contrary—with more parties involved in negotiating each Council decision, for example. It is also self-defeating to continue pursuing related proposals that are predicated on either removing, or extending, the veto.[52]

Taken together, this speculation tells a different story: that if the first tool for accountability of the Council is the voices of the E10—or even an E15—better they be elected in contemplation of those voices genuinely being raised on behalf of the UN's membership, and with formal recognition of the idea that there is more to their responsibilities than pursuit of national interests.[53] Then, reshaping election processes to be oriented to what they are expected to do when holding elected office is part of the means by which an omnipresent monitor of Council productiveness, and accountability towards enhancing that, might be achieved.

That would fundamentally shift the debate about how many elected members the Council should have, or how long they ought to be allowed to serve. In particular, states seeking re-election in future would be required to formally demonstrate how they showed respect for the assigned duties and

51 In the terms discussed at the annual workshop for newly elected Council members: 'Non-permanent members needed to remember why the larger membership had elected them in the first place'—see *Letter dated 14 February 2019 from the Permanent Representative of Finland to the United Nations addressed to the President of the Security Council* S/2019/144 (15 February 2019), 18. As will have been apparent in earlier discussion, I suggest this would be greatly assisted by being subject to rules about what they may, might, or must, consider in casting their votes, for example, or having some conduct standards to meet in how they 'represent' the wider membership of the UN.

52 If decades of debate on *Charter* reform is any sort of indication—see discussion in Chapter 2.2.

53 As the E10 showed that they could do on, for example, ensuring implementing Resolution 1267 and appointing the next Secretary General, for example—see discussion in Chapter 6.2.2 and 6.2.3.

responsibilities when previously in office—all the more crucial if *Charter* change proved to be possible in making terms longer and/or 'renewable' (that is, immediate re-election would be possible). Such obligations first need to be determined and this could be done by Assembly decisions.[54]

Standards for E10 conduct may not bind P5 members without their agreement, and that may not be readily forthcoming—but one might well wonder to what extent P5 states will expend political capital to argue against the relevance and utility of such standards to their decision-making, when application of those standards is evidenced in the conduct of their non-permanent colleagues.

> *Debate in the Assembly will then turn to where Assembly members might best impact the work of the Council, whether elected to the Council or not. For example, Singapore has made its mark as 'penholder for penholding'. Having campaigned successfully for election on the idea that every E10 member should take the lead on some substantive issues, and that penholding provides a gateway to doing that, during its second ever Council term Singapore made good on the idea by coordinating involvement of all the E10. Similarly, the penholder for finalising Rules of Procedure for the Council, New Zealand, is widely anticipated to be returning for another E10 term. Well regarded as prime mover for prompt and successful conclusion of that project, New Zealand is a strong contender to lead the periodic review of the Rules, with this iteration slated to involve the adoption of substantive standards for voting in the Council by elected members. As penholder on the humanitarian track of several Council agenda items, E10 member Jordan has been sharing its experiences on past projects to recruit interest from like-minded states—those who might do more to help craft novel approaches to persistent humanitarian fallout from crisis situations, even when not serving as an E10 member. Uruguay has completed its work as penholder on review of tribunal processes for peacekeeping, by framing three case studies to be considered by the International Court of Justice for advice on further improving the arrangements. The initiative to hold open, topical consultations on this with troop contributing countries was warmly welcomed, especially by those states who have yet to serve on the Council.*

54 Of course, should the unlikely day come when the UN is morphed into a world government, that effort might well pay an extra dividend.

Penholding is a relatively recent work practice in Council, and a role the P5 still needs more 'encouragement' to share with the E10.[55] Otherwise, the P5 are left as the de facto arbiters of the Council's direction, unless and until the E10 marshals its presence to provide a modicum of leadership in the business coming before the Council. Further engendering E10 penholding is an example of creating the opportunities to do that. This is well-known as a sore point in Council dynamics,[56] and E10 intentions to follow through on this might be read from recent initiatives.[57] That much said, small to medium states have already been an interesting influence on major issues by this means—showing a cross section of states might be influential in shaping the Council's work,[58] especially by focus on selected issues combined with the political will to take the lead.[59]

---

55 See above Chapter 5, n 162; see also above Chapter 5, n 80.

56 Again receiving attention at the annual workshop for newly elected Council members in 2018—see *Letter dated 14 February 2019 from the Permanent Representative of Finland to the United Nations addressed to the President of the Security Council* S/2019/144 (15 February 2019), 11—where it was noted that in terms of working methods 'the most contentious issues continued to relate to who should hold the pen and chair subsidiary bodies', for example, and that 'who held the pen remained a sensitive matter [and] there should be greater clarity on the rules' (ibid, 13), moreover that 'delegations should be able to take the pen without humiliation or opposition' (ibid).

57 In small things and in large. See, for example:
   a) Julian Borger 'Curtains opened on UN security council for first time since attack on Che Guevara' *The Guardian* (online) 5 April 2019 <https://www.theguardian.com/world/2019/apr/04/un-security-council-curtains-germany-che-guevara>, reporting on an initiative of Germany in the capacity of President of the Security Council for April 2019; and
   b) *Letter dated 13 November 2018 from the representatives of Belgium, the Plurinational State of Bolivia, Côte d'Ivoire, the Dominican Republic, Equatorial Guinea, Ethiopia, Germany, Indonesia, Kazakhstan, Kuwait, the Netherlands, Peru, Poland, South Africa and Sweden to the United Nations addressed to the President of the Security Council* S/2018/1024 (15 November 2018), which addresses a collective initiative of all serving and incoming E10 members (15 states in total), wherein they formally expressed a renewed call for 'equal distribution of work among all members of the Security Council', including specifically in relation to E10 members being more involved in penholding and in chairing subsidiary bodies.

58 Which would be an extension of the thought leadership and agenda-shaping initiatives that a variety of E10 members took in relation to, for example, Resolution 1267—see Chapter 6.2.2, or Resolution 2504—see above Chapter 6, n 190 to 195, and associated text.

59 Of which, the efforts of Australia, Jordan, and Luxembourg on humanitarian access to the Syria people are a very clear example in recent times. See above Chapter 5, n 163 to 170 inclusive, and associated text. See also above n 50 and 56, (including the examples discussed therein).

On the whole, this 'future-scape' may lean towards optimism as far as asking the Council to be the architect of its own regulation, and asking the Assembly to collate and direct its collective will in a way seen only occasionally over the course of UN history. Recent achievements of E10 members give reason to believe that this speculative and perhaps somewhat utopian 'future-scape' is not, however, unduly naïve or an entirely forlorn hope. Rather it is one where at least a 'judicious reformer',[60] who holds back from glum cynicism, could imagine the E10 (or the E15, perhaps) being activated as a genuine voice of those they are already said to 'represent'. This would be achieved, in important part, by holding those states to their task as 'representatives' when this is expressed as duties or obligations associated with holding E10 office.

The tipping point towards owning a more accountable way of doing the Council's business thus is acknowledging explanations are owed when, and simply because, the Council has significant powers and potentially wields vast power over all the world—but, in practice, only if allowed to do so by those empowering it via the *Charter*.

7.3 Navigating between Naïveté and Cynicism

A key premise in the research behind this book is two-fold: that the Purposes and Principles of the *Charter* can be better served by a more productive Security Council, and that such ends can be sought through a more accountable Council without resort to *Charter* reform.

Accordingly, I have purposefully circumnavigated other projects with similar interests—including instituting judicial review of Council decisions (as a right of states or perhaps also accessible by certain non-state actors), for example, or changing the decision rights of Council members (particularly the veto).

One reason for this approach is that these are certainly important possibilities, but *Charter* reform does not yet appear to be in prospect. Crucially, however, another reason is that until conduct standards are established, such projects still have genuine challenges to face in finding their underpinnings—particularly in relation to what it is that the Council should account for. Without such conduct standards, it is not certain, for example, that a court would have a sufficient basis on which to proceed, whoever might bring a cause to it.

This also has implications for suggestions about increasing the number of Council seats, as it does not follow that a larger Council is more

60 See Cassese, above Chapter 1, n 5, xvii.

'representative'—beyond the arithmetic fact of its size being made more proportional to the present size of the UN's membership. Instead, I have taken it that a more 'representative' Council is better evidenced in how its members do their work—including by embracing the need to explain or justify the Council's conduct against agreed standards. Important aspects of this include what Council members may, might, or must, consider in doing its work, or how some or all Council members are otherwise entitled or obliged in a 'representative' capacity. Put another way, the idea of 'representative' lacks form without identified duties and obligations, but when those are given, they become a vector via which to account for conduct—as true around the Council as elsewhere.

Conceptualising the Council as exercising public power, to seek standards for its conduct, other projects draw lessons and analogies from the accountabilities of government, or governance when portrayed as a close substitute. Again, these are important possibilities, but I would observe that what the Council is supposed to do, and how, pivots on the manifold and manifest significance of Council power seen in its capacity to affect others—distinct from, and possibly independent of, the Council's specific nature and thus the precise nature of the power that it may wield.

In that overall light, one question I have asked is how legal accountability, though pursued outside a court, might assist.

From a 'bare bones' meaning of accountability—to explain or justify conduct—the point of orienting it to the legal status and institutional stature of the Council was that I sought ways to enhance those arrangements around the Council. Thus my aim for Council accountability is to consider the extent to which it is meeting, or is even equipped to meet, its Functions for maintaining international peace and security under the *Charter*, and, as a principal organ, its general duty to keep faith with the *Charter* to aid both in realising that design of the UN as a legal person, and in the pursuit of its organisational Purposes.

To such ends, the Council is a social construct created with particular functions: it is a decision-making body so its contribution is metered according to whether and how it deliberates on, and concludes, the decisions that are central to its raison d'être. When no other institution is so empowered, this may create an obligation to make those decisions. In any case, the extent to which decisions that it does make are then carried out is the nub of the Council's real capacity for delivering on the responsibilities assigned to it. What follows on from Council decisions is crucial in this, because not every decision unfolds in practice as it was anticipated to do so when planning, and doing good cannot be entirely divorced from the possibility of causing harm anyhow.

In a prevailing organisational ecosystem, a decision-maker's outputs (expressed as determinations, decisions, recommendations, directions, and so on) provide leadership to others with their own contribution to make. Placed to lead the way, a decision-maker doing nothing may add to harms that, by doing something, it could have diminished or avoided (though the reverse might also be true). Either way, to decide what matters to international peace and security, and have its decisions matter by being effective, the Council thus needs an evolving suite of capabilities and capacities: the Council needs to equip itself in light of both its *Charter* Functions and the outcomes of its work in the fluid environment of geopolitics. This stands to foster its ability to function under the *Charter* design and imperfections that it has, but also accords with what to some would be the fundamental need for the UN, as a legal person, to obtain the ways and means to meet its legal obligations—and to do so both now and in the face of exigencies in changing circumstances.

To aid that evolution, I identified a structured series of accountability questions that would reveal the Council's progress on a matter put before it, and rehearsed their application in illustrative case examples. As a future habit of the Council, such assessments may be informative even if they were made in a bare, formalist fashion, and only in light of established legal obligations. However, my view is different and two-fold: it seems that such assessments are better made in contemplation of qualities that states empowering the Council find to be valuable in its decisions, and that states' perceptions of Council legitimacy would likely embrace standards that are not limited to concrete legal obligations. That is, my view acknowledges that the Council was bestowed rights to make legally binding decisions, but states are volunteers in committing to the *Charter* and do not mortgage their sovereignty to its design, so they retain an independent interest in what the Council does, how, and how well.

Of course, this also points to the reality that identifying those qualities or standards for Council conduct is itself a question resistant to formal resolution (as shown in reform discourse around the Council), so my further conclusion is that identifying such qualities is also likely to be better negotiated progressively, as part of an accountability process. That is, part of the practicality of any suggestion is the chances of it being digestible in the relevant geopolitical setting, where largely unproductive reform efforts, but recent progress in changing Council work practice, together suggest that change is more amenable in smaller steps—but also that being seen to take those small steps is an indispensable and salutary part of obtaining the major change wanted in the larger scheme of things.

Again, to my eye this suggests that if conduct standards are articulated, tested, and polished, in the course of Council work, and the process of accounting for that, the hurdle to their formal adoption may be lowered, particularly if what E10 initiatives have achieved in recent times provides a reasonable indication.

My approach prioritises accounting for things that only the Council may do, or for which only the Council has been granted powers, though it anticipates the Council should address—in some fashion or another—all the matters sent its way. This certainly puts at the top of the agenda those activities directly and proximately linked to maintaining or restoring international peace and security, most especially when regulating the threat or use of force in international relations. Equally, that does not exclude other matters where the Council might plausibly take an interest before a crisis develops, or those linked via multiple connections or steps, leaving them less proximate to international peace and security. Done well, agenda-setting means that those matters which cannot, and should not, be put at the top of the list still need not fall to the floor as detritus from an overburdened Council. This more suggests the Council's agenda itself needs attention as a distinct accountability—that is, as an integral part of ongoing development of Council working methods to ensure its effectiveness.

As do other decision-making bodies, the Council remains susceptible to acquiring unhelpful habits when it is not pressed to explain itself in line with relevant standards, to those others to whom it is connected via rules that provide such standards. On the other hand, a routine of general conformity with prevailing rules—still allowing for interpretive differences and an occasional bit of wriggle room—is the basis for the legitimacy of a decision-making body, because it is part of, and enabled by, the rules system which it inhabits—especially if it has a leadership role as an author of such rules.

Beyond lawfulness of its decisions in the legal order of which it is a part, Council legitimacy thus also needs to satisfy expectations that others have some right to harbour. Whether arising from delegation or representation, or from some admixture, these need to be acknowledged and addressed towards maintaining a sufficiently legitimate standing of the Council. Expectations that member states have about the Council will, most immediately, remain a consideration in whether they respond, willingly or well, to the Council's calls to action.

Information is a necessity for accountability, so such expectations usually begin with transparency and openness. However, I caution against formalistic responses on those because, for example, recording a plethora of facts without critique just becomes part of a debate on the Council's endeavours, rather than an answer to explain or justify its outputs and outcomes.

Noting its idiosyncratic placing in the international legal order, relevant actors quite likely also share expectations that the Council should demonstrate proportionality in its decisions, and evidence good faith and respect for the rule of law in all that it does. Though not the only characteristics that may be interesting in aiding Council productiveness, these are examples of some that could become standards against which Council conduct is explained—where satisfactory explanations engender approbation and enhance perceptions of Council legitimacy that can, in their turn, be put to work in implementing Council projects, thus showing them to be feasible.

How such characteristics are agreed as relevant to the Council also speaks to the greater challenge—that legitimacy does not flow from an introspective monologue on how things are going. Thus, Council review of its own productiveness will not suffice in lieu of an accountability dialogue that encompasses an external perspective on how effective the Council has been.

It is open to the Council to decide on whether and how to recognise some external actor for such purposes. If the Council will not, in its collective voice, recognise such an external actor (not least, but not only, due to a veto of a related proposal) then this may still be obtained to some degree by an Assembly decision—that is, by UN member states acting collectively to force such a voice into the Council's way of working. I have modelled this element here as being the E10, because they are already said to be 'representatives' of those empowering the Council, and might well become so in their conduct even without *Charter* reform. That conduct might also develop further by embracing a capacity to engage with other voices raised on behalf of those affected by the Council.

Further in that direction: as a compact between states, established at a certain time and under certain conditions, the *Charter* has not benefitted much from adjustments to legal arrangements around the Council, such as to reflect transitions of geopolitics arising from decolonisation, the disintegration of the USSR, or rearrangement of national economic fortunes over the course of seven decades, or, indeed, what may come to pass in the wake of unplanned-for calamities—such as the COVID-19 pandemic, for example. My observations additionally suggest that a considerably larger, more multivariate constellation of actors now interacts with the Council, including in various ways not foreseen by the *Charter*. The Council thus must rely on others to turn the ink on paper of its decisions into a walking, talking reality, but that interaction functions in a way at least arguably accompanied by expectations that the Council should explain itself on a routine basis.

Concomitantly, if states are expected to answer for the Council's directions and how they have been carried out, so the Council should answer the questions put to it. This arises simply because of the spinning point of the relationship between the Council and states: its voluntarist nature. As a pervasive example, even though states have no legal obligation to contribute peacekeeping troops in response to Council requests, it may suit their national interests to do so from time to time. Accordingly, their response, such as each may be, is created at least partly by the Council's powers of persuasion in crafting the mandate, but that is then aided and abetted by the Council's willingness to answer questions from (potential) contributors towards eliciting their action.

That is not to say that the Council is hostage to the dictates of contributors: failed, or even just less than fully productive, Council projects, or the UN's name being sullied by conduct connected to the Council, will hardly enhance Council effectiveness overall. Instead, the onus is on the Council to be persuasive in both *designing* and *regulating* these activities, as well as then being thorough in the implementation of both.

As it is for a broad sweep of decision-making bodies, in the end legitimacy is lifeblood to the Council's purpose, and indispensable for feasibility of its projects, but the largest determinant of its legitimacy is likely to be its own conduct—including as is shown in being productive in making decisions then ensuring due implementation.

This prompts two closing points on the potential for the Council to become more productive by being more accountable.

Firstly, discussion herein highlights where the Council departs, for the better, from its otherwise Herculean labours: the Council does not labour alone and nor does it need to.

Legitimate standing, among those whose support the Council needs to be effective, is more likely to see its purposes realised, and, I suggest, will be all the better for being mediated and moderated in an accountability dialogue of authentic and purposive engagement. Having been bestowed power to further its Functions under the *Charter*, however, the onus is also on the Council to make this so.

In a scheme towards that end, I have suggested that the elected members of the Council now have more to say, and more right to say it, than others not already enfranchised in Council work by the *Charter* design. In a larger, more variegated, and complicated array of actors that the Council now needs to address, I observe that the E10 has already shown useful form as a group capable of harnessing a range of resources to such purpose. From there, I suggest that this capacity might be bent further to the UN's Purposes by more formality in obliging the elected, non-permanent members in terms of the characteristics of their conduct in the Council's work, to be evidenced via their ongoing work practice.

As far as the *Charter* provides the E10 the power to be powerful, collectively, via their votes, but P5 members do not feel obliged to consider views other than their own in casting their votes, then elected members may be taken to have a proportionally greater obligation to ensure that they do when casting theirs. This extends as far as the E10's essential function is agreed as somehow being to represent those states empowering the Council—that is, the larger body of UN members—in the machinery and workings of the Council.

Finally, it may be correct to observe that the Council is as accountable as it wants to be, and that structural imperfections of the *Charter* system impede it from deciding to be more accountable on its own initiative—perhaps due to threat or reality of the veto power. I suggest it is more important, however, that the dialogic nature of accountability, and the socially constructed nature of the Council, together mean that it is also only as *un*accountable as those empowering the Council let it be.

Further, it seems to me that—notwithstanding the almost unassailable position of the P5—the arbiter of that is the E10.

Through concerted use of their voting power, the E10 can be custodians of Council effectiveness at least until a veto arises. In keeping with the *Charter* design, the Assembly has a golden opportunity to play a more active part in obtaining Council accountability in the future, albeit working via the E10 in concerted fashion rather than asserting a direct supervisory influence. By articulating tasks, standards, duties, and so on, by which the Assembly would oblige those representatives that it elects, and holding them to that articulation, Council productiveness might be advanced in the process of the E10's election, and through E10 terms of office, without the need for *Charter* reform—and, indeed, may be educative in terms of reforms that would have better prospects for success after having been rehearsed in this way

Index

www.ingramcontent.com/pod-product-compliance
Lightning Source LLC
Chambersburg PA
CBHW071227230926
51849CB00001B/47
9789004444294